Logical Effort:

Designing Fast CMOS Circuits

Ivan Sutherland is currently Vice President and Fellow at Sun Microsystems Laboratories. He earned EE degrees from Carnegie Mellon University, the California Institute of Technology, and MIT and later taught at Harvard University, the University of Utah, and the California Institute of Technology. His 1963 Ph.D. thesis, Sketchpad, laid the foundation for interactive computer graphics. With Bob Sproull, he built the first "virtual reality" system in the late 1960s and has worked on integrated circuit design for the past 20 years. He cofounded Evans and Sutherland in 1968 and Advanced Technology Ventures in 1980 then joined Sun as VP and Fellow in 1990 after 10 years as an independent consultant. Ivan is a member of both the National Academy of Engineering and the National Academy of Sciences, and is a Fellow of the ACM. He holds both the ACM Turing and the IEEE Von Neumann awards.

Bob Sproull is also Vice President and Fellow at Sun Microsystems Laboratories, and leads its Application Technologies Center. Since undergraduate days, he has been building hardware and software for computer graphics, such as an early device-independent graphics package, clipping hardware, page description languages, laser printing software, and window systems. He has also been involved in VLSI design, especially of asynchronous circuits and systems. Before joining Sun, he was a principal with Sutherland, Sproull, & Associates, an associate professor at Carnegie Mellon University, and a member of the Xerox Palo Alto Research Center. He is coauthor of the early text, *Principles of Interactive Computer Graphics*, and is a member of both the National Academy of Engineering and the U.S. Air Force Scientific Advisory Board.

David Harris is assistant professor in the Engineering Department at Harvey Mudd College and a consultant at Sun. He received S.B. degrees in electrical engineering and mathematics and an M. Eng. in electrical engineering and computer science from MIT in 1994, and a Ph.D. in electrical engineering from Stanford University in 1999. His professional interests include high-speed circuit and logic design, microprocessors, and teaching. When not building chips, he can usually be found climbing mountains.

Logical Effort:

Designing Fast CMOS Circuits

Ivan Sutherland

Bob Sproull

David Harris

M K◀® Morgan Kaufmann Publishers, Inc.
San Francisco, California

Senior Editor   Denise E. M. Penrose
Director of Production and Manufacturing   Yonie Overton
Production Editor   Edward Wade
Editorial Coordinator   Meghan Keeffe
Cover Design   Ross Carron Design
Cover, Title, and Chapter Opener Illustrations   Duane Bibby
Text Design, Technical Illustration, and Composition   Windfall Software, using ZzTEX
Copyeditor   Gary Morris
Proofreader   Jennifer McClain
Indexer   Steve Rath
Printer   Courier Corp.

Designations used by companies to distinguish their products are often claimed as trademarks or registered trademarks. In all instances where Morgan Kaufmann Publishers, Inc. is aware of a claim, the product names appear in initial capital or all capital letters. Readers, however, should contact the appropriate companies for more complete information regarding trademarks and registration.

Morgan Kaufmann Publishers, Inc.
Editorial and Sales Office
340 Pine Street, Sixth Floor
San Francisco, CA 94104-3205
USA
Telephone   415-392-2665
Facsimile   415-982-2665
Email   *mkp@mkp.com*
WWW   *http://www.mkp.com*
Order toll free 800-745-7323

Library of Congress Cataloging-in-Publication Data

Sutherland, Ivan, date
    Logical effort : designing fast CMOS circuits / Ivan
Sutherland, Bob Sproull, David Harris.
        p.   cm.
    Includes bibliographical references and index.
    ISBN 1-55860-557-6
    1. Metal oxide semiconductors, Complementary—Design and
construction.   2. Logic design.   3. Delay faults (Semiconductors)
I. Sproull, Bob.   II. Harris, David.   III. Title.
TK7871.99.M44S88   1999
621.3815′2—dc21   98-53860
                                                        CIP

Contents

12 —— Conclusions   205

APPENDICES

A —— Cast of Characters   217

B —— Reference Process Parameters   221

C —— Solutions to Selected Exercises   223

The method of logical effort evolved in three stages. It began in 1985 while I was living in London. Bob Sproull and I were engaged in research on fast asynchronous circuits involving mostly Muller C-elements and XOR functions. In trying to improve the speed of our circuits I resorted to calculus for lack of circuit simulation tools. Instead of computing I had to think about the problem, a formula for success that I recommend highly. Fortunately, both Muller C-elements and XOR functions are symmetric with respect to zero and one, and the usual circuits for them are correspondingly symmetric in N and P transistors. Their delay equations revealed a simple similarity between logic delay and electrical delay. It was only later that we learned to treat less symmetric functions like NAND and NOR.

I recall well the period of about a week during which the idea of logical effort emerged. At first I had only hints that the equations were telling me something interesting; I could smell value before simplicity emerged. I wrote a memo to Bob Sproull trying to describe the concept, but the formulation was still unclear and the idea had no name.

With more understanding I was able to name the idea "logical effort." Logical effort described the increased cost inherent in the circuit topology necessary to implement a logic function. I was pleased that more complex logic functions had higher logical effort than simple ones, and that the logical effort of compound circuits was the product of their individual logical efforts. With the name logical effort assigned and precisely defined, the idea became useable. The name electrical effort came afterward, assigning a name to a problem whose solution—namely gain—was very well understood.

The second phase of evolution took place in the late 1980s. I had returned to the United States, and worked with Bob Sproull to prepare the class notes on which this text is based. Bob carried the mathematics further than I had, finding ways to deal with parasitic delays that I had previously ignored. He tidied our notation, fixed my prose, and augmented my rough notes so that we could teach a coherent course to our industrial sponsors. We had almost a book but lacked the energy to finish it. In 1991 Bob and I published a short paper about logical effort [8].

Years later, David Harris faced the problem of teaching junior circuit designers and graduate students at Stanford University how to design circuits and size transistors. Teaching is often the best way to learn; he was forced to develop coherent explanations for his intuitive approach to sizing. His explanations proved to be a rediscovery of logical effort, which suggests that logical effort may be fundamental to circuit topology. David gradually discovered more properties of circuits, especially regarding the logical effort of newer circuit families such as domino logic. When David and I met, we found that many of his results were already in the unpublished logical effort course notes. Because he and his students wanted a good reference text for logical effort, David undertook the task of polishing the course notes into book form. Youth has such energy.

Ivan Sutherland

The method of logical effort is a way of thinking about delay in MOS circuits. It seeks to determine quickly a circuit's maximum possible speed and how to achieve it. It provides insight into how both the sizes of different transistors and the circuit topology itself affect circuit delay.

We offer two new names for causes of delay in MOS circuits, *electrical effort* and *logical effort*. The similarity of these names reflects a remarkable symmetry between the effort required to drive an electrical load and the effort required to perform a logic function; the two forms of effort present identical and interchangeable sources of delay. Identifying these concepts leads to a formulation that simplifies circuit analysis and allows a designer to analyze alternative circuit designs quickly.

Electrical effort is a new name for the problem overcome by electrical gain. It has long been known that the fastest driver for a large electrical load is a multistage amplifier whose gain is distributed among stages of exponentially increasing size. Thinking of what amplifiers do as compensating for electrical effort paves the way to understanding how they similarly compensate for logical effort.

Logical effort describes the cost of computation inherent in the circuit topology that implements each logic function. Logic functions incur a cost not only because they involve many transistors, but also because MOS transistors in series are poorer conductors of electricity than individual transistors of the same size. Both factors conspire to make logic function blocks less good than inverters at electrical amplification. Logical effort quantifies this weakness, enabling us to reason about which of several alternate topologies will be best.

Critics of this method observe that it achieves no more than conventional RC analysis and that experienced designers know how to optimize circuits for speed. Indeed, the best designers, whether by intuition or experience, design circuits that match closely those derived by the method of logical effort. However, we have seen many instances where experienced designers devise poor circuits. Even the best designers can become mired in detailed transistor sizing simulations and fail to find structural changes to a circuit that will lead to major performance improvements. Because of its simplicity, the method of logical effort bridges the gap between structural design and detailed simulation.

We wrote this book for those who design MOS integrated circuits. It assumes a knowledge of static CMOS digital circuits, elementary electronics, and modest mathematical skill. Although some of the derivations use calculus, only algebra is required to apply the method. The novice designer will find simple techniques for designing high-speed circuits. The experienced designer will find new ways to think about old design techniques. Both will gain new rules of thumb that lead to high-speed circuits. The techniques of logical effort help us analyze and optimize large circuits quickly.

How to Use this Book

There are many ways to use this text. We believe it will be of interest to practicing circuit, logic, and CAD designers, students, and researchers. Junior circuit designers will learn new techniques and reduce their dependence on tedious circuit simulation, while veteran designers will discover new ways to look at concepts they may have developed intuitively through experience. We believe that logic designers interested in high-speed chips must have a thorough understanding of delay in CMOS gates. Logical effort provides simple but powerful models for thinking about this delay and comparing alternative topologies. Similarly, we believe good tool developers need a thorough understanding of the problems being faced by their users, and we hope this book will offer them such insight.

Chapter 1 stands alone as an introduction to logical effort. A road map at the end of the chapter describes the more advanced topics presented later in the book. A course on VLSI design may use the first four chapters as supplemental reading to provide examples of applying logical effort and to develop the basic theory behind the method. Experienced circuit designers and students in advanced circuit classes will be interested in the later chapters, which apply logical effort to common circuit problems. We conclude with Chapter 12, a concise review of the method of logical effort and of important insights gained from the method.

About the Exercises

In our experience, it is very difficult to learn anything without practice. We have provided a number of exercises at the end of each chapter intended for self-study as well as for formal classes in logical effort.

The problems are rated in difficulty on a logarithmic scale, similar to that used by Knuth and Hennessy. A rough guide is listed below. Your mileage may vary.

[10]   1 minute (read and understand)

[20]   15–20 minutes

[30]   2 hours or more (especially if the TV is on)

[50]   research problem

Solutions to the odd-numbered problems are presented in the back of the book. Please use them wisely; do not turn to the answer until you have made a genuine effort to solve the problem yourself. Solutions to the even-numbered problems are available to instructors on the logical effort Web page (see the following section).

About the Web Site

The Morgan Kaufmann Web page *www.mkp.com/Logical_Effort* is dedicated to and offers several tools to assist with logical effort.

Some features on this Web page include

- A detailed example of logical effort applied to the design of a multiplier.

- Solutions to even-numbered exercises, available to instructors.

- The Perl script used in Chapter 5 to characterize the logical effort of gates. The script takes a SPICE netlist of the gates, a process file, and a list of input stimuli for each gate. It measures the logical effort and parasitic delay of each gate using the test setup described in Chapter 5.

- A Java tool to design wide NAND, NOR, AND, and OR gates. It takes the number of inputs and the electrical effort of the path and computes the minimum-delay tree, as discussed in Section 11.1. This tool can be used from a form-based interface on the Web, or downloaded for use on your computer.

If you discover an error in this book, please contact the publisher by email at lebugs@mkp.com. The first person to report a technical error will be awarded a $1.00 bounty upon its implementation in future printings of the book. Please check the errata page at *www.mkp.com/Logical_Effort* to see if a particular bug has already been reported and corrected.

Acknowledgments

Many people have helped us develop the method of logical effort and prepare this book. We wish to thank five companies that sponsored the original research: Austek Microsystems, Digital Equipment Corporation, Evans and Sutherland Computer Corporation, Floating Point Systems, and Schlumberger. We are grateful to Apple Computer for its support as we began to edit our course notes. We also thank the engineers and designers from those firms who served as students during our early attempts to teach this material and whose penetrating questions contributed to a clearer presentation of the ideas. We thank Carnegie Mellon University, Stanford University, and the Imperial College of London University for the office space, computing support, and collegial thinking they have provided.

Thanks are due to Sun Microsystems Laboratories for encouragement and support as we brought this book into final form, Our colleagues Ian W. Jones, Erik L. Brunvand, Bob Proebsting, Mark Horowitz, and Peter Single contributed in several ways to the work. More recently, we thank our students at Stanford University, HAL Computer, UC Berkeley, and Intel Corporation for bringing fresh life and interest to logical effort. Thanks are also due to those who partici-pated in the review process: Peter Ashenden of the University of Adelaide, Peter Beerel and Massoud Pedram of the University of Southern California, Dileep Bhandarkar of Intel, Lynn Conway of the University of Michigan, Steve Kang and Farid Najm of the University of Illinois, Urbana-Champaign, Jaeha Kim of Stanford University, and Wayne Wolf of Princeton University.

We have been very happy working with our publisher, Morgan Kaufmann. We would especially like to thank our editor, Denise Penrose, editorial coordinator, Meghan Keeffe, and production editor, Edward Wade, for their devotion to quality and good sense of humor.

Jaeha Kim did a remarkably thorough job hunting down errors in the text and solutions; the remaining mistakes are ours. Sally Harris worked tirelessly to prepare illustrations. Finally, we offer special thanks to our friends and colleagues Bob Spence and the late Charles Molnar for ideas, encouragement, and moral support.

The Method of Logical Effort————1

Designing a circuit to achieve the greatest speed or to meet a delay constraint presents a bewildering array of choices. Which of several circuits that produce the same logic function will be fastest? How large should a logic gate's transistors be to achieve least delay? And how many stages of logic should be used to obtain least delay? Sometimes, adding stages to a path reduces its delay!

The *method of logical effort* is an easy way to estimate delay in a CMOS circuit. We can select the fastest candidate by comparing delay estimates of different logic structures. The method also specifies the proper number of logic stages on a path and the best transistor sizes for the logic gates. Because the method is easy to use, it is ideal for evaluating alternatives in the early stages of a design and provides a good starting point for more intricate optimizations.

This chapter describes the method of logical effort and applies it to simple examples. Chapter 2 explores more complex examples. These two chapters together provide all you need to know to apply the method of logical effort to a wide class of circuits. We devote the remainder of this book to derivations that show why the method of logical effort works, to some detailed optimization techniques, and to the analysis of special circuits such as domino logic and multiplexers.

1.1 ——— Introduction

To set the context of the problems addressed by logical effort, we begin by reviewing a simple integrated circuit design flow. We will see that topology selection and gate sizing are key steps of the flow. Without a systematic approach, these steps are extremely tedious and time-consuming. Logical effort offers such an approach to these problems.

Figure 1.1 shows a simplified chip design flow illustrating the logic, circuit, and physical design stages. The design starts with a specification, typically in textual form, defining the functionality and performance targets of the chip. Most chips are partitioned into more manageable blocks so that they may be divided among multiple designers and analyzed in pieces by CAD tools. Logic designers write register transfer level (RTL) descriptions of each block in a language like Verilog or VHDL and simulate these models until they are convinced the specification is correct. Based on the complexity of the RTL descriptions, the designers estimate the size of each block and create a floorplan showing relative placement of the blocks. The floorplan allows wire-length estimates and provides goals for the physical design.

Given the RTL and floorplan, circuit design may begin. There are two general styles of circuit design: custom and automatic. *Custom* design trades additional human labor for better performance. In a custom methodology, the circuit designer has flexibility to create cells at a transistor level or choose from a library of predefined cells. The designer must make many decisions: Should I use static CMOS, transmission gate logic, domino circuits, or other circuit families? What circuit topology best implements the functions specified in the RTL? Should I use NAND, NOR, or complex gates? After selecting a topology and drawing the schematics, the designer must choose the size of transistors in each logic gate. A larger gate drives its load more quickly, but presents greater input capacitance to the previous stage and consumes more area and power. When the schematics are complete, functional verification checks that the schematics correctly implement the RTL specification. Finally, timing verification checks that the circuits meet the performance targets. If performance is inadequate, the circuit designer may try to resize gates for improved speed, or may have to

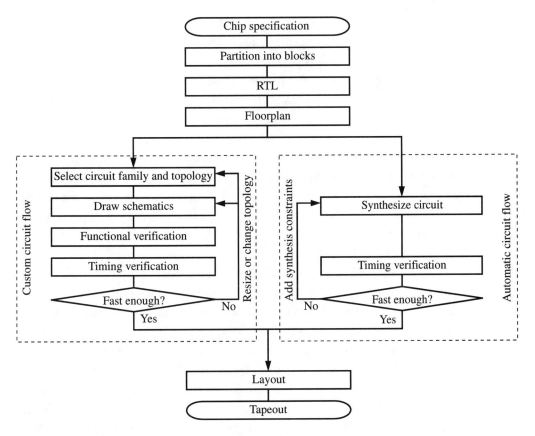

Figure 1.1 — Simplified chip design flow.

change the topology entirely, exploiting parallelism to build faster structures at the expense of more area or switching from static cmos to faster domino gates.

Automatic circuit design uses synthesis tools to choose circuit topologies and gate sizes. Synthesis takes much less time than manually optimizing paths and drawing schematics, but is generally restricted to a fixed library of static cmos cells and produces slower circuits than those designed by a skilled engineer. Advances in synthesis and manufacturing technology continue to expand the set of problems that synthesis can acceptably solve, but for the foreseeable future, high-end designs will require at least some custom circuits. Synthesized circuits are normally logically correct by construction, but timing verification is still necessary. If performance is inadequate, the circuit designer may set directives for the synthesis tool to improve critical paths.

When circuit design is complete, layout may begin. Layout may also be custom or may use automatic place and route tools. Design rule checkers (DRC) and layout versus schematic (LVS) checks are used to verify the layout. Postlayout timing verification ensures the design still meets timing goals after including more accurate capacitance and resistance data extracted from the layout; if the estimates used in circuit design were inaccurate, the circuits may have to be modified again. Finally, the chip is "taped out" and sent for manufacturing.

One of the greatest challenges in this design flow is meeting the timing specifications, a problem known as *timing convergence.* If speed were not a concern, circuit design would be much easier, but if speed were not a concern, the problem could be solved more cost-effectively in software.

Even experienced custom circuit designers often expend a tremendous amount of frustrating effort to meet timing specifications. Without a systematic approach, most of us fall into the "simulate and tweak" trap of making changes in a circuit, throwing it into the simulator, looking at the result, making more changes, and repeating. Because circuit blocks often take half an hour or more in simulation, this process is very time-consuming. Moreover, the designer often tries to speed up a slow gate by increasing its size. This can be counterproductive if the larger gate now imposes greater load on the previous stage, slowing the previous stage more than improving its own delay! Another problem is that without an easy way of estimating delays, the designer who wishes to compare two topologies must draw, size, and simulate a schematic of each. This process takes a great deal of time and discourages such comparisons. The designer soon realizes that a more efficient and systematic approach is needed and over the years develops a personal set of heuristics and mental models to assist with topology selection and sizing.

Users of synthesis tools experience similar frustrations with timing convergence, especially when the specification is near the upper limit of the tool's capability. The synthesis equivalent of "simulate and tweak" is "add constraints and resynthesize"; as constraints fix one timing violation, they often introduce a new violation on another path. Unless the designer looks closely at the output of the synthesis and understands the root cause of the slow paths, adding constraints and resynthesizing may never converge on an acceptable result.

This book is written for those who are concerned about designing fast chips. It offers a systematic approach to topology selection and gate sizing that captures many years of experience and offers a simple language for quantitatively discussing such problems. In order to reason about such questions, we need a simple delay model that's fast and easy to use. The models should be accurate enough that if it predicts circuit *a* is significantly faster than circuit *b*, then circuit *a* really is faster; the absolute delays predicted by the model are not as important because a better simulator or timing analyzer will be used for timing verification. This chapter begins by discussing such a simple model of delay and introduces terms that describe how the complexity of the gate, the load capacitance, and the parasitic capacitance contribute to delay. From this model, we introduce a numeric "path effort" that allows the designer to compare two multistage topologies easily without sizing or simulation. We also describe procedures for choosing the best number of stages of gates and for selecting each gate size to minimize delay. Many examples illustrate these key ideas and show that using fewer stages or larger gates may fail to produce faster circuits.

1.2 —— Delay in a Logic Gate

The method of logical effort is founded on a simple model of the delay through a single MOS logic gate.[1] The model describes delays caused by the capacitive load that the logic gate drives and by the topology of the logic gate. Clearly, as the load increases, the delay increases, but delay also depends on the logic function of the gate. Inverters, the simplest logic gates, drive loads best and are often used as amplifiers to drive large capacitances. Logic gates that compute other functions require more transistors, some of which are connected in series, making them poorer than inverters at driving current. Thus a NAND gate has more delay than an inverter with similar transistor sizes that drives the same load. The method of logical effort quantifies these effects to simplify delay analysis for individual logic gates and multistage logic networks.

---

1. The term "gate" is ambiguous in integrated circuit design, signifying either a circuit that implements a logic function such as NAND or the gate of a MOS transistor. We hope to avoid confusion by referring to "logic gate" or "transistor gate" unless the meaning is clear from context.

The first step in modeling delays is to isolate the effects of a particular integrated circuit fabrication process by expressing all delays in terms of a basic *delay unit* τ particular to that process.[2] τ is the delay of an inverter driving an identical inverter with no parasitics. Thus we express absolute delay as the product of a unitless delay of the gate d and the delay unit that characterizes a given process:

$$d_{abs} = d\tau \tag{1.1}$$

Unless otherwise indicated, we will measure all times in units of τ. In a typical 0.6μ process τ is about 50 ps. This and other typical process parameters are summarized in Appendix B.

The delay incurred by a logic gate is comprised of two components, a fixed part called the *parasitic delay* p and a part that is proportional to the load on the gate's output, called the *effort delay* or *stage effort* f. (Appendix A lists all of the notation used in this book.) The total delay, measured in units of τ, is the sum of the effort and parasitic delays:

$$d = f + p \tag{1.2}$$

The effort delay depends on the load and on properties of the logic gate driving the load. We introduce two related terms for these effects: the *logical effort* g captures properties of the logic gate, while the *electrical effort* h characterizes the load. The effort delay of the logic gate is the product of these two factors:

$$f = gh \tag{1.3}$$

The logical effort g captures the effect of the logic gate's topology on its ability to produce output current. It is independent of the size of the transistors in the circuit. The electrical effort h describes how the electrical environment of the logic gate affects performance and how the size of the transistors in the gate determines its load-driving capability. The electrical effort is defined by:

$$h = \frac{C_{out}}{C_{in}} \tag{1.4}$$

---

2. This definition of τ differs from that used by Mead and Conway [7].

Table 1.1 — Logical effort for inputs of static CMOS gates, assuming $\gamma = 2$. γ is the ratio of an inverter's pullup transistor width to pulldown transistor width. Chapter 4 explains how to calculate the logical effort of these and other logic gates.

Gate type	1	2	3	4	5	n
Inverter	1					
NAND		4/3	5/3	6/3	7/3	$(n+2)/3$
NOR		5/3	7/3	9/3	11/3	$(2n+1)/3$
Multiplexer		2	2	2	2	2
XOR (parity)		4	12	32		

where C_{out} is the capacitance that loads the output of the logic gate and C_{in} is the capacitance presented by the input terminal of the logic gate. Electrical effort is also called *fanout* by many CMOS designers. Note that fanout, in this context, depends on the load capacitance, not just the number of gates being driven.

Combining Equations 1.2 and 1.3, we obtain the basic equation that models the delay through a single logic gate, in units of τ:

$$d = gh + p \qquad (1.5)$$

This equation shows that logical effort g and electrical effort h both contribute to delay in the same way. This formulation separates τ, g, h, and p, the four contributions to delay. The process parameter τ represents the speed of the basic transistors. The parasitic delay p expresses the intrinsic delay of the gate due to its own internal capacitance, which is largely independent of the size of the transistors in the logic gate. The electrical effort, h, combines the effects of external load, which establishes C_{out}, with the sizes of the transistors in the logic gate, which establish C_{in}. The logical effort g expresses the effects of circuit topology on the delay free of considerations of loading or transistor size. Logical effort is useful because it depends only on circuit topology.

Logical effort values for a few CMOS logic gates are shown in Table 1.1. Logical effort is defined so that an inverter has a logical effort of 1. An inverter driving an exact copy of itself experiences an electrical effort of 1. Therefore, an

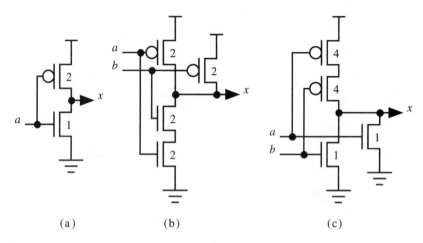

Figure 1.2—Simple gates: inverter (a), two-input NAND gate (b), and two-input NOR gate (c). The numbers indicate relative transistor widths.

inverter driving an exact copy of itself will have an effort delay of 1, according to Equation 1.3.

The logical effort of a logic gate tells how much worse it is at producing output current than is an inverter, given that each of its inputs may present only the same input capacitance as the inverter. Reduced output current means slower operation, and thus the logical effort number for a logic gate tells how much more slowly it will drive a load than would an inverter. Equivalently, logical effort is how much more input capacitance a gate must present in order to deliver the same output current as an inverter. Figure 1.2 illustrates simple gates with relative transistor widths chosen for roughly equal output currents. The inverter has three units of input capacitance while the NAND has four. Therefore, the NAND gate has a logical effort $g = 4/3$. Similarly, the NOR gate has $g = 5/3$. Chapter 4 estimates the logical effort of other gates, while Chapter 5 shows how to extract logical effort from circuit simulations.

It is interesting but not surprising to note from Table 1.1 that more complex logic functions have larger logical effort. Moreover, the logical effort of most logic gates grows with the number of inputs to the gate. Larger or more complex logic gates will thus exhibit greater delay. As we shall see later, these properties make it worthwhile to contrast different choices of logical structure. Designs that minimize the number of stages of logic will require more inputs for each logic gate and thus have larger logical effort. Designs with fewer inputs and thus less logical effort per stage may require more stages of logic. In Section 1.4, we will see how the method of logical effort expresses these trade-offs.

The electrical effort h is just a ratio of two capacitances. The load driven by a logic gate is the capacitance of whatever is connected to its output; any such load will slow down the circuit. The input capacitance of the circuit is a measure of the size of its transistors. The input capacitance term appears in the denominator of Equation 1.4 because bigger transistors in a logic gate will drive a given load faster. Usually most of the load on a stage of logic is the capacitance of the input or inputs of the next stage or stages of logic that it drives. Of course, the load also includes the stray capacitance of wires, drain regions of transistors, and so on. We shall see later how to include stray load capacitances in our calculations.

Electrical effort is usually expressed as a ratio of transistor widths rather than actual capacitances. We know that the capacitance of a transistor gate is proportional to its area; if we assume that all transistors have the same minimum length, then the capacitance of a transistor gate is proportional to its width. Because most logic gates drive other logic gates, we can express both C_{in} and C_{out} in terms of transistor widths. If the load capacitance includes stray capacitance due to wiring or external loads, we shall convert this capacitance into an equivalent transistor width. If you prefer, you can think of the unit of capacitance as the capacitance of a transistor gate of minimum length and unit width.

The parasitic delay of a logic gate is fixed, independent of the size of the logic gate and of the load capacitance it drives, because wider transistors providing greater output current have correspondingly greater diffusion capacitance. This delay is a form of overhead that accompanies any gate. The principal contribution to parasitic delay is the capacitance of the source or drain regions of the transistors that drive the gate's output. Table 1.2 presents crude estimates of parasitic delay for a few logic gate types; note that parasitic delays are given as multiples of the parasitic delay of an inverter, denoted as p_{inv}. A typical value for p_{inv} is 1.0 delay units, which is used in most of the examples in this book. p_{inv} is a strong function of process-dependent diffusion capacitances, but 1.0 is representative and is convenient for hand analysis. These estimates omit stray capacitance between series transistors, as will be discussed in more detail in Chapters 3 and 5.

The delay model of a single logic gate, as represented in Equation 1.5, is a simple linear relationship. Figure 1.3 shows this relationship graphically: delay appears as a function of electrical effort for an inverter and for a two-input NAND

Table 1.2—Estimates of parasitic delay of various logic gate types, assuming simple layout styles. A typical value of p_{inv}, the parasitic delay of an inverter, is 1.0.

Gate type	Parasitic delay
Inverter	p_{inv}
n-input NAND	np_{inv}
n-input NOR	np_{inv}
n-way multiplexer	$2np_{inv}$
XOR, XNOR	$4p_{inv}$

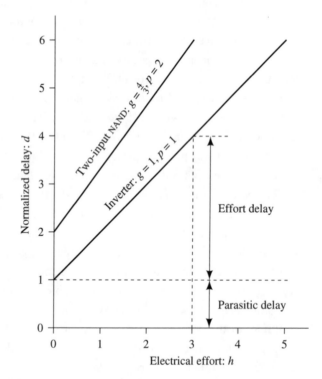

Figure 1.3—Plots of the delay equation for an inverter and a two-input NAND gate.

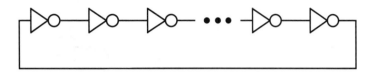

Figure 1.4—A ring oscillator of N identical inverters.

gate. The slope of each line is the logical effort of the gate; its intercept is the parasitic delay. The graph shows that we can adjust the total delay by adjusting the electrical effort or by choosing a logic gate with a different logical effort. Once we have chosen a gate type, however, the parasitic delay is fixed, and our optimization procedure can do nothing to reduce it.

EXAMPLE 1.1 Estimate the delay of an inverter driving an identical inverter, as in the ring oscillator shown in Figure 1.4.

SOLUTION Because the inverter's output is connected to the input of an identical inverter, the load capacitance, C_{out}, is the same as the input capacitance. Therefore the electrical effort is $h = C_{out}/C_{in} = 1$. Because the logical effort of an inverter is 1, we have, from Equation 1.5, $d = gh + p = 1 \times 1 + p_{inv} = 2.0$. This result expresses the delay in *delay units*; it can be scaled by τ to obtain the absolute delay, $d_{abs} = 2.0\tau$. In a 0.6μ process with $\tau = 50$ ps, $d_{abs} = 100$ ps.

The ring oscillator shown in Figure 1.4 can be used to measure the value of τ. Because N, the number of stages in the ring, is odd, the circuit is unstable and will oscillate. The delay of each stage of the ring oscillator is expressed by:

$$\frac{1}{2NF} = d\tau = (1 + p_{inv})\tau \qquad (1.6)$$

where N is the number of inverters, F is the oscillation frequency, and the 2 appears because a transition must pass twice around the ring to complete a single cycle of the oscillation. If a value for p_{inv} is known, this equation can be used to determine τ from measurements of the frequency of the ring oscillator. Chapter 5 shows a method for measuring both τ and p_{inv}. ∎

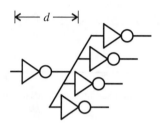

Figure 1.5 — An inverter driving four identical inverters.

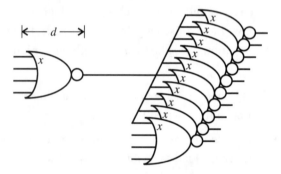

Figure 1.6 — A four-input NOR gate driving 10 identical gates.

EXAMPLE 1.2   Estimate the delay of a fanout-of-4 (FO4) inverter, as shown in Figure 1.5.

SOLUTION   Because each inverter is identical, $C_{out} = 4C_{in}$, so $h = 4$. The logical effort $g = 1$ for an inverter. Thus the FO4 delay, according to Equation 1.5, is $d = gh + p = 1 \times 4 + p_{inv} = 4 + 1 = 5$. It is sometimes convenient to express times in terms of FO4 inverter delays because most designers know the FO4 delay in their process and can use it to estimate the absolute performance of your circuit in their process.   ■

EXAMPLE 1.3   A four-input NOR gate drives 10 identical gates, as shown in Figure 1.6. What is the delay in the driving NOR gate?

SOLUTION   If the capacitance of one input of each NOR gate is x, then the driving NOR has $C_{in} = x$ and $C_{out} = 10x$, and thus the electrical effort is $h = 10$. The logical effort of the four-input NOR gate is $9/3 = 3$, obtained from Table 1.1. Thus the delay is $d = gh + p = 3 \times 10 + 4 \times 1$, or 34 delay units. Note that when the load is large, as in this example, the parasitic delay is insignificant compared to the effort delay.   ∎

1.3 —— Multistage Logic Networks

The method of logical effort reveals the best number of stages in a multistage network and how to obtain the least overall delay by balancing the delay among the stages. The notions of logical and electrical effort generalize easily from individual gates to multistage paths.

The logical effort along a path compounds by multiplying the logical efforts of all the logic gates along the path. We use the uppercase symbol G to denote the *path logical effort*, so that it is distinguished from g, the logical effort of a single gate in the path. The subscript i indexes the logic stages along the path.

$$G = \prod g_i \qquad (1.7)$$

The electrical effort along a path through a network is simply the ratio of the capacitance that loads the last logic gate in the path to the input capacitance of the first gate in the path. We use an uppercase symbol H to indicate the electrical effort along a path.

$$H = \frac{C_{out}}{C_{in}} \qquad (1.8)$$

In this case, C_{in} and C_{out} refer to the input and output capacitances of the path as a whole, as may be inferred from context.

We need to introduce a new kind of effort, named *branching effort*, to account for fanout within a network. So far we have treated fanout as a form of electrical effort: when a logic gate drives several loads, we sum their capacitances, as in Example 1.3, to obtain an electrical effort. Treating fanout as a form of electrical effort is easy when the fanout occurs at the final output of a network. This method is less suitable when the fanout occurs within a logic network because we know that the electrical effort for the network depends only on the ratio of its output capacitance to its input capacitance.

When fanout occurs within a logic network, some of the available drive current is directed along the path we are analyzing, and some is directed off that path. We define the branching effort b at the output of a logic gate to be

$$b = \frac{C_{on-path} + C_{off-path}}{C_{on-path}} = \frac{C_{total}}{C_{useful}} \qquad (1.9)$$

where $C_{on-path}$ is the load capacitance along the path we are analyzing and $C_{off-path}$ is the capacitance of connections that lead off the path. Note that if the path does not branch, the branching effort is one. The branching effort along an entire path B is the product of the branching effort at each of the stages along the path.

$$B = \prod b_i \qquad (1.10)$$

Armed with definitions of logical, electrical, and branching effort along a path, we can define the *path effort F*. Again, we use an uppercase symbol to distinguish the path effort from the stage effort f associated with a single logic stage. The equation that defines path effort is reminiscent of Equation 1.3, which defines the effort for a single logic gate:

$$F = GBH \qquad (1.11)$$

Note that the path branching and electrical efforts are related to the electrical effort of each stage:

$$BH = \frac{C_{out}}{C_{in}} \prod b_i = \prod h_i \qquad (1.12)$$

The designer knows C_{in}, C_{out}, and branching efforts b_i from the path specification. Sizing the path consists of choosing appropriate electrical efforts h_i for each stage to match the total BH product.

Although it is not a direct measure of delay along the path, the path effort holds the key to minimizing the delay. Observe that the path effort depends only on the circuit topology and loading and not upon the sizes of the transistors used in logic gates embedded within the network. Moreover, the effort is unchanged if inverters are added to or removed from the path, because the logical effort of an inverter is one. The path effort is related to the minimum achievable delay along the path, and permits us to calculate that delay easily. Only a little more work yields the best number of stages and the proper transistor sizes to realize the minimum delay.

The path delay D is the sum of the delays of each of the stages of logic in the path. As in the expression for delay in a single stage (Equation 1.5), we shall distinguish the *path effort delay* D_F and the *path parasitic delay* P:

$$D = \sum d_i = D_F + P \tag{1.13}$$

The path effort delay is simply

$$D_F = \sum g_i h_i \tag{1.14}$$

and the path parasitic delay is

$$P = \sum p_i \tag{1.15}$$

Optimizing the design of an N-stage logic network proceeds from a very simple principle that we will prove in Chapter 3: *The path delay is least when each stage in the path bears the same stage effort.* This minimum delay is achieved when the stage effort is

$$\hat{f} = g_i h_i = F^{1/N} \tag{1.16}$$

We use a hat over a symbol to indicate an expression that achieves minimum delay.

Combining these equations, we obtain the principal result of the method of logical effort, which is an expression for the minimum delay achievable along a path:

$$\hat{D} = NF^{1/N} + P \tag{1.17}$$

From a simple computation of its logical, branching, and electrical efforts we can obtain an estimate of the minimum delay of a logic network. Observe that when $N = 1$, this equation reduces to Equation 1.5.

To equalize the effort borne by each stage on a path, and therefore achieve the minimum delay along the path, we must choose appropriate transistor sizes for each stage of logic along the path. Equation 1.16 shows that each logic stage should be designed with electrical effort

$$\hat{h}_i = \frac{F^{1/N}}{g_i} \tag{1.18}$$

From this relationship, we can determine the transistor sizes of gates along a path. Start at the end of the path and work backward, applying the capacitance transformation:

$$C_{in_i} = \frac{g_i C_{out_i}}{\hat{f}} \tag{1.19}$$

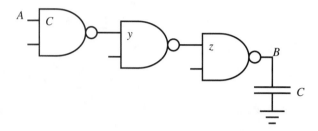

Figure 1.7—A logic network consisting of three two-input NAND gates.

This determines the input capacitance of each gate, which can then be distributed appropriately among the transistors connected to the input. The mechanics of this process will become clear in the following examples.

EXAMPLE 1.4   Consider the path from A to B involving three two-input NAND gates shown in Figure 1.7. The input capacitance of the first gate is C, and the load capacitance is also C. What is the least delay of this path, and how should the transistors be sized to achieve least delay? (The next example will use the same circuit with a different electrical effort.)

SOLUTION   To compute the path effort, we must compute the logical, branching, and electrical efforts along the path. The path logical effort is the product of the logical efforts of the three NAND gates, $G = g_0 g_1 g_2 = 4/3 \times 4/3 \times 4/3 = (4/3)^3 = 2.37$. The branching effort is $B = 1$, because all of the fanouts along the path are one, that is, there is no branching. The electrical effort is $H = C/C = 1$. Hence, the path effort is $F = GBH = 2.37$. Using Equation 1.17, we find the least delay achievable along the path to be $\hat{D} = 3(2.37)^{1/3} + 3(2p_{inv}) = 10.0$ delay units.

This minimum delay can be realized if the transistor sizes in each logic gate are chosen properly. First compute the stage effort $\hat{f} = 2.37^{1/3} = 4/3$. Starting with the output load C, apply the capacitance transformation of Equation 1.19 to compute input capacitance $z = C \times (4/3)/(4/3) = C$. Similarly, $y = z \times (4/3)/(4/3) = z = C$. Hence we find that all three NAND gates should have the same input capacitance, C. In other words, the transistor sizes in the three gates will be the same. This is not a surprising result: all stages have the same load and the same logical effort, and hence bear equal effort, which is the condition for minimizing path delay.

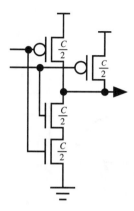

Figure 1.8—A schematic of a NAND gate from Example 1.4.

A schematic of the NAND gate is shown in Figure 1.8, assuming PMOS transistors have half the mobility of NMOS transistors. Selecting transistor sizes will be discussed further in Chapter 4. Since each input drives both a PMOS and NMOS transistor with capacitance $C/2$, the capacitance of each input is C, as desired. ∎

EXAMPLE 1.5 Using the same network as in the previous example, Figure 1.7, find the least delay achievable along the path from A to B when the output capacitance is $8C$.

SOLUTION Using the result from Example 1.4 that $G = (4/3)^3$ and the new electrical effort $H = 8C/C = 8$, we compute $F = GBH = (4/3)^3 \times 8 = 18.96$, so the least path delay is $\hat{D} = 3(18.96)^{1/3} + 3(2p_{inv}) = 14.0$ delay units. Observe that although the electrical effort in this example is eight times the electrical effort in the earlier example, the delay is increased by only 40%.

Now let us compute the transistor sizes that achieve minimum delay. The stage effort $\hat{f} = 18.96^{1/3} = 8/3$. Starting with the output load $8C$, apply the capacitance transformation of Equation 1.19 to compute input capacitance $z = 8C \times (4/3)/(8/3) = 4C$. Similarly, $y = z \times (4/3)/(8/3) = z/2 = 2C$. To verify the calculation, calculate the capacitance of the first gate $y \times (4/3)/(8/3) = y/2 = C$, matching the design specification. Each successive logic gate has twice the input capacitance of its predecessor. This is achieved by making the transistors in a gate twice as wide as the corresponding

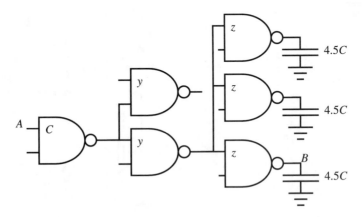

Figure 1.9—A multistage logic network with internal fanout.

transistors in its predecessor. The wider transistors in successive stages are better able to drive current into the larger loads.   ∎

EXAMPLE 1.6   Optimize the circuit in Figure 1.9 to obtain the least delay along the path from A to B when the electrical effort of the path is 4.5.

SOLUTION   The path logical effort is $G = (4/3)^3$. The branching effort at the output of the first stage is $(y + y)/y = 2$, and at the output of the second stage it is $(z + z + z)/z = 3$. The path branching effort is therefore $B = 2 \times 3 = 6$. The electrical effort along the path is specified to be $H = 4.5$. Thus $F = GBH = 64$, and $\hat{D} = 3(64)^{1/3} + 3(2p_{inv}) = 18.0$ delay units.

To achieve this minimum delay, we must equalize the effort in each stage. Since the path effort is 64, the stage effort should be $(64)^{1/3} = 4$. Starting from the output, $z = 4.5C \times (4/3)/4 = 1.5C$. The second stage drives three copies of the third stage, so $y = 3z \times (4/3)/4 = z = 1.5C$. We can check the math by finding the size of the first stage $2y \times (4/3)/4 = (2/3)y = C$, as given in the design spec.   ∎

EXAMPLE 1.7   Size the circuit in Figure 1.10 for minimum delay. Suppose the load is 20 microns of gate capacitance and that the inverter has 10 microns of gate capacitance.

SOLUTION   Assuming minimum-length transistors, gate capacitance is proportional to gate width. Hence, it is convenient to express capacitance in terms of microns of gate width, as given in this problem.

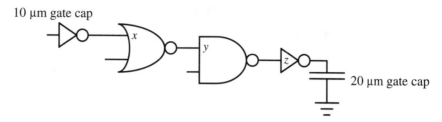

10 μm gate cap

20 μm gate cap

Figure 1.10—A multistage logic network with a variety of gates.

The path has logical effort $G = 1 \times (5/3) \times (4/3) \times 1 = 20/9$. The electrical effort is $H = 20/10 = 2$, and the branching effort is 1. Thus, $F = GBH = 40/9$, and $\hat{f} = (40/9)^{1/4} = 1.45$.

Start from the output and work backward to compute sizes: $z = 20 \times 1/1.45 = 14$, $y = 14 \times (4/3)/1.45 = 13$, and $x = 13 \times (5/3)/1.45 = 15$. These input gate widths are divided among the transistors in each gate. Notice that the inverters are assigned larger electrical efforts than the more complex gates because they are better at driving loads. Also note that these calculations do not have to be very precise. We will see in Section 3.6 that sizing a gate too large or too small by a factor of 1.5 still results in circuits within 5% of minimum delay. Therefore, it is easy to use "back-of-the-envelope" hand calculations to find gate sizes to one or two significant figures.

Note that the parasitic delay does not enter into the procedure for calculating transistor sizes to obtain minimum delay. Because the parasitic delay is fixed, independent of the size of the logic gate, adjustments to the size of logic gates cannot alter parasitic delay. In fact, we can ignore parasitic delay entirely unless we want to obtain an accurate estimate of the time required for a signal to propagate through a logic network, or if we are comparing two logic networks that contain different types of logic gates or different numbers of stages and therefore exhibit different parasitic delays.   ∎

EXAMPLE 1.8   Consider three alternative circuits for driving a load 25 times the input capacitance of the circuit. The first design uses one inverter, the second uses three inverters in series, and the third uses five in series. All three designs compute the same logic function. Which is best, and what is the minimum delay?

SOLUTION   In all three cases, the path logical effort is 1, the branching effort is 1, and the electrical effort is 25. Equation 1.17 gives the path delay $D = N(25)^{1/N} + Np_{inv}$ where $N = 1, 3$, or 5. For $N = 1$, we have $\hat{D} = 26$ delay units; for $N = 3$, $\hat{D} = 11.8$; and for $N = 5$, $\hat{D} = 14.5$. The best choice is $N = 3$. In this design, each stage will bear an effort of $(25)^{1/3} = 2.9$, so each inverter will be 2.9 times larger than its predecessor. This is the familiar geometric progression of sizes that is found in many textbooks.   ■

This example shows that the fastest speed obtainable depends on the number of stages in the circuit. Since the path delay varies markedly for different values of N, it is clear we need a method for choosing N to yield the least delay; this is the topic of the next section.

1.4 —— Choosing the Best Number of Stages

The delay equations of logical effort, such as Equation 1.17, can be solved to determine the number of stages, $\hat{N}$, that achieves the minimum delay. Although we will defer the solution technique until Chapter 3, Table 1.3 presents some results. The table shows, for example, that a single stage is fastest only if the path effort F is 5.83 or less. If the path effort lies between 5.83 and 22.3, a two-stage design is best. If it lies between 22.3 and 82.2, three stages are best. The table confirms that the right number of stages to use in Example 1.8, which has $F = 25$, is three. As the effort gets very large, the stage effort approaches 3.59.

If we use Table 1.3 to select the number of stages that gives the least delay, we may find that we must add stages to a network. We can always add an even number of stages by attaching pairs of inverters to the end of the path. Because we can't add an odd number of inverters without changing the logic function of the network, we may have to settle for a somewhat slower design or alter the logic network to accommodate an inverted signal. If a path uses a number of stages that is not quite optimal, the overall delay is usually not increased very much; what is disastrous is a design with half or twice the best number of stages.

The table is accurate only when we are considering increasing or decreasing the number of stages in a path by adding or removing inverters, because the table assumes that stages being added or removed have a parasitic delay equal to that of an inverter. Chapter 3 explains how other similar tables can be produced. When we are comparing logic networks that use different logic gate types or different

Table 1.3 — Best number of stages to use for various path efforts. For example, for path efforts between 3920 and 14200, seven stages should be used; the stage effort will lie in the range 3.3–3.9 delay units. The table assumes $p_{inv} = 1.0$.

Path effort F	Best number of stages, $\hat{N}$	Minimum delay $\hat{D}$	Stage effort, f, range
0		1.0	
	1		0–5.8
5.83		6.8	
	2		2.4–4.7
22.3		11.4	
	3		2.8–4.4
82.2		16.0	
	4		3.0–4.2
300		20.7	
	5		3.1–4.1
1090		25.3	
	6		3.2–4.0
3920		29.8	
	7		3.3–3.9
14200		34.4	
	8		3.3–3.9
51000		39.0	
	9		3.3–3.9
184000		43.6	
	10		3.4–3.8
661000		48.2	
	11		3.4–3.8
2380000		52.8	
	12		3.4–3.8
8560000		57.4	

numbers of stages of logic, it is necessary to evaluate the delay equations to determine which design is best.

EXAMPLE 1.9   A string of inverters in a 0.6μ process drives a signal that goes off-chip through a pad. The capacitance of the pad and its load is 40 pF, which is equivalent to about 20,000 microns of gate capacitance. Assuming the load on the input should be that of an inverter with 7.2 microns of input capacitance, what is the fastest inverter string?

SOLUTION   As in Example 1.8, the logical and branching efforts are both 1, but the electrical effort is $20,000/7.2 = 2777$. Table 1.3 specifies a six-stage design.

The stage effort will be $\hat{f} = (2777)^{1/6} = 3.75$. Thus the input capacitance of each inverter in the string will be 3.75 times that of its predecessor. The path delay will be $\hat{D} = 6 \times 3.75 + 6 \times p_{inv} = 28.5$ delay units. This corresponds to an absolute delay of $28.5\tau = 1.43$ ns, assuming $\tau = 50$ ps.   ∎

This example finds the best ratio of the sizes of succeeding stages to be 3.75. Many texts teach us to use a ratio of $e = 2.718$, but the reasoning behind the smaller value fails to account for parasitic delay. As the parasitic delay increases, the size ratio that achieves least delay rises above e, and the best number of stages to use decreases. Chapter 3 explores these issues further and presents a formula for the best stage effort.

In general, the best stage effort $\hat{f}$ is between 3 and 4. Targeting a stage effort of 4 is convenient during design and gives delays within 1% of minimum delay for typical parasitics. Thus, the number of stages $\hat{N}$ is about $\log_4 F$. We will find that stage efforts between 2 and 8 give delays within 35% of minimum and efforts between 2.4 and 6 give delays within 15% of minimum. Therefore, choosing the right stage effort is not critical.

We will also see in Chapter 3 that an easy way to estimate the delay of a path is to approximate the delay of a stage with effort of 4 as that of an FO4 inverter. We found in Example 1.2 that an FO4 inverter has a delay of 5 units. Therefore, the delay of a circuit with path effort F is about $5 \log_4 F$, or about $\log_4 F$ FO4 delays. This is somewhat optimistic because it neglects the larger parasitic delay of complex gates.

1.5 ——— Summary of the Method

The method of logical effort is a design procedure for achieving the least delay along a path of a logic network. It combines into one calculation the effort required to drive large electrical loads and to perform logic functions. The principle expressions of logical effort are summarized in Table 1.4. The procedure is:

1. Compute the path effort $F = GBH$ along the path of the network you are analyzing. The path logical effort G is the product of the logical efforts of the logic gates along the path; use Table 1.1 to obtain the logical effort of each individual logic gate. The branching effort B is the product of the branching effort at each stage along the path. The electrical effort H is the ratio of the

Table 1.4—Summary of terms and equations for concepts in the method of logical effort.

Term	Stage expression	Path expression
Logical effort	g (Table 1.1)	$G = \prod g_i$
Electrical effort	$h = C_{out}/C_{in}$	$H = C_{out-path}/C_{in-path}$
Branching effort	—	$B = \prod b_i$
Effort	$f = gh$	$F = GBH = \prod f_i$
Effort delay	f	$D_F = \sum f_i$ minimized when $f_i = F^{1/\hat{N}}$
Number of stages	1	N (Table 1.3)
Parasitic delay	p (Table 1.2)	$P = \sum p_i$
Delay	$d = f + p$	$D = D_F + P$

capacitance loading the last stage of the network to the input capacitance of the first stage of the network.

2. Use Table 1.3 or estimate $\hat{N} \approx \log_4 F$ to find out how many stages $\hat{N}$ will yield the least delay.

3. Estimate the minimum delay, $\hat{D} = \hat{N}F^{1/\hat{N}} + \sum p_i$, using values of parasitic delay obtained from Table 1.2. If you are comparing different architectural approaches to a design problem, you may choose to stop the analysis here.

4. Add or remove stages if necessary until N, the number of stages in your circuit, is approximately $\hat{N}$.

5. Compute the effort to be borne by each stage: $\hat{f} = F^{1/N}$.

6. Starting at the last logic stage in the path, work backward to compute transistor sizes for each of the logic gates by applying the equation $C_{in} = (g_i/\hat{f})C_{out}$ for each stage. The value of C_{in} for a stage becomes C_{out} for the previous stage, perhaps modified to account for branching effort.

This design procedure finds the circuit with the least delay along a particular path, without regard to area, power, or other limitations that may be as important as delay. In some cases, compromises will be necessary to obtain practical designs. For example, if this procedure is used to design drivers for a high-capacitance bus, the drivers may be too big to be practical. You may compromise by using a larger stage delay than the design procedure calls for, or even by making the delay in the last stage much greater than in the other stages; both of these approaches reduce the size of the final driver at the expense of delay.

The method of logical effort achieves an *approximate* optimum. Because it ignores a number of second-order effects, such as stray capacitances between series transistors within logic gates, a circuit designed with the procedure given above can sometimes be improved by careful simulation with a circuit simulator and subsequent adjustment of transistor sizes. However, in our experience the method of logical effort alone obtains designs that are within 10% of the minimum.

Another limitation of logical effort is the fact that circuits with complex branches or interconnect have no closed-form best design. Chapters 9 and 10 address these issues and provide approximations useful when gate or wire loads dominate, but in some cases, iteration is still necessary.

One of the strengths of the method of logical effort is that it combines into one framework the effects on performance of capacitive load, of complexity of the logic function being computed, and of the number of stages in the network. For example, if you redesign a logic network to use high fan-in logic gates in order to reduce the number of stages, the logical effort increases, thus blunting the improvement. Although many designers recognize that large capacitive loads must be driven with strings of drivers that increase in size geometrically, they are not sure what happens when logic is mixed in, as occurs often in tristate drivers. The method of logical effort addresses all of these design problems.

1.6 —— A Look Ahead

The information presented in this chapter is sufficient to attack almost any design. The next chapter applies the method to a variety of circuits of practical importance. Chapter 3 exposes the model behind the method and derives the equations presented in this chapter. Chapter 4 shows how to compute the logical effort of a logic gate and exhibits a catalog of logic gate types. Chapter 5 describes how to measure various parameters required by the method, such as p_{inv} and τ. The remaining chapters explore refinements to the method and more intricate design problems. Chapters 6 and 7 describe how to unbalance or skew a gate to favor a particular input or transition at the expense of the others. Chapter 8 applies logical effort to other circuit families, including pseudo-NMOS, domino, and transmission gates. Chapters 9 and 10 tackle the problems of circuits that fork and branch in irregular fashions. Chapter 11 uses logical effort to gain insights on wide structures including many-input gates, decoders, and multiplexers. The conclusion in Chapter 12 summarizes the method of logical effort and many insights provided by the method. It gives a design procedure to apply logical effort and compares the procedure with other approaches to path design. Finally, it reviews some of the limitations of logical effort that are important to the designer. Even if you skip the middle chapters on a first reading, we still recommend you glance at the conclusion.

You may also wish to refer to the appendices from time to time. We recognize that the notation of logical effort can be confusing at first, so Appendix A contains a complete list of all the symbols with definitions. Appendix B summarizes nominal process parameters for the 0.6μ process used in examples throughout the book and Appendix C contains solutions to the odd-numbered exercises.

1.7 —— Exercises

The bracketed numbers to the left of each exercise indicate the degree of difficulty for each. Please see About the Exercises in the Preface for a ratings guide.

[20] **1-1** Consider the circuits shown in Figure 1.11. Both have a fanout of 6, that is, they must drive a load six times the capacitance of each of the inputs. What is the path effort of each design? Which will be fastest? Compute the sizes x and y of the logic gates required to achieve least delay.

[20] **1-2** Design the fastest circuit that computes the NAND of four inputs with a fanout of 6. Consider a four-input NAND gate by itself, a four-input NAND gate followed by two additional inverters, and a tree formed by 2 two-input NAND gates whose outputs are connected to a two-input NOR gate followed by an

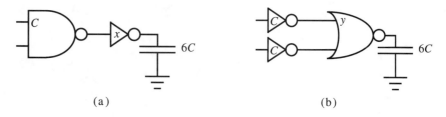

(a)   (b)

Figure 1.11 — Two circuits for computing the AND function of two inputs.

inverter. Estimate the shortest delay achievable for each circuit. If the fanout were larger, would other circuits be better?

[10]   **1-3**   A three-stage logic path is designed so that the effort borne by each stage is 10, 9, and 7 delay units, respectively. Can this design be improved? Why? What is the best number of stages for this path? What changes do you recommend to the existing design?

[10]   **1-4**   A clock driver must drive 500 minimum-size inverters. If its input must be a single minimum-size inverter, how many stages of amplification should be used? If the input to the clock driver comes from outside the integrated circuit via an input pad, could fewer stages be used? Why?

[15]   **1-5**   A particular system design of interest will have eight levels of logic between latches. Assuming that the most complex circuits involve four-input NAND gates with fanouts of three in all eight levels of logic and that latching overhead is negligible, estimate the minimum clock period.

[20]   **1-6**   A long metal wire carries a signal from one part of a chip to another. Only a single unit load may be imposed on the signal source. At its destination the signal must drive 20 unit loads. The distributed wire capacitance is equivalent to 100 unit loads; assume the wire has no resistance. Design a suitable amplifier. You may invert the signal if necessary. Should the amplifier be placed at the beginning, middle, or end of the wire?

Design Examples ———————————— **2**

This chapter presents a number of design examples worked out in detail. To clarify the presentation, some of the designs are simpler than cases that are likely to arise in practice. The last design, however, is taken from an actual problem confronted by designers.

As you read through the examples, focus not only on how we apply the mechanics of the method of logical effort, but also on the insights into circuit structure that the concepts of logical effort permit. Perhaps the greatest strength of the method of logical effort is in simplifying analysis of structural variants.

All of these examples assume we are using CMOS logic gates with $p_{inv} = 1.0$. Values for the logical effort and parasitic delay of logic gates are obtained from Tables 1.1 and 1.2, respectively. The best number of stages to accommodate a given path effort is obtained from Table 1.3.

2.1 ——— The AND Function of Eight Inputs

Ben Bitdiddle is developing the ALPHANOT microprocessor and needs an eight-input AND gate. He is considering three options for the structure of the circuit shown in Figure 2.1. Which one is best?

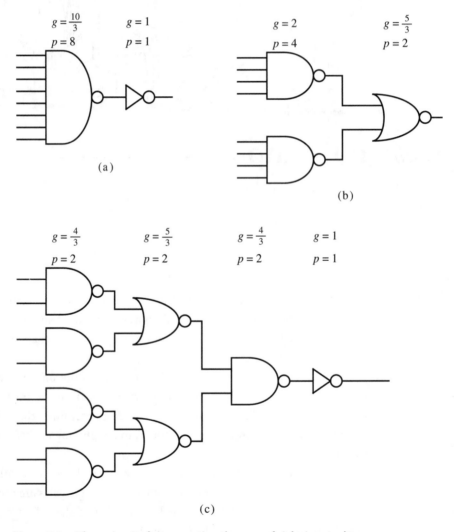

Figure 2.1 — Three circuits for computing the AND of eight inputs: {8-NAND, inverter} (a), {4-NAND, 2-NOR} (b), and {2-NAND, 2-NOR, 2-NAND, inverter} (c).

Before beginning the analysis of these three circuits, let us pause to introduce a notation that we will use in this book. To describe a path through a network, it suffices to list the logic gates that lie along the path. The circuit shown in Figure 2.1(a) can be described by the path {8-NAND, inverter}. Similarly, Figure 2.1(b) shows {4-NAND, 2-NOR} and 2.1(c) shows {2-NAND, 2-NOR, 2-NAND, inverter}. Often the networks are symmetric, so that all paths through the network have the same description, as is the case with all three circuits in Figure 2.1.

Let us start the analysis by computing the logical effort of each of the three alternatives. In Case *a*, the path logical effort is the product of the logical effort of an eight-input NAND gate, which is 10/3, and that of an inverter, which is 1, so $G = 10/3 \times 1 = 3.33$. In Case *b*, the logical effort is the product of 6/3, the logical effort of a four-input NAND gate, and 5/3, the logical effort of a two-input NOR gate, for a total of $10/3 = 3.33$—the same as case *a*. The logical effort in the last case is computed as $(4/3) \times (5/3) \times (4/3) \times 1 = 2.96$. Because we know that logical effort is related to delay, we might conclude that the last case is the fastest because it yields the lowest logical effort.

Logical effort is not the only consideration, however, because the size of the load will also influence the speed of the circuit. In particular, the circuits have different numbers of stages, and the method of logical effort shows that minimum delay is obtained only when the number of stages is chosen to accommodate the effort, both logical and electrical. So we can't decide which circuit will achieve the least delay until we know the electrical effort and can determine the best number of stages.

The delay equation, Equation 1.17, tells us how the minimum delay that can be obtained from each circuit is related to the electrical effort H the circuit bears. These equations also include the effect of the parasitic delays, obtained by summing the parasitic delays of each of the logic gates along the path:

$$\hat{D} = N(GBH)^{1/N} + P$$

Case *a* $\qquad \hat{D} = 2(3.33H)^{1/2} + 9.0$ (2.1)

Case *b* $\qquad \hat{D} = 2(3.33H)^{1/2} + 6.0$ (2.2)

Case *c* $\qquad \hat{D} = 4(2.96H)^{1/4} + 7.0$ (2.3)

Let us illustrate the effect of electrical effort on circuit choice by solving two problems, one with $H = 1$ and one with $H = 12$. Table 2.1 shows the results of evaluating the delay equations for the three circuits with different electrical

Table 2.1 — Delays for computing the AND of eight inputs for two different values of electrical effort.

	$H = 1$			$H = 12$		
Case	$NF^{1/N}$	P	$\hat{D} = NF^{1/N} + P$	$NF^{1/N}$	P	$\hat{D} = NF^{1/N} + P$
a	3.65	9.0	12.65	12.64	9.0	21.64
b	3.65	6.0	9.65	12.64	6.0	18.64
c	5.25	7.0	12.25	9.77	7.0	16.77

efforts. The table shows that for $H = 1$, the designs with two stages (Cases a and b) have less effort delay than the design with four stages (Case c). Of the two-stage designs, Case b is faster because it has less parasitic delay. When the electrical effort increases to $H = 12$, the design with the larger number of stages is best.

These results agree with the predictions for the best number of stages to use for a given path effort. Because the logical effort of all three circuits is approximately 3, we find that the path effort when $H = 1$ is $F = GBH \approx 3$, while when $H = 12$, $F \approx 36$. Table 1.3 shows that when $F = 3$, a one-stage design will be best, while when $F = 36$, a three-stage design will be best. Clearly, Cases a and b best approximate a one-stage design. It is not immediately obvious whether a two-stage or four-stage path is closest to the three-stage design recommended by the table, but usually it is better to err by one stage too many, as happens in this example where Case c is the fastest. Note that this reasoning ignores the effects of parasitic delay when the logic gate types in the competing circuits are different, as they are in this case. While this method yields approximate answers, a precise answer requires comparing the delay equations for each circuit, as we did in Table 2.1.

This example shows that the choice of circuit to use depends on the size of the load. Because there is a relationship between the load and the best number of stages, we must know the size of the load capacitance in relation to the size of the input capacitance in order to choose the best circuit structure.

2.1.1   Calculating gate sizes

The different circuits for computing the AND of eight inputs can illustrate the calculation of gate sizes along a path. Let us start with electrical effort H of 12, which calls for the design in Figure 2.1(c). Let us assume that the input capacitance is 4 units, so the load capacitance is $4H = 48$ units. From our earlier analysis, we know that each stage should bear an effort $\hat{f} = F^{1/4} = (2.96 \times 12)^{1/4} = 2.44$. Let us work backward along the path, starting with the inverter at the right. At each gate, we apply the capacitance transformation of Equation 1.19 to find the input capacitance given the output load.

The inverter at the right should have $C_{in} = 48 \times 1/2.44 = 19.66$. This becomes the load for the third stage, which therefore should have $C_{in} = 19.66 \times (4/3)/2.44 = 10.73$. This in turn becomes the load for the NOR in the second stage, which should have $C_{in} = 10.73 \times (5/3)/2.44 = 7.33$. Finally, we can use this as the load on the NAND gate in the first stage, which should have $C_{in} = 7.33 \times (4/3)/2.44 = 4.0$. This agrees with the specified input capacitance, so our calculation checks.

If Ben Bitdiddle were building a full-custom chip, he could select transistor sizes for each gate to match the input capacitances we have just computed. This will be discussed further in Section 4.3. If Ben were using an existing cell library, he could simply select the gates from the library that have input capacitances closest to the computed values. We will see in Section 3.6 that modest deviation from the computed sizes still gives excellent performance, so he should not be concerned if his library does not have a cell of exactly the desired size. Even for a full-custom design, it is necessary to adjust transistor sizes to the nearest available size, such as an integer.

Since rounding will occur anyway and precision in sizing is not very important, experienced designers often perform logical effort calculations mentally, keeping results to only one or two significant figures.

Now let us consider electrical effort of unity, which calls for the design of Figure 2.1(b). We will again assume that the input capacitance is 4 units, so now the output capacitance is also 4 units. To obtain the fastest operation, each stage should bear an effort $\hat{f} = F^{1/2} = (3.33 \times 1)^{1/2} = 1.83$.

Working backward, the NOR gate in the second stage should have $C_{in} = 4 \times (5/3)/1.83 = 3.64$. This is the load on the first stage NAND gate, which must have input capacitance of 4. Notice that the NAND has an electrical effort $3.64/4 = 0.91$ less than 1! This result may seem somewhat alarming at first, but it simply means that the load on the gate's output must be less than the load presented at its input, in order that the gate be sufficiently lightly loaded that it can operate in the required time. In other words, since we're equalizing effort in each stage, a stage with large logical effort g must have small electrical effort h.

2.2 ——— Decoder

Ben Bitdiddle is now responsible for memory design on the Motoroil 68W86, an embedded processor targeting automotive applications. He must design a decoder for a 16-word register file. Each register is 32 bits wide, and each bit cell presents a total load, gate and wire, equal to 3 unit-sized transistors. True and complement versions of the four address bits are available and can each drive 10 unit-sized transistors.

The decoder could be designed with a few stages of high fan-in gates or with many stages of simple gates. The best topology depends on the effort of the path. Unfortunately, the path effort depends on the logical effort, which depends in turn on the topology!

Because a decoder is a relatively simple structure, we can make an initial estimate of the path effort by assuming the logical effort is unity. The electrical effort is $32 \times 3/10 = 9.6$. The branching effort is 8 because the true and complement address inputs each control half of the outputs. Path effort is $9.6 \times 8 = 76.8$. Hence, we should use about $\log_4 76.8 = 3.1$ stages. Because we neglected logical effort, the actual number of stages will be slightly higher than the number we have estimated. Figure 2.2 shows a three-stage circuit, while Exercise 2.3 considers a four-stage circuit.

The three-stage circuit uses 16 four-input NAND gates. Because each address input must drive eight of the NAND gates, yet can handle only a relatively small input capacitance, we use an inverter to power up the signal. How do we size the decoder, and what is its delay?

Because the logical effort is $1 \times 2 \times 1 = 2$, the actual path effort is 154 and the stage effort is $f = (154)^{1/3} = 5.36$. Working from the output, the final inverter must have input capacitance $z = (32 \times 3) \times 1/5.36 = 18$, and the NAND gate must have input capacitance $y = 18 \times 2/5.36 = 6.7$. The delay is $3f + P = 3 \times 5.36 + 1 + 4 + 1 = 22.1$. These results are summarized in Case 1 of Table 2.2.

2.2.1   Generating complementary inputs

Now suppose the inputs were available only in true polarity and that Ben must produce his own complementary versions. To match the previous example in spirit, let the true signals drive a load of 20 unit-sized transistors. The new decoder is shown in Figure 2.3.

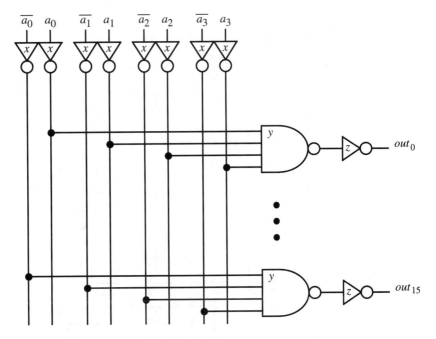

Figure 2.2—Three-stage 4:16 decoder circuit.

Table 2.2—Sizes and delays of decoder designs.

Case	x	y	z	u	v	P	D
1	10	6.7	18			6	22.1
2	10	6.7	18	10	23.2	7	22.4
3	11.2	9.8	21.6	8.8	26.2	7	21.8

The inverter strings used to compute true and complement versions of the input are called *forks* and are discussed further in Chapter 9. The two-inverter and one-inverter legs of the fork must drive the same load, a NAND gate, in the same amount of time. Computing the best sizes for circuits that fork can require iteration. Fortunately, we can make simple approximations that produce good results.

Suppose we keep $x = u = 10$ and use the final AND gate sizes y and z we computed earlier. How do we select v for minimum delay? We recall that the stage efforts of inverters u and v should be equal and are therefore

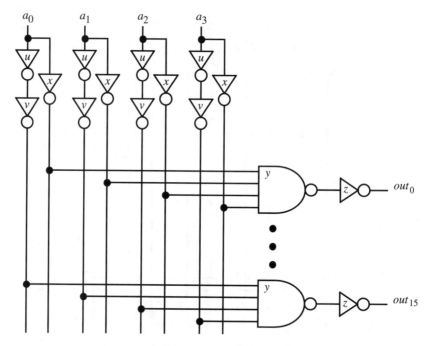

Figure 2.3 — 4:16 decoder with one polarity of input.

$\sqrt{5.36} = 2.32$ because they must together bear the same effort as the one-inverter path. Therefore, we can assign $v = 10\sqrt{5.36} = 23.2$. The delay of the decoder via the two-inverter leg is now $2.32 \times 2 + 5.36 \times 2 + 1 + 1 + 4 + 1 = 22.4$. These results are summarized in Case 2 of Table 2.2. This topology is less than 2% slower than the original design, so the approximation worked well.

If we were concerned about every picosecond of delay, we could try tweaking some of the sizes. For example, the circuit may be improved by dedicating more than half of the address input capacitance to one leg of the fork. Also, the circuit may be improved by choosing a stage effort for the second two stages between the efforts used for the one-inverter and two-inverter legs of the fork. We found the best sizes by writing the delay equations in a spreadsheet and letting it solve for minimum delay. The results are summarized in Case 3 of Table 2.2. The delay improvement is tiny and was probably not worth the effort.

Ben Bitdiddle, faced with designing bizillions of transistors, would rather not waste time tweaking sizes for tiny speedups. How could he have found in advance that his design was good enough? We will show in Section 3.4 that the best possible delay is $\rho \log_\rho F + P$, where the best stage effort ρ is about 4. Therefore, a lower bound on the delay of the circuit in Figure 2.2 is $4 \log_4 154 + 1 + 4 + 1 = 20.5$.

2.3 —— Synchronous Arbitration

Ben Bitdiddle transferred yet again to the Pentagram Processor project. The Pentagram has five separate function units that share a single on-chip bus mediated by a sinister arbitration circuit that determines which function unit may use the bus on each cycle (Figure 2.4). The operation of the bus and the arbitration circuits are synchronous: during one clock cycle, each function unit presents its *request* signal R_i to the arbitration circuit, and the arbitration circuit computes a *grant* signal G_i indicating which function unit may use the bus on the next clock cycle. While the bus is being used during one cycle, the arbitration circuit determines which function unit may use the bus during the next cycle. The five function units have fixed priority, with Unit 1 having the highest priority and Unit 5 the lowest.

   The speed of the arbitration circuit is critical, because each unit requires a portion of the clock cycle to compute the request signals, and the remainder of the clock cycle must be sufficient to compute the arbitration results. Moreover, because the function units are physically large, the capacitance of the wiring between the units will retard the circuit. The critical delay for the circuit will be the time from the arrival of the request signals until delivery of the last grant signal.

   This example explores the proper number of stages in the path and the effect of fixed wire loading. It is somewhat complex and may be skipped on a first reading.

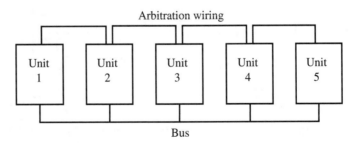

Figure 2.4— The physical arrangement of five units connected by a common bus and arbitration circuitry. The units are sufficiently large that the wires between them have significant stray capacitance.

2.3.1   The original circuit

A designer proposed the circuit shown in Figure 2.5 for arbitration. It relies on a *daisy chain* to compute which unit should gain access to the bus. The signal C_i represents the chain, and is interpreted as "C_i is true exactly when unit i and all higher-priority units are *not* requesting service." The designer then

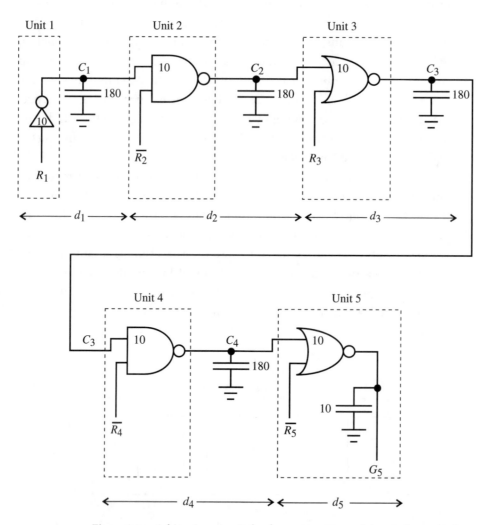

Figure 2.5—Arbitration circuit for five units, using a daisy-chain method. Unit 1 has highest priority, and Unit 5 lowest. Only the critical path is shown; additional circuitry is required to compute grant signals for Units 1 through 4.

formulated the following Boolean equations to express what each function unit must compute:

$$C_0 = \textbf{true} \tag{2.4}$$

$$C_i = C_{i-1} \wedge \overline{R_i} \tag{2.5}$$

$$G_i = C_{i-1} \wedge R_i \tag{2.6}$$

Working from the assumption that minimizing the number of stages would improve speed, the designer manipulated these equations so that only one gate would be required for each stage of the daisy chain:

$$\overline{C_i} = \overline{C_{i-1} \wedge \overline{R_i}} \tag{2.7}$$

$$C_i = \overline{\overline{C_{i-1}} \vee R_i} \tag{2.8}$$

Thus the gates on the daisy chain alternate between NAND and NOR gates, and the daisy-chain signal alternates between true and complement forms. Figure 2.5 shows all of the circuitry on the critical path from R_1 to G_5, but omits much of the rest. We assume that the request signals are available in true or complement form, that the grant signal can be computed in complementary form, that each R_i and G_i is loaded with 10 units of capacitance, and that the daisy-chain wire leading from one function unit to the next has a stray capacitance of 180 units.

Let us start by estimating the speed of the circuit shown in the figure. We will analyze the stage delay d_i in each of the five stages. For each stage, we determine the electrical and logical effort, which we multiply to obtain the effort delay. The results are shown in Table 2.3: the overall effort delay is 103, and parasitic delay is 9, for a total delay of 112.

Table 2.3 illustrates some of the defects in the circuit design of Figure 2.5. We know that overall delay is least when the effort delay is the same in every stage,

Table 2.3 — Delay computations for the circuit in Figure 2.5.

Stage	C_{in}	C_{out}	$h = C_{out}/C_{in}$	g	$f = gh$	p
1	10	190	19	1	19	1.0
2	10	190	19	4/3	25.3	2.0
3	10	190	19	5/3	31.7	2.0
4	10	190	19	4/3	25.3	2.0
5	10	10	1	5/3	1.7	2.0
Total delay					103	9.0

but in this design the delays vary between 1.7 and 32. This observation suggests that we have used the wrong number of stages in the design.

Let us compute the effort along the path. The electrical effort is 1, because both the input capacitance of R_1 and the output capacitance of G_5 are 10. There are four sites along the path at which the branching effort is $(180 + 10)/10 = 19$, because of the stray capacitance of the wiring; thus the branching effort is 19^4. The logical effort is the product of the logical efforts of the gates, or $1 \times (4/3) \times (5/3) \times (4/3) \times (5/3) = 4.94$. The path effort is therefore $F = GBH = 4.94 \times 19^4 \times 1 = 643785$. Table 1.3 shows that we should be using 10 stages, rather than the 5 in the present design. This is a big error, which suggests there is room for dramatic improvement.

A simple improvement is to enlarge the NAND gates along the daisy chain. If the input capacitance of each gate input were 90 rather than 10, the branching effort would be reduced to 3^4 and the total effort becomes $F = 4.94 \times 81 \times 1 = 400$. This calls for a five-stage design, with an estimated delay of $5(400)^{1/5} + 9p_{inv} = 25.6$, which is a vast improvement over the estimate of 112 for the original design. However, this change increases the load on each of the request signals, which will add more delay as well as more area.

2.3.2 Improving the design

Because the best design would use 10 stages of logic, an improved circuit should use 2 stages of logic for each function unit, rather than 1. Each unit should contain a logic gate and an inverter, which permits the daisy-chain signal to have a constant polarity and makes all arbitration units identical. Figure 2.6 shows the new structure: the logic in the box at the center of the figure is the logic associated with Units 2, 3, and 4 of the arbitration. The logic of the arbitration problem allows the first and last units to differ, because C_0 is always true and C_6 is unnecessary.

The transistor sizes shown in the figure as variables w, x, y, and z are all determined by the method of logical effort. Let us start by analyzing the critical path in the middle units, namely, the path from C_{i-1} to C_i. The load capacitance on this path is the stray capacitance, 180, plus $x + z$, the input capacitance of the two NAND gates in the next unit. For the critical path, $H = C_{out}/C_{in} = (180 + x + z)/x$. The logical effort along this path is the logical effort of the NAND gate, which is $4/3 \times 1 = 4/3$. For the design to be fast, we know that we should target a stage effort of about 4, as discussed in Section 1.4. Because we

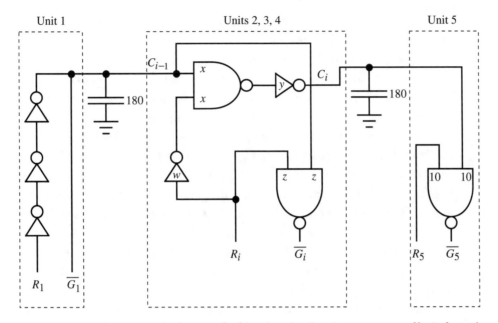

Figure 2.6 — An improved arbitration circuit, using two stages of logic for each unit.

are using a two-stage design, the two stages should bear an effort of $4 \times 4 = 16$. So we have the equation:

$$F = GH \tag{2.9}$$

$$16 = \frac{4}{3} \frac{(180 + x + z)}{x} \tag{2.10}$$

To solve this equation, we will assume that z is small compared to $180 + x$, and can be neglected. Solving, we obtain $x = 16.4$.

We can now calculate y in two ways. The NAND gate stage should have an effort delay of 4, so:

$$f = gh \tag{2.11}$$

$$4 = \left(\frac{4}{3}\right)\left(\frac{y}{x}\right) \tag{2.12}$$

Because $x = 16.4$, we can solve for y to obtain $y = 49$. Alternatively, we can consider the delay in the inverter stage, which has electrical effort approximately

$(180 + x)/y$, so we obtain a delay equation $4 = (180 + x)/y$. Solving for y, we obtain a value of 49, the same answer.

Now let us turn to calculating z and w. Even though paths leading from R_i or to G_i are not on the critical path of the entire arbitration chain, let us try to give them reasonable performance as well. For the inverter to have a stage delay of 4, we must have $x/w = 4$, so $w = 4.1$. Given the stipulation that R_i offer a load of 10 units of capacitance, we must have $z = 10 - w = 5.9$. This will mean that the effort delay in the generation of $\overline{G_i}$ will be $gh = (4/3)(10/5.9) = 2.3$. Is this delay reasonable? If it were much greater than 4, the gate would have very slow rise/fall times. If it were much less than 4, the gate would probably be presenting too much load on its inputs. In Section 3.5, we will see that stage efforts in the range of 2–8 give good results, so 2.3 is acceptable.

Let us now turn to the first and last units of the design. The last unit need only generate $\overline{G_5}$. As a consequence, we make the NAND gate as fast as possible by making it as large as allowed, given the constraint on the load capacitance of R_5. The first unit needs to compute $C_1 = \overline{R_1}$, but must drive a considerable load. The load is 10 units for the connection to $\overline{G_1}$, 180 units for the wiring capacitance, and $x + z = 22.3$ units for the input capacitance of Unit 2, for a total of 212. Thus the electrical effort is $H = 212/10 = 21$. Because the logical effort of the inverters is 1, the path effort F is also 21. Table 1.3 tells us that two stages of logic are required to bear this effort, but we need an odd number of inversions. Shall we use one or three inverters? The effort is closer to the range for three inverters than one, so we use three. Another way of choosing the number of stages is to compute $N = \log_4 F = 2.2$, and then round N to 3, the nearest odd number of stages.

The stage effort delay will be $H^{1/N} = 21.2^{1/3} = 2.8$. We know that the input capacitance of the first inverter is 10 units, so the input capacitance of the second will be $10 \times 2.8 = 28$, and that of the third will be $10 \times 2.8 \times 2.8 = 78$.

Now that the design is finished, let us compute the delay we expect along the critical path from R_1 to $\overline{G_5}$. This calculation is largely a matter of recalling the stage delays used to obtain the transistor sizes. The calculation appears in Table 2.4. The path effort delay is 33.7 and the parasitic delay is 14, for a total of 47.7. The improved circuit is more than twice as fast as the original. The designer of the original tried to achieve speed by minimizing the number of logic gates in the circuit, but a far faster circuit uses twice the number of gates!

Table 2.4 — Delay computations for the circuit in Figure 2.6.

Unit	Number of stages	Stage effort delay	Path effort delay	Path parasitic delay
1	3	2.8	8.4	1×3
2	2	4	8.0	$2 + 1$
3	2	4	8.0	$2 + 1$
4	2	4	8.0	$2 + 1$
5	1	1.3	1.3	2
Total delay			33.7	14

Also notice that in this circuit the fixed wiring capacitance still dominates the loading. Therefore, larger gates could have been used in the daisy chain, only slightly increasing total loading on the C_i signals while significantly reducing stage effort. Finding exact solutions to problems with fixed loading usually requires iteration, but the essential idea is to enlarge gates on the node with fixed capacitance until their input capacitance becomes a significant portion of the node capacitance.

2.3.3 Restructuring the problem

Changing its structure can make the arbitration circuit even faster. The weakness of the current design is the daisy chain, which bears a large stray capacitive load. The four segments of the chain are in series with logic, so that the electrical and logical efforts compound to produce a very large path effort that leads to large delays.

An alternative structure transmits the four request signals R_i, $i = 1, 2, 3, 4$ to all units and places logic in each unit to compute the grant signals. Figure 2.7 shows this structure but omits Units 2 and 4, which are much like Unit 3. Note that the capacitive load on the four broadcast signals is four times the load on each of the daisy-chain signals because the broadcast signals are four times as long.

Let us consider the effort along the path from R_1 to $\overline{G_5}$. The electrical effort is 1, because the load on R_1 is 10 units and the load on $\overline{G_5}$ is also 10 units. The logical effort is the logical effort of the five-input NAND gate, which is 7/3. The branching effort is $(720 + 4x)/x$, where x is the input capacitance of the NAND

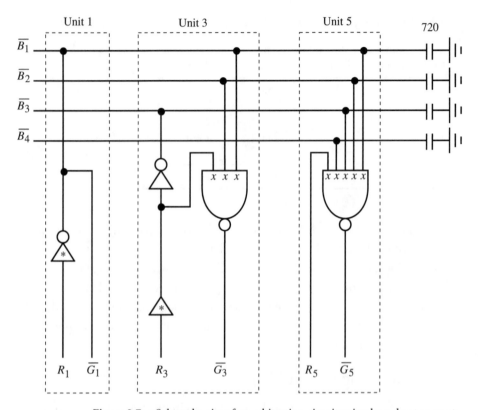

Figure 2.7 — Selected units of an arbitration circuit using broadcast requests.

gate. The path effort is thus $F = GBH = (7/3) \times (720 + 4x)/x \times 1$. To obtain least delay, we should minimize this effort by choosing x as large as possible, but excessive values will lead to layout problems. Also as x becomes comparable to the load capacitance it drives, there is little benefit to increasing x. Although large x theoretically would reduce the branching effort, the delay driving the load is already small. We will choose a modest value, $x = 10$, in part because R_5 can then drive the NAND gate directly, and in part because this is a convenient number. Thus $F = 177.3$, which from Table 1.3 suggests a four-stage design. Since the NAND gate represents one stage, we shall use three inverters to amplify R_1 for driving the broadcast wires.

Even though we have yet to compute transistor sizes, we can estimate the delay of this design. The effort delay in each stage will be $\hat{f} = F^{1/N} = 177.3^{1/4} = 3.6$, for a total delay of $4 \times 3.6 = 14.4$. The parasitic delay will be 3×1.0 for the three inverters and 5×1.0 for the NAND gate, for a total of 8.0. The overall delay is thus $\hat{D} = 14.4 + 8.0 = 22.4$. This represents a further improvement over the previous designs, at the expense of additional long wires. The restructured design operates the long wires concurrently, whereas the slower daisy-chain design operates its main wires sequentially.

2.4 —— Summary

The design examples in this chapter illustrate a number of points about designing for high speed.

- Tree structures are an attractive way to combine a great many inputs, especially when the electrical effort is large. These structures show up in adders, decoders, comparators, and so on. Chapter 11 shows further design examples of tree structures.

- Forks are used to produce true and complement versions of a signal. The input capacitance is divided among the legs so that the effort delay is equalized.

- Minimizing the number of gates is not always a good idea. The circuit of Figure 2.6 uses twice as many gates in the critical path as the circuit of Figure 2.5, but is substantially faster. The best number of stages depends on the overall path effort.

- Because delay grows only as the logarithm of the capacitive load, it is almost always wise to consolidate load in one part of the circuit rather than to distribute it around. Thus the broadcast scheme in Figure 2.7 is better than the daisy-chain method. Section 10.4 considers this problem further.

- When a path has a large fixed load, such as wire capacitance, using a large receiving gate on the node will make the path faster because the larger gates will provide much more current yet only slightly increase the total node capacitance. In other words, the larger receiver reduces the branching effort of the path.

- While the parasitic delay is important to estimate the actual delay of a design, it rarely enters directly into our calculations. Rather, it enters indirectly into the choice of the best number of stages and, equivalently, the best effort borne by each stage.

2.5 —— Exercises

[20]   **2-1**   Compare the delays of the three cases in Figure 2.1 by plotting three curves on one graph, one curve for each of the delays predicted by Equations 2.1 to 2.3. The graph should show total delay as a function of electrical effort H up to $H = 200$. Consider also a case similar to Case c, but with two more inverters connected to the output. Write the delay equation for this case, and add its plot to the graph. What does the graph show?

[20]   **2-2**   Find the network that computes the OR function of six inputs in least time, assuming an electrical effort of 140. The network may use NAND and NOR gates with up to four inputs, as well as inverters.

[20]   **2-3**   Because we did not include logical effort in the estimate of the number of decoder stages, we may have underestimated the best number of stages. Suppose the decoder design with true and complement inputs from Figure 2.2 were modified to use four stages instead of three by adding another input inverter. Find the best size for each stage and the delay of the decoder. Is it better or worse than the three-stage design? Is the difference significant?

[15]   **2-4**   The critical path for the middle units of the arbitration circuit in Figure 2.6 is from C_{i-1} to C_i. This suggests that the sizes of the gates associated with R_i and G_i can be made as small as we wish, for example, $w = z = 1$. Is this a good idea? Why or why not?

[10]   **2-5**   The design in Figure 2.6 uses a NAND gate in each stage. Why not use a NOR gate?

[25]   **2-6**   The design in Figure 2.6 uses some rather large transistors. Suppose that the largest inverter or logic gate you may use has an input capacitance of 30 units. How fast a design can you obtain?

[30]   **2-7**   Suppose you are told to design an arbitration circuit like the ones described in Section 2.3, with the requirement that its overall delay be no more than 60 units. Which structure would you choose? Show a detailed design.

Deriving the Method of Logical Effort — 3

The method of logical effort follows directly from a simple model of logic gates in which delays result from charging and discharging capacitors through resistors. The capacitors model transistor gates and stray capacitances; the resistors model networks of transistors connected between the power supply voltages and the output of a logic gate. The derivations presented in this chapter provide a physical basis for the following notions:

- The logical effort, electrical effort, and parasitic delay are parameters of a linear equation that gives the delay in a logic gate.

- The least delay along a path of logic gates is obtained when each logic gate bears the same effort.

- The number of stages to use in a path for least delay can be computed knowing only the effort along the path and, remarkably, the parasitic delay of an inverter.

- The extra delay incurred by using the wrong number of stages is small unless the error in the number of stages is large.

These results validate the method of logical effort.

3.1 —— Model of a Logic Gate

An electrical model that approximates the behavior of a single static CMOS logic gate is shown in Figure 3.1. The figure shows an input signal loaded by a capacitance C_{in}, the capacitance of the transistor gates connected to the input terminal. The voltages on the input terminals, of which only one is shown in the figure, determine which transistors will conduct and which will not. If the upper switch conducts, it connects the output of the logic gate to the positive power supply, through a *pullup* resistance R_{ui} that models the resistance of the pullup network of transistors that conduct current from the positive supply to the output terminal. Alternatively, the bottom switch may conduct, connecting the output of the logic gate to ground through a *pulldown* resistance R_{di}. The output of the logic gate is loaded by two capacitances: C_{pi}, a parasitic capacitance associated with components of the logic gate itself; and a load capacitance C_{out} that represents the load presented to the logic gate by the input capacitance of

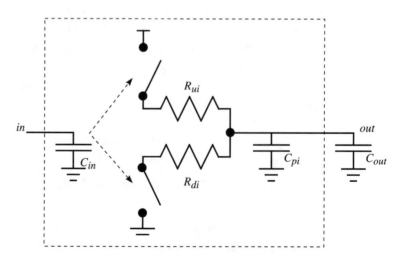

Figure 3.1 — Conceptual model of a CMOS logic gate, showing only one input. The output is driven HIGH or LOW through a resistor.

logic gates it drives and by the stray capacitance of the wiring connected to the gate's output terminal.

The logic gate is modeled by the four quantities C_{in}, R_{ui}, R_{di}, and C_{pi}, which are related in various ways depending on the particular logic function, the performance of the transistors in the CMOS process used, and so on. Because we are interested in choosing transistor sizes to obtain minimum delay, we shall view a logic gate as a scaled version of a *template circuit*. To obtain a particular logic gate, we scale the widths of all transistors in the template by a factor α. The template will have input capacitance C_t, equal pullup and pulldown resistances R_t, and parasitic capacitance C_{pt}. Thus the four quantities in the model are related to corresponding template properties and the scale factor α:

$$C_{in} = \alpha C_t \tag{3.1}$$

$$R_i = R_{ui} = R_{di} = \frac{R_t}{\alpha} \tag{3.2}$$

$$C_{pi} = \alpha C_{pt} \tag{3.3}$$

Scaling the template changes the widths of all transistors by the factor α, leaving the transistor lengths unchanged. Scaling a transistor's width increases its gate capacitance by the scale factor, but decreases its resistance by the scale factor. The relationships shown in these equations also reflect an assumption that the pullup and pulldown resistances are equal, so as to obtain equal rise and fall times when the output of the logic gate changes. This restriction makes circuits slightly slower overall; it will be relaxed in Chapter 7.

The model shown in Figure 3.1 relates easily to the design of an inverter, such as the template shown in Figure 3.2. Figure 3.1 models the n-type pulldown

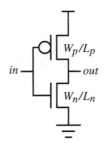

Figure 3.2 — A design for an inverter. The transistors are labeled with the ratio of the width to length of the transistor.

transistor, with width W_n and length L_n, by the switch and resistor R_{di} that form a path from the output to ground. The switch and resistor R_{ui} that form a path to the positive power supply model, the p-type transistor, with width W_p and length L_p. The capacitance formed by the gates of both transistors, which is proportional to the area of the transistor gates, loads the input signal:

$$C_t = \kappa_1 W_n L_n + \kappa_1 W_p L_p \qquad (3.4)$$

where κ_1 is a constant that depends on the fabrication process. The resistances are determined by:

$$1/R_t = \frac{\kappa_2 \mu_n W_n}{L_n} = \frac{\kappa_2 \mu_p W_p}{L_p} \qquad (3.5)$$

where κ_2 is a constant that depends on the fabrication process, and the μ's characterize the relative mobilities of carriers in n- and p-type transistors. Note that this equation implies a constraint on the design of the inverter template to ensure that pullup and pulldown resistances are equal, namely, $\mu_n W_n / L_n = \mu_p W_p / L_p$.

The model of Figure 3.1 also relates easily to logic gates other than inverters. Each input is loaded by the capacitance of the transistor gates it drives. The circuit of the logic gate is a network of source-to-drain connections of transistors such that the output of the logic gate can be connected either to the power supply or to ground, depending on the voltages present on the input signals that control the transistors in the network. The pullup and pulldown resistances shown in the model are the effective resistances of the network when the pullup or pulldown path is active. We shall defer until Chapter 4 a detailed analysis of popular logic gates and their correspondence to the model.

3.2 ———— Delay in a Logic Gate

The delay in a logic gate modeled by Figure 3.1 is just the RC delay associated with charging and discharging the capacitance attached to the output node:

$$d_{abs} = \kappa R_i (C_{out} + C_{pi}) \qquad (3.6)$$

$$= \kappa \left(\frac{R_t}{\alpha} \right) C_{in} \left(\frac{C_{out}}{C_{in}} \right) + \kappa \left(\frac{R_t}{\alpha} \right) (\alpha C_{pt})$$

$$= (\kappa R_t C_t) \left(\frac{C_{out}}{C_{in}} \right) + \kappa R_t C_{pt} \qquad (3.7)$$

where κ is a constant characteristic of the fabrication process that relates RC time constants to delay. The third equation follows from the first by rearranging terms and substituting values for R_i, C_{in}, and C_{pi} obtained from Equations 3.1 to 3.3. It is a characteristic of our formulation that the scale factor α is absent in the final form; it is hidden in C_{in}.

We can rewrite Equation 3.7 to obtain the key equations of logical effort:

$$d_{abs} = \tau(gh + p) \tag{3.8}$$

$$\tau = \kappa R_{inv} C_{inv} \tag{3.9}$$

$$g = \frac{R_t C_t}{R_{inv} C_{inv}} \tag{3.10}$$

$$h = \frac{C_{out}}{C_{in}} \tag{3.11}$$

$$p = \frac{R_t C_{pt}}{R_{inv} C_{inv}} \tag{3.12}$$

where C_{inv} is the input capacitance of the inverter template, and R_{inv} is the resistance of the pullup or pulldown transistor in the inverter template.

Equation 3.8 gives the delay of a logic gate in terms of logical effort g, electrical effort h, and parasitic delay p. This equation expresses absolute delay, unlike its counterpart, Equation 1.5, where delay is measured in *delay units*. Absolute delay and delay units are related by the time, τ, that is characteristic of the fabrication process. It is the delay of an ideal inverter with electrical effort of 1 and no parasitic delay. With more accurate transistor models and a reformulation of Equation 3.6, we could develop an analytic value for τ, expressed in terms of transistor length and width, gate oxide thickness, mobility, and other process parameters. We shall use an alternative approach, extracting the value of τ from suitable test circuits (see Section 5.1).

The logical effort, given by Equation 3.10, is determined by the circuit topology of the template for the logic gate, and is independent of the scale factor α. In effect, the logical effort compares the characteristic RC time constant of a logic gate with that of an inverter. Note that we choose the logical effort of an inverter to be 1.

The electrical effort, defined by Equation 3.11, is just the ratio of the load capacitance of the logic gate to the capacitance of a particular input. This is the same as the definition in Equation 1.4. Observe that the size of the transistors used in the logic gate influences the electrical effort, because it determines the gate's input capacitance. This is the only remnant of the scale factor α.

Finally, Equation 3.12 defines the parasitic delay of the logic gate. Because this equation is independent of the logic gate's scale α it represents a fixed delay associated with the operation of the gate, irrespective of its size or load. Observe that for an inverter, the parasitic delay p is the ratio of the parasitic capacitance to the input capacitance.

The linear relationship between delay and load expressed in Equation 3.8 is a more general result than the formulation of our model might suggest. Although our derivation has assumed that transistors behave like resistors, we would obtain the same linear relationship if we had assumed that transistors are current sources. In fact, our result is correct for any model of transistor behavior that combines a current source and a resistor, and thus handles both the linear and saturated regions of transistor behavior. If we use a resistor model of transistors, their output current follows an exponential waveform that distorts only by stretching linearly in time for different values of capacitance and transistor width. If we use a current source model of the transistors, their output current follows a sawtooth waveform that also distorts only by stretching in time for different values of capacitance and width.

Actually, Equation 3.8 requires only that delay grow linearly with load and diminish linearly as the widths of transistors are scaled. The exponential behavior of the output voltage in the simple model is described by a differential equation relating the rate of change of output voltage to the value of the output voltage. As the output voltage approaches its final value, its rate of change decreases because of the smaller current provided by the resistors. If any of the parameters we have assumed to be constant vary instead with output voltage, the differential equation becomes more complex, but its solution retains the same character. For example, if the capacitance of the transistor gates that form the driven load depends on their voltage, as it really does, the behavior of the output voltage will depart from exponential, but it will not change its general character. Similarly, if the current through the transistors depends on their drain-to-source voltage, as it really does, the behavior of the output voltage will be distorted from exponential, but again will not change its general character.

Some effects that the model ignores have little effect on its application to the method of logical effort. One of the most important is the variation in output current because of different input gate voltages, which leads to variations in the delay of a logic gate due to different rise times of input signals. Long input rise times increase the delay of the logic gate because the pullup and pulldown networks are not switched fully on or off while the input voltage is near the switching threshold. If all rise times are equal, our simple model again holds because all logic gates will exhibit identical charging current waveforms and thus the same output voltage waveforms. Because the method of logical effort leads to nearly equal rise times by equalizing effort borne by all logic gates, we are justified in omitting rise time effects from Equation 3.8.

Further evidence to support the model is obtained from detailed circuit simulations, described in Section 5.1. Although the delay model is very simple, it is quite accurate when suitably calibrated. It is, indeed, the basis of models used by most static timing analyzers.

3.3 —— Minimizing Delay along a Path

The delay model for a single logic gate leads to a method for minimizing the delay in a sequence of logic gates connected in series. The key result is that path delay is minimized when the effort borne by each logic gate along the path is the same.

Consider the two-stage path in Figure 3.3. The path's input capacitance is C_1, the input capacitance of the first stage. Capacitance C_3 loads the second stage. According to Equation 3.8, the total delay, measured in units of τ, is

$$D = (g_1 h_1 + p_1) + (g_2 h_2 + p_2) \qquad (3.13)$$

While the logical efforts g_1 and g_2 and parasitic delays p_1 and p_2 in this equation are fixed, the electrical efforts in each stage can be adjusted to minimize the

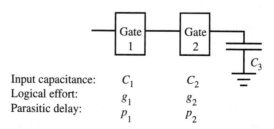

Input capacitance:	C_1	C_2
Logical effort:	g_1	g_2
Parasitic delay:	p_1	p_2

Figure 3.3 — Generic two-stage path.

delay. The electrical efforts are constrained, however, by the input capacitance C_1 and the load capacitance C_3, which are fixed:

$$h_1 = \frac{C_2}{C_1}$$

$$h_2 = \frac{C_3}{C_2}$$

and because the branching effort is 1:

$$h_1 h_2 = \frac{C_3}{C_1} = H$$

The path electrical effort H is a given constant that we cannot adjust. Substituting $h_2 = H/h_1$ into Equation 3.13, we obtain

$$D = (g_1 h_1 + p_1) + \left(\frac{g_2 H}{h_1} + p_2 \right) \tag{3.14}$$

To minimize D, we take the partial derivative with respect to the only variable h_1, set the result equal to zero, and solve for h_1:

$$\frac{\partial D}{\partial h_1} = g_1 - \frac{g_2 H}{h_1^2} = 0 \tag{3.15}$$

$$g_1 h_1 = g_2 h_2 \tag{3.16}$$

Thus, delay is minimized when each stage bears the same effort, which is the product of the logical effort and the electrical effort. This result is independent of the scale of the circuits and of the parasitic delays. It does not say that the delays in the two stages will be equal—the delays will differ if the parasitic delays differ.

This result generalizes to paths with any number of stages (Exercise 3-3) and to paths that include branching effort. The fastest design always equalizes effort in each stage.

Let us now see how to compute the effort in each stage. We have for a path of length N:

$$h_1 h_2 \cdots h_N = BH \tag{3.17}$$

where the path electrical effort H is the ratio of the load on the last stage to the input capacitance of the first stage, and the branching effort B is the product of the branching efforts at each stage. Define the path logical effort to be

$$g_1 g_2 \cdots g_N = G \tag{3.18}$$

Multiplying these two equations together, we obtain the path effort F:

$$(g_1 h_1)(g_2 h_2) \cdots (g_N h_N) = GBH = F \tag{3.19}$$

To obtain minimum delay, the N factors on the left must be equal, so that each stage bears the same effort $\hat{f} = gh$. Thus the equation can be rewritten as:

$$\hat{f}^N = F \tag{3.20}$$

or

$$\hat{f} = F^{1/N} \tag{3.21}$$

Given G, B, H, and N for the path, we can compute F and therefore the stage effort $\hat{f}$ that achieves least delay. (Recall that our notation places a hat over a quantity chosen to achieve least path delay.) Now we can solve for the electrical effort h_i of each stage: $h_i = \hat{f}/g_i$. To calculate transistor sizes, we work backward or forward along the path, choosing transistor sizes to obtain the required electrical effort in each stage. This is the procedure outlined in Section 1.3.

The path delay obtained by this optimization procedure is

$$\hat{D} = \sum (g_i h_i + p_i) = NF^{1/N} + P \tag{3.22}$$

Although the parasitic delays do not affect the procedure for designing the path to obtain least delay, they do affect the actual delay obtained. We will see in the next section that parasitic delay also influences the best number of stages in a path.

3.4 — Choosing the Length of a Path

Although equalizing the effort borne by each stage in a path minimizes delay for a given path, the delay can sometimes be reduced further by adjusting the number of stages in the path. This optimization is also a straightforward result of our delay model.

Consider a path of logic gates containing n_1 stages, to which we append n_2 additional inverters to obtain a path with a total of $N = n_1 + n_2$ stages. Let us assume that we may alter the original n_1 stages only by scaling because they perform necessary logic functions, but we may alter the number n_2 of inverters if necessary to reduce delay. Although preserving the correct logic function requires adding only an even number of inverters, we will assume that changes to the logic function could accommodate an odd number of inverters. We will assume that the path effort $F = GBH$ is known: the logical and branching efforts are properties of the n_1 logic stages that will not be altered by adding inverters, and the electrical effort is determined by the input and load capacitances required.

The minimum delay of the N stages is the sum of the delay in the logic stages and in the inverter stages:

$$\hat{D} = NF^{1/N} + \left(\sum_{i=1}^{n_1} p_i \right) + (N - n_1)p_{inv} \qquad (3.23)$$

The first term is the delay obtained by distributing effort equally among the N stages, as shown in the preceding section. The second term is the parasitic delay of the logic stages, and the third term is the parasitic delay of the inverters. Differentiating this expression with respect to N and setting the result to zero, we obtain

$$\frac{\partial \hat{D}}{\partial N} = -F^{1/N} \ln(F^{1/N}) + F^{1/N} + p_{inv} = 0 \qquad (3.24)$$

Let us define the solution to this equation to be $\hat{N}$, the number of stages to use to obtain least delay. If we define $\rho = F^{1/\hat{N}}$ to be the effort borne by each stage when the number of stages is chosen to minimize delay, the solution of the equation can be expressed as:

$$p_{inv} + \rho(1 - \ln \rho) = 0 \qquad (3.25)$$

In other words, the fastest design is one in which each stage along a path bears an effort equal to ρ, where ρ is a solution of Equation 3.25. Thus we call ρ the *best stage effort*.

It is important to understand the relationship between ρ and $\hat{f}$, both of which appear to specify the stage effort required to achieve least delay. The expressions for $\hat{f}$, such as Equation 3.21, determine the best stage effort when the number of stages, N, is known. By contrast, the value ρ, which is a constant independent of the properties of a path, represents the stage effort that will result when a path uses the number of stages required to achieve least delay.

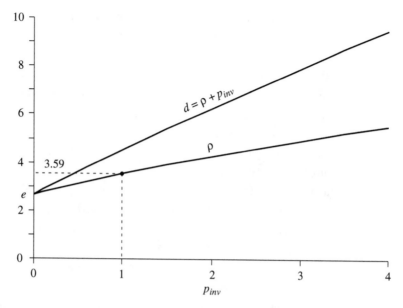

Figure 3.4 — Best effort per stage, ρ, and corresponding best stage delay $\rho + p_{inv}$, as a function of p_{inv}. Calculated from Equation 3.25.

Equation 3.25 shows that the best effort, ρ, is a function of the parasitic delay of an inverter. This result has an intuitive explanation. The stray capacitance of the logic gates in the network is fixed—you can't do much about it, and it simply adds a fixed delay to the path. Adjusting the sizes of the logic gates will change their effort delay, but not the delay contribution due to their parasitic delay. When you add an inverter as a gain element in the hope of speeding up the circuit, you need to know its actual delay, including parasitic contributions, to compare the delay of the extra inverter to the improvement in delay of the rest of the circuit. As p_{inv} grows, adding inverters becomes less advantageous because their extra stray load blunts the improvement they might otherwise offer. Therefore, the best number of stages diminishes.

Although Equation 3.25 has no closed-form solution, it is not hard to solve for values of ρ given values of p_{inv}. Figure 3.4 shows the solution as a function of an inverter's parasitic delay. Note that if we assume that the parasitic delay of an inverter is zero, then $\rho = e = 2.718$; this is the familiar result when parasitic delay is ignored [7]. Although Equation 3.25 is nonlinear, the equation

$$\rho \approx 0.71 p_{inv} + 2.82 \qquad (3.26)$$

fits it well over the range of reasonable inverter parasitics. For most of our examples, we shall assume that $p_{inv} = 1.0$ and thus that $\rho = 3.59$.

The quantity ρ is sometimes called the *best step-up ratio*, because it is the ratio of the sizes of successive inverters in a string of inverters designed to drive a large capacitive load. Figure 3.4 shows the stage delay obtained when the best step-up ratio is used. From Equation 3.8, the stage delay is the sum of the effort and the parasitic delay.

Actual designs will require us to choose a step-up ratio that differs somewhat from ρ because the design must use an integral number of stages. Given the path effort F, we must find the number of stages $\hat{N}$ that gives the least delay; this result will have a stage delay close to ρ. Table 3.1 shows how to select $\hat{N}$, given the effort F and several values of the parasitic delay of an inverter. The values of F in the table satisfy $\hat{N}(F^{1/\hat{N}} + p_{inv}) = (\hat{N} + 1)(F^{1/(\hat{N}+1)} + p_{inv})$. These are the values of path effort for which the best $\hat{N}$-stage design exhibits just as much delay as the best $(\hat{N} + 1)$-stage design.

Some designs fail to speed up when inverters are added. For example, if the path effort is 10 and there are three stages of logic, the logic network already has more stages than the optimum, which is two stages. In this case, consolidating the three stages of logic into two may result in a speedup.

Equations 3.20 and 3.21 allow us to derive equations that approximate the number of stages and delays when F is large. Using the fact that $F = \rho^{\hat{N}}$, we find

$$\hat{N} \approx \frac{\ln F}{\ln \rho} = \log_\rho F \tag{3.27}$$

$$\hat{D} \approx \hat{N}\rho + \sum p_i \tag{3.28}$$

As the effort gets large, we see that the stage delay approaches $\rho + p$. For an inverter chain, these two equations combine to read

$$\hat{D} \approx \frac{\ln F}{\ln \rho}(\rho + p_{inv}) \tag{3.29}$$

When a stage effort of 4 is used, this reduces to $\hat{D} = \log_4 F$ fanout-of-4 (FO4) inverter delays, where an FO4 delay is 5τ. We will see in the next section that delay is almost independent of stage effort for stage efforts near optimal, so this delay formula is a good estimate of the delay of an inverter chain using any reasonable stage effort. Moreover, it is a handy estimate of the delay of any circuit

Table 3.1 — Table of ranges of path effort F and the best number of stages $\hat{N}$.

$\hat{N}$	$p_{inv} = 0.0$	$p_{inv} = 0.6$	$p_{inv} = 0.8$	$p_{inv} = 1.0$
	0	0	0	0
1				
	4.0	5.13	5.48	5.83
2				
	11.4	17.7	20.0	22.3
3				
	31.6	59.4	70.4	82.2
4				
	86.7	196	245	300
5				
	237	647	848	1090
6				
	648	2130	2930	3920
7				
	1770	6980	10100	14200
8				
	4820	22900	34700	51000
9				
	13100	74900	120000	184000

with path effort F. Paths with more complex gates will have higher parasitics, but effort delay usually dominates, which makes the estimate useful for quickly comparing different circuit topologies by computing only the path effort. Finally, FO4 delays are a useful way to express delay in a process-independent way because most designers know the delay of an FO4 inverter in their process and can therefore estimate how your circuit will scale to their process.

3.5 —— Using the Wrong Number of Stages

It is interesting to ask how much worse the delay for a properly optimized circuit gets if we use the wrong number of stages. The answer, as shown in Figure 3.5, is that delay is quite insensitive to the number of stages, provided the deviation from optimum is not too large.

To develop the curve in the figure, we start by assuming that the number of stages is wrong by a factor s, that is, the number of stages is $s\hat{N}$, where $\hat{N}$ is the best number to use. The delay can be expressed as a function of N:

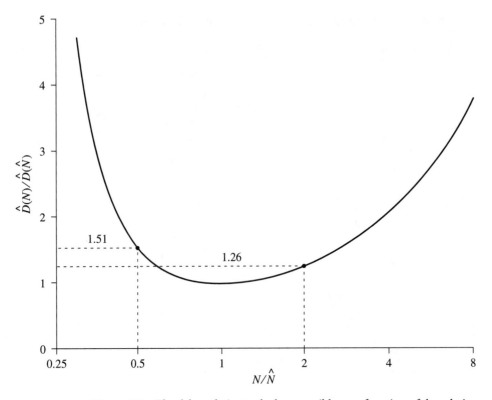

Figure 3.5 — The delay relative to the best possible, as a function of the relative error in the number of stages used, $N/\hat{N}$. Assumes $p_{inv} = 1$.

$$D(N) = N(F^{1/N} + p) \tag{3.30}$$

where we assume the parasitic delay of each stage is the same. Let r be the ratio of the delay when using $s\hat{N}$ stages to the delay when using the best number of stages, $\hat{N}$:

$$r = \frac{D(s\hat{N})}{D(\hat{N})} \tag{3.31}$$

Since $\hat{N}$ is best, we know that $F = \rho^{\hat{N}}$. Solving for r, we obtain

$$r = \frac{s(\rho^{1/s} + p)}{\rho + p} \tag{3.32}$$

This is the relationship plotted in Figure 3.5 for $p = 1$ and thus $\rho = 3.59$.

As the graph shows, doubling the number of stages from optimum increases the delay only 26%. Using half as many stages as the optimum increases the delay 51%. Thus we should not slavishly stick to exactly the correct number of stages, and it is slightly better to err in the direction of using more stages than the optimum. A stage or two more or less in a design with many stages will make little difference, provided proper transistor sizes are used. Only in designs with very few stages does a change of one or two stages make a large difference.

A designer often faces the problem of deciding whether it would be beneficial to change the number of stages in an existing circuit. Calculating the stage effort quickly reveals any potential benefit. If the effort is between 2 and 8, the design is within 35% of best delay. If the effort is between 2.4 and 6, the design is within 15% of best delay. Therefore, there is little benefit in modifying a circuit unless the stage effort is grossly high or low. It is easy for a CAD system to compute the stage effort of each gate and flag those outside the reasonable range.

Targeting a stage effort of 4 is convenient because 4 is a round number and it is easy to compute the desired number of stages mentally. For values of p_{inv} between 0.7 and 2.5, a stage effort of 4 produces delays within 2% of minimum.

A final reason to avoid excessively large stage efforts is that gates with such large efforts have very slow rise and fall times. In submicron processes, such gates are susceptible to "hot electron" problems, in which energetic electrons are blasted into the gate oxide and gradually change the transistor threshold voltages until the circuit fails. The greatest damage occurs to NMOS transistors in saturation. The transistors remain in saturation for the longest time when the input rise time or output fall time are slow. Customers get cranky when components fail after several years in the field, so designers usually keep stage efforts below about 8–12, depending on their process and supply voltage, to obtain acceptable edge rates [5].

3.6 —— Using the Wrong Gate Size

It is also interesting to ask how much worse the delay for a properly optimized circuit gets if some of the gates are the wrong size. For example, a standard cell library has only a discrete set of gate sizes, so it is not always possible to use exactly the desired size.

Consider the effect of missizing a stage in a string of inverters. The string in Figure 3.6 has a best stage effort of 4, but the middle inverter is missized so that

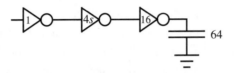

Figure 3.6—A string of inverters with a missized middle stage.

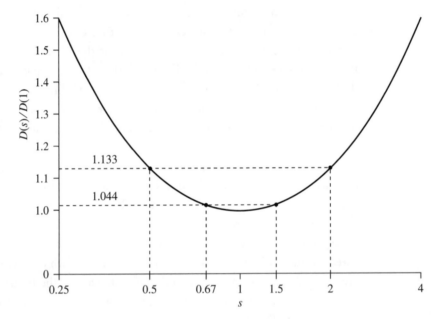

Figure 3.7—The relative delay compared to the best possible, as a function of s, the size error of a stage. Assumes $p_{inv} = 1$.

it has an actual stage effort of $4/s$ while the predecessor has an actual stage effort of $4s$.

Figure 3.7 plots the delay of the string relative to the best possible delay, as a function of s. The figure shows that for values of s from 0.5 to 2, the actual delay is within 15% of minimum, and for values of s from 2/3 to 1.5, the actual delay is within 5% of minimum. Therefore, the designer has a great deal of freedom to select gate sizes different from those specified by the logical effort computation. This is the reason that standard cell libraries with a limited repertoire of gate sizes can achieve acceptable performance.

Because minor errors in gate sizes have almost no effect on overall delay, a designer can save time by making "back-of-the-envelope" calculations of sizes to one or two significant figures [8]. With practice, most logical effort calculations can be done mentally.

3.7 ——— Summary

This chapter has presented all of the major results of the method of logical effort. These are summarized as follows:

- The absolute delay in a single logic gate is modeled as

$$d = \tau(gh + p) \tag{3.33}$$

The next chapter shows how to estimate or measure the logical effort and parasitic delay of logic gates for a particular fabrication process, and how to measure τ.

- A path has least delay when each logic gate bears the same effort. This result leads to the equation for delay along a path:

$$D = NF^{1/N} + \sum p_i \tag{3.34}$$

where F is the path effort.

- Delay along a path is least when each stage bears effort ρ, a quantity calculated from the parasitic delay of an inverter (Equation 3.25 and Figure 3.6). This in turn determines the best number of stages to use, for any path effort (Table 3.1). In practice, the stage effort deviates slightly from ρ because the number of stages, N, must be an integer.

- A good approximation for ρ is 4. Any stage effort from 2 to 8 gives reasonable results, and any value from 2.4 to 6 gives nearly optimal results, so you can be sloppy about sizing and still have a good design.

- You can estimate the delay of a path from the path effort as $\log_4 F$ FO4 inverter delays.

3.8 ——— Exercises

[25] **3-1** Show that modeling transistors as current sources leads to the same basic results (Equations 3.8 through 3.12).

[30] **3-2** Using process parameters from your favorite CMOS process, estimate values for κ and τ.

[30] **3-3** Generalize the result of Section 3.3 to show that the least delay in a path of N stages results when all stages bear the same effort.

[20] **3-4** One impediment to scaling each stage precisely is the resolution of widths supported by the lithographic equipment used in fabrication. Suppose the process could support only three distinct widths of each transistor type (n and p), but that you could choose these widths. What would you choose? How might you get the effect of widths greater than those chosen?

[15] **3-5** If a logic string must be increased in length, extra inverters can be added either before or after the logic gates, or between them. What practical considerations would cause you to choose one location over the other?

Calculating the Logical —————— 4
Effort of Gates

The simplicity of the theory of logical effort follows from assigning to each kind of logic gate a number—its logical effort—that describes its drive capability relative to that of a reference inverter. The logical effort is independent of the actual size of the logic gate, allowing us to postpone detailed calculations of transistor sizes until after we finish the logical effort analysis.

Two quantities characterize each logic gate: its logical effort and its parasitic delay. We can determine these parameters in three ways:

- Using a few process parameters, we can estimate logical effort and parasitic delay as described in this chapter. The results are sufficiently accurate for most design work.

- Using test circuit simulations, we can estimate the logical effort and parasitic delay of various logic gates. This technique is explained in Chapter 5.

- Using fabricated test structures, we can physically measure logical effort and parasitic delay.

Before turning to methods of calculating logical effort, we present a discussion of different definitions and interpretations of logical effort. While these are all equivalent, in some sense, each offers a different perspective to the design task and each leads to different intuitions.

4.1 —— Definitions of Logical Effort

Logical effort captures enough information about a logic gate's topology—the network of transistors that connect the gate's output to the power supply and to ground—to determine the delay of the logic gate. Here are three equivalent concrete definitions of logical effort.

DEFINITION 4.1   The logical effort of a logic gate is defined as the number of times worse it is at delivering output current than would be an inverter with identical input capacitance.

Any topology required to perform logic makes a logic gate less able to deliver output current than an inverter with identical input capacitance. At the very least, a logic gate must have more transistors than an inverter, and so to maintain equal input capacitance, its transistors must be narrower on average and thus less able to conduct current than those of an inverter with identical input capacitance. If its topology requires transistors in parallel, a conservative estimate of its performance will assume that not all of them conduct at once, and therefore that they will not deliver as much current as could an inverter with identical input capacitance. If its topology requires transistors in series, it cannot possibly deliver as much current as could an inverter with identical input capacitance. Whatever the topology of a simple logic gate, its ability to deliver output current must be worse than an inverter with identical input capacitance. Logical effort is a measure of how much worse.

DEFINITION 4.2   The logical effort of a logic gate is defined as the ratio of its input capacitance to that of an inverter that delivers equal output current.

This alternative definition is useful for computing the logical effort of a particular topology. To compute the logical effort of a logic gate, pick transistor sizes for it that make it as good at delivering output current as a standard inverter, and then tally up the input capacitance of each input terminal. The ratio of this input capacitance to that of the standard inverter is the logical effort of that input to the logic gate. The logical effort of a logic gate will depend slightly on the mobility ratio in the fabrication process used to build it. These calculations appear in detail later in this chapter.

DEFINITION 4.3   The logical effort of a logic gate is defined as the slope of the gate's delay vs. fanout curve divided by the slope of an inverter's delay vs. fanout curve.

This alternative definition suggests an easy way to measure the logical effort of any particular logic gate by experiments with real or simulated circuits of various fanouts.

4.2 —— Grouping Input Signals

Because logical effort relates the input capacitance to the output drive current available, a natural question arises: for a logic gate with multiple inputs, how many of the input signals should we consider when computing logical effort? It is useful to define several kinds of logical effort, depending on how input signals are grouped. In each case, we define an *input group* to contain the input signals that are relevant to the computation of logical effort:

- Logical effort *per input*, in which logical effort measures the effectiveness of a single input in controlling output current. The input group is the single input in question. All of the discussion in preceding chapters uses logical effort per input.

- Logical effort of a *bundle*, a group of related inputs. For example, a multiplexer requires true and complement select signals; this pair might be grouped into a bundle. Because bundles of complementary pairs of signals occur frequently in CMOS circuits, we adopt a special notation: $s*$ stands for a bundle containing the true signal s and the complement signal $\bar{s}$. The input group of a bundle contains all the signals in the bundle.

- *Total* logical effort, the logical effort of all inputs taken together. The input group contains all the input signals of the logic gate.

Terminology and context determine which kind of logical effort applies. We always use the adjective "total" when we mean total logical effort, while we distinguish the other two cases by the signals associated with them in context. "The total logical effort of a two-input NAND gate" is the logical effort of both inputs taken together, while "the logical effort of a two-input NAND gate" is the logical effort per input of one of its two inputs.

We define the logical effort of an input group analogously to the logical effort per input, shown in the previous section. The analog of Definition 4.2 is: the logical effort g_b of an input group b is just

$$g_b = \frac{C_b}{C_{inv}} = \frac{\sum_b C_i}{C_{inv}} \tag{4.1}$$

where C_b is the combined input capacitance of every signal in the input group b, and C_{inv} is the input capacitance of an inverter designed to have the same drive capabilities as the logic gate whose logical effort we are calculating.

A consequence of Equation 4.1 is that the logical efforts associated with input groups sum in a straightforward way. The total logical effort is the sum of the logical effort per input of every input to the logic gate. The logical effort of a bundle is the sum of the logical effort per input of every signal in the bundle. Thus a logic gate can be viewed as having a certain total logical effort that can be allocated to its inputs according to their contribution to the gate's input capacitance.

4.3 ———— Calculating Logical Effort

Definition 4.2 provides a convenient method for calculating the logical effort of a logic gate. We have but to design a gate that has the same current drive characteristics as a reference inverter, calculate the input capacitances of each signal, and apply Equation 4.1 to obtain the logical effort.

Because we compute the logical effort as a ratio of capacitances, the units we use to measure capacitance may be arbitrary. This observation simplifies the calculations enormously. First, assume that all transistors are of minimum length, so that a transistor's size is completely captured by its width, w. The capacitance of the transistor's gate is proportional to w, and its ability to produce output current, or conductance, is also proportional to w. In most CMOS processes, pullup transistors must be wider than pulldown transistors to have the same conductance. $\mu = \mu_n/\mu_p$ is the ratio of PMOS to NMOS width in an inverter for equal conductance. Because circuit designers often depart from this ideal ratio, we use another symbol γ to denote the actual ratio of PMOS to NMOS widths in an inverter. For simplicity, we will often assume that $\gamma = \mu = 2$. Under this

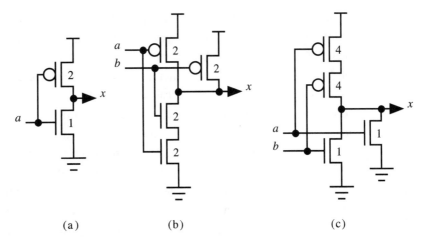

Figure 4.1 — Simple gates: the reference inverter (a), a two-input NAND gate (b), and a two-input NOR gate (c).

assumption, an inverter will have a pulldown transistor of width w and a pullup transistor of width $2w$, as shown in Figure 4.1(a), so the total input capacitance can be said to be $3w$. In this chapter, we will also find general expressions for logical effort as a function of γ. In Chapter 7, we will consider the benefits of choosing $\gamma \neq \mu$.

Let us now design a two-input NAND gate so that it has the same drive characteristics as an inverter with a pulldown of width 1 and a pullup of width 2. Figure 4.1(b) shows such a NAND gate. Because the two pulldown transistors of the NAND gate are in series, each must have twice the conductance of the inverter pulldown transistor so that the series connection has a conductance equal to that of the inverter pulldown transistor. Therefore, these transistors are twice as wide as the inverter pulldown transistor. This reasoning assumes that transistors in series obey Ohm's law for resistors in series. By contrast, each of the two pullup transistors in parallel need be only as large as the inverter pullup transistor to achieve the same drive as the reference inverter. Here we assume that if either input to the NAND gate is LOW, the output must be pulled HIGH, and so the output drive of the NAND gate must match that of the inverter even if only one of the two pullups conducts.

We find the logical effort of the NAND gate in Figure 4.1(b) by extracting capacitances from the circuit schematic. The input capacitance of one input signal is the sum of the width of the pulldown transistor and the pullup transistor, or $2 + 2 = 4$. The input capacitance of the inverter with identical output drive is $C_{inv} = 1 + 2 = 3$. According to Equation 4.1, the logical effort per input of the two-input NAND gate is therefore $g = 4/3$. Observe that both inputs of the NAND gate have identical logical efforts. Section 4.4 considers gates that are topologically asymmetric for which inputs inherently have different logical efforts. Chapter 6 futher considers deliberately asymmetric gate designs favoring the logical effort of one input at the expense of another.

We designed the NOR gate in Figure 4.1(c) in a similar way. To obtain the same pulldown drive as the inverter, pulldown transistors one unit wide suffice. Obtaining the same pullup drive requires transistors four units wide because two of them in series must be equivalent to one transistor two units wide in the inverter. Summing the input capacitance on one input, we find that the NOR gate has logical effort $g = 5/3$. This is larger than the logical effort of the NAND gate because pullup transistors are less effective at generating output current than pulldown transistors. Were the two types of transistors similar, that is, $\gamma = 1$, both NAND and NOR gates would both have a logical effort of 1.5.

All of the sizing calculations in this monograph compute the input capacitance of gates. This capacitance is distributed among the transistors in the gate in the same proportions as are used when computing logical effort. For example, Figure 4.2 shows an inverter, NAND, and NOR gate, each with input capacitance equal to 60 unit-sized transistors.

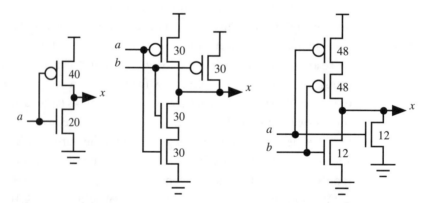

Figure 4.2 — Simple gates with input capacitance of 60 unit-sized transistors.

When designing logic gates to produce the same output drive as the reference inverter, we are modeling CMOS transistors as pure resistors. If the transistor is off, the resistor has no conductance; if the transistor is on, it has a conductance proportional to its width. To determine the conductance of a transistor network, the conductances of the transistors are combined using the standard rules for calculating the conductance of a resistor network containing series and parallel resistor connections. While this model is only approximate, it characterizes logic gate performance well enough to design fast structures. More accurate values for logical effort can be obtained by simulating or measuring test circuits, as discussed in Chapter 5.

An important limitation of the model is that it does not account for velocity saturation. The velocity of carriers, and hence the current through a transistor, normally scales linearly with the electric field across the channel. When the field reaches a critical value, carrier velocity begins to saturate and no longer increases with field strength. The field across a single transistor is proportional to V_{DD}/L. In submicron processes, V_{DD} is usually scaled with L so that an NMOS transistor in an inverter is on the borderline of velocity saturation. PMOS transistors have lower mobility and thus are less prone to velocity saturation. Also, series NMOS transistors have a lower field across each transistor and therefore are less velocity saturated. Velocity saturation increases the effective resistance of all NMOS transistors, but has less of an impact on series transistors than on a single transistor. The important result to remember is that because logical effort is normalized to the resistance of a reference inverter with a single transistor, more complex gates with series NMOS transistors have slightly lower logical effort than our model predicts.

4.4 ——— Asymmetric Logic Gates

Unlike the NAND and NOR gates, not all logic gates induce the same logical effort per input for all inputs. Equal logical effort per input is a consequence of the symmetries of the logic gates we have studied thus far. In this section, we will analyze an example in which the logical effort differs for different inputs.

Figure 4.3 shows one form of and-or-invert gate with an asymmetric configuration. The transistor widths in this gate have been chosen so that the output drive matches the reference inverter in Figure 4.1(a): the pulldown structure is equivalent to a single pulldown transistor of width 1, and the pullup structure

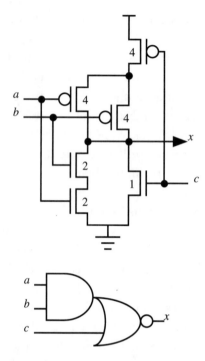

Figure 4.3 — An asymmetric and-or-invert gate.

is equivalent to a single pullup transistor of width 2. The total logical effort of the gate, computed using Equation 4.1, is 17/3.

Let's calculate the logical effort of the individual inputs of the and-or-invert gate. The logical effort per input for inputs a and b is $6/3 = 2$. The logical effort of the asymmetric input c is 5/3. The c input has a slightly lower logical effort than the other inputs, reflecting the fact that the c input presents less capacitive load than the other inputs. Input c is "easier to drive" than the other two inputs.

Asymmetries in the logical effort of inputs arise in several different ways. The and-or-invert gate is topologically asymmetric, giving rise to unequal logical efforts of its inputs. Topologically symmetric gates, such as NAND and NOR, can have unequal transistor sizes to make them asymmetric so as to reduce the logical effort on some inputs, and thus reduce the logical effort along critical paths in a network. Other gates, such as XOR, have both asymmetric and symmetric forms, as discussed in Section 4.5.4. Chapter 6 explores further the deliberate design of asymmetric gates.

4.5 —— Catalog of Logic Gates

The techniques for calculating logical effort are used in this section to develop Table 4.1, a catalog of the logical efforts of common gates. The expressions are slightly more general than those exhibited in Chapter 1 in two ways. First, the expressions apply to logic gates with an arbitrary number of inputs, n. Second, they use a parameter for the ratio of p-type to n-type transistor widths,

Table 4.1 — Summary of calculations of the logical effort of logic gates.

Gate type	Logical effort	Formula	$n = 2$ $\gamma = 2$	$n = 3$ $\gamma = 2$	$n = 4$ $\gamma = 2$
NAND	Total	$\frac{n(n+\gamma)}{1+\gamma}$	8/3	5	8
	Per input	$\frac{(n+\gamma)}{1+\gamma}$	4/3	5/3	2
NOR	Total	$\frac{n(1+n\gamma)}{1+\gamma}$	10/3	7	12
	Per input	$\frac{1+n\gamma}{1+\gamma}$	5/3	7/3	3
Multiplexer	Total	$4n$	8	12	16
	$d, s*$	2, 2	2, 2	2, 2	2, 2
XOR, XNOR, parity	Total	$n^2 2^{n-1}$	8	36	128
(symmetric)	Per bundle	$n2^{n-1}$	4	12	32
XOR, XNOR, parity	Total		8	24	48
(asymmetric)	Per bundle		4, 4	6, 12, 6	8, 16, 16, 8
Majority	Total			12	
(symmetric)	Per input			4	
Majority	Total			10	
(asymmetric)	Per input			4, 4, 2	
C-element	Total	n^2	4	9	16
	Per input	n	2	3	4
Latch	Total	4			
(dynamic)	$d, \phi*$	2, 2			
Upper bounds	Total	$\frac{\gamma n^2 2^n}{1+\gamma}$	32/3	48	512/3
	Per bundle	$\frac{\gamma n 2^n}{1+\gamma}$	16/3	16	128/3

so as to permit calculation of logical effort for gates fabricated with various CMOS processes. Whereas the reference inverter in Figure 4.1(a) has a pullup-to-pulldown width ratio of 2:1, a ratio of γ:1 is used throughout this section. Each logic gate has a pulldown drive equivalent to an n-type transistor of width 1 and a pullup drive equivalent to a p-type transistor of width γ.

4.5.1 NAND gate

A NAND gate with n inputs, designed to have the same output drive as the reference inverter, will have a series connection of pulldown transistors, each of width n, and a parallel connection of pullup transistors, each of width γ. Using Equation 4.1, the total logical effort is

$$g_{tot} = \frac{n(n + \gamma)}{1 + \gamma} \tag{4.2}$$

The logical effort per input is just $1/n$ of this value, because the input capacitance is equally distributed among the n inputs.

Table 4.1 includes the expressions for logical effort and calculations for several common cases: $\gamma = 2$, $n = 2, 3, 4$. Note from the equation that the logical effort changes only slightly for a wide range of γ: when γ ranges from 1 to 3, the total logical effort for $n = 2$ ranges from 3 to 2.5.

4.5.2 NOR gate

The n-input NOR gate consists of a parallel connection of pulldown transistors, each of width 1, and a series connection of pullup transistors, each of width $n\gamma$. The total logical effort is therefore

$$g_{tot} = \frac{n(1 + n\gamma)}{1 + \gamma} \tag{4.3}$$

Again, the logical effort per input is just $1/n$ of this value. Table 4.1 includes examples of the logical effort of a NOR gate. For CMOS processes in which $\gamma > 1$, the logical effort of a NOR gate is greater than that of a NAND gate. If the CMOS fabrication process were perfectly symmetric, so that we could choose $\gamma = 1$, then the logical effort of NAND and NOR gates would be equal.

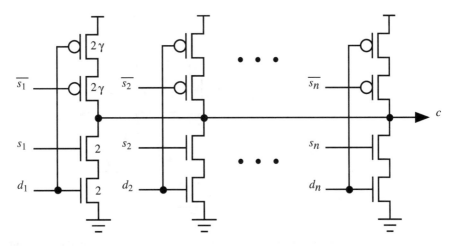

Figure 4.4 — An *n*-way multiplexer. Each arm of the multiplexer has a data input d_i and a select bundle $s*_i$.

4.5.3   Multiplexers, tristate inverters

An *n*-way inverting multiplexer appears schematically in Figure 4.4. There are *n* data inputs, $d_1 \ldots d_n$, and *n* bundles of complementary select signals, $s *_1 \ldots s*_n$. Each data input drives a four-transistor *select arm*, which in turn drives the output *c*. To select input *i*, only bundle $s*_i$ is driven TRUE, which enables current to flow through the pullup or pulldown structures in the select arm associated with d_i.

The total logical effort of a multiplexer is $n(4 + 4\gamma)/(1 + \gamma) = 4n$. The logical effort per data input is just $(2 + 2\gamma)/(1 + \gamma) = 2$, and the logical effort per select bundle is also 2. Note that the logical effort per input of a multiplexer is independent of the number of inputs. Although this property suggests that large, fast multiplexers could be built, stray capacitance in large multiplexers limits their growth. This problem is analyzed fully in Chapter 11. Also, increasing the number of multiplexer inputs tends to increase the logical effort of the select generation logic.

A single multiplexer arm is sometimes called a *tristate inverter*. When a multiplexer is distributed along a bus, the individual arms often appear separately as tristate inverters. Note that the logical efforts of the *s* and $\bar{s}$ inputs may differ.

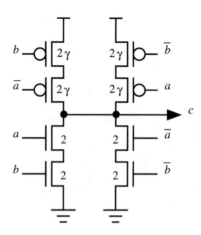

Figure 4.5 — A two-input XOR gate, with input bundles $a*$ and $b*$, and output c.

4.5.4   XOR, XNOR, and parity gates

Figure 4.5 shows an XOR gate with two inputs, $a*$ and $b*$, and output c. The gate has two bundled inputs; the $a*$ bundle contains a complementary pair a and $\bar{a}$, and the $b*$ bundle contains b and $\bar{b}$. The total logical effort of the gate is $(8 + 8\gamma)/(1 + \gamma) = 8$. The logical effort per input is just $1/4$ this amount, or 2. The logical effort per input bundle is just the sum of the logical effort per input of the two inputs in the bundle, or 4.

The structure shown in Figure 4.5 can be generalized to compute the parity of n inputs. As an example, Figure 4.6(a) shows a three-input XOR gate. The n-input gate will have 2^{n-1} pulldown chains, each with n transistors in series, each of width n. There will be 2^{n-1} pullup chains, each with n transistors in series, each of width $n\gamma$. Thus the total logical effort will be $2^{n-1}n(n + n\gamma)/(1 + \gamma) = n^2 2^{n-1}$. The logical effort per input will be $1/(2n)$ times this figure, or $n2^{n-2}$, and the logical effort per input bundle will be $1/n$ times the total logical effort, or $n2^{n-1}$.

For $n = 3$ or more, symmetric structures such as the one shown in Figure 4.6(a) fail to yield least logical effort. Figure 4.6(b) shows a way to share some of the transistors from the separate pullup and pulldown chains to reduce the logical effort. Repeating the calculation, we see that the total logical effort is 24, which is a substantial reduction from 36, the total logical effort of the symmetric structure in Figure 4.6(a). In the asymmetric version, bundles $a*$ and $c*$

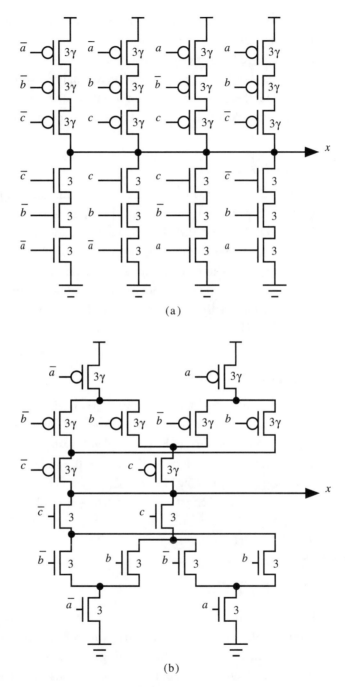

Figure 4.6—Two designs for three-input parity gates: a symmetric design (a) and an asymmetric design with reduced logical effort (b).

have a logical effort per bundle of 6. Bundle $b*$ has a logical effort of 12, which is the same as in the symmetric version because no transistors connected to b or $\bar{b}$ are shared in the asymmetric gate.

The XOR and parity gates can be altered slightly to produce an inverted output suitable for the XNOR function: simply interchange the a and $\bar{a}$ connections. Note that this transformation does not change any of the logical effort calculations.

4.5.5   Majority gate

Figure 4.7 shows two designs for an inverting three-input majority gate. Its output is LOW when two or more of its inputs are HIGH. The symmetric design is shown in Figure 4.7(a). The total logical effort is $(12 + 12\gamma)/(1 + \gamma) = 12$, distributed evenly among the inputs. The logical effort per input is therefore 4. Figure 4.7(b) shows an asymmetric design, which shares transistors as does the XOR design in Figure 4.6(b). The total logical effort of this design is 10, distributed unevenly among the inputs. Input a has a logical effort of 2, while inputs b and c each have logical efforts of 4.

4.5.6   Adder carry chain

Figure 4.8 shows one stage of a ripple-carry chain in an adder. The stage accepts carry C_{in} and delivers a carry out in inverted form on $\overline{C}_{out}$. The inputs g and $\bar{k}$ come from the two bits to be summed at this stage. The signal g is HIGH if this stage generates a new carry, forcing $\overline{C}_{out} = 0$. Similarly, $\bar{k}$ is LOW if this stage kills incoming carries, forcing $\overline{C}_{out} = 1$.

The total logical effort of this gate is $(5 + 5\gamma)/(1 + \gamma) = 5$. The logical effort per input for C_{in} is 2; for the g input it is $(1 + 2\gamma)/(1 + \gamma)$; and for the $\bar{k}$ input it is $(2 + \gamma)/(1 + \gamma)$.

4.5.7   Dynamic latch

Figure 4.9 shows a dynamic latch: when the clock signal ϕ is HIGH and its complement $\bar{\phi}$ is LOW, the gate drives its output q to the complement of the input d. The total logical effort of this gate is 4; the logical effort per input for d is 2, and the logical effort of the $\phi*$ bundle is also 2. Altering the latch to make it statically stable increases its logical effort slightly (see Exercise 4-1).

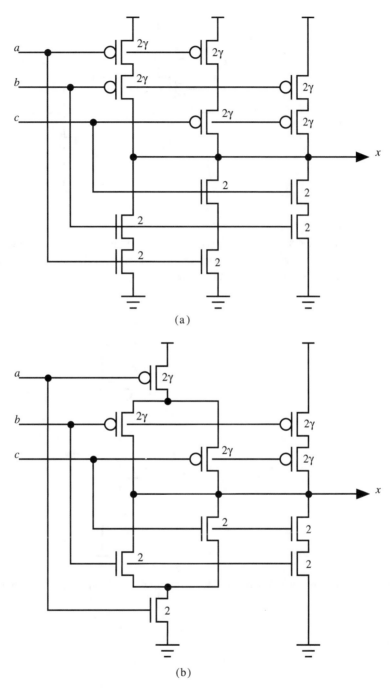

Figure 4.7 — Two designs for three-input majority gates: a symmetric design (a) and an asymmetric design with reduced logical effort (b).

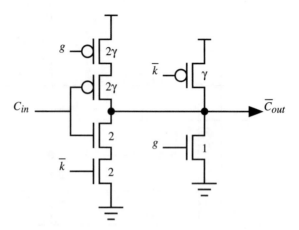

Figure 4.8—A carry propagation gate. The carry arrives on C_{in} and leaves on $\overline{C}_{out}$. The g input is HIGH if a carry is generated at this stage, and the $\overline{k}$ input is LOW if a carry is killed at this stage.

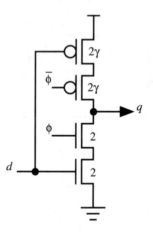

Figure 4.9—A dynamic latch with input d and output q. The clock bundle is $\phi*$.

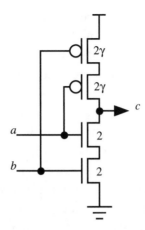

Figure 4.10—A two-input inverting dynamic Muller C-element. The inputs are a and b, and the output is c.

4.5.8   Dynamic Muller C-element

Figure 4.10 shows an inverting dynamic Muller C-element with two inputs. Although this gate is rarely seen in designs for synchronous systems, it is a staple of asynchronous system design. The behavior of the gate is as follows: When both inputs are HIGH, the output goes LOW; when both inputs are LOW, the output goes HIGH. When the inputs differ, the output retains its previous value—the C-element thus retains state. The total logical effort of this gate is 4, equally divided between the two inputs.

An n-input C-element can be formed in the obvious way, by making series pullup and pulldown chains of n transistors each. The width of a pulldown transistor is n, and the width of a pullup transistor is $n\gamma$. The total logical effort is thus $n(n + n\gamma)/(1 + \gamma) = n^2$, and the logical effort per input is just n.

4.5.9   Upper bounds on logical effort

It is easy to establish an upper bound for the logical effort of a gate with n inputs. For any truth table, construct a gate with 2^n arms, each consisting of a series connection of n transistors, each of which receives the true or complement form of a different input. For entries in the truth table that produce a LOW output, the series transistors in the corresponding arm are all n-type pulldown transistors, and the series string spans ground and the logic gate output. The transistor gates in the string receive inputs in such a way that the series connection conducts current when the input conditions for the truth table entry are met. For entries in the truth table that produce a HIGH output, the series transistors are all p-type pullups and the series string spans the positive power supply and the logic gate output. The transistor gates receive the complement of the appropriate input. To design such a gate to have the same output drive as the reference inverter, each n-type transistor must have width n, and each p-type transistor must have width γn. To compute the worst-case logical effort, assume that $\gamma \geq 1$ and inputs are connected only to p-type transistors, which are larger than n-type transistors and so offer more load. Thus the worst-case input capacitance is $\gamma n^2 2^n$, and the worst-case logical effort is therefore $\gamma n^2 2^n / (1 + \gamma)$.

This result shows that in the worst case, the logical effort of a logic gate grows exponentially with the number of inputs. These bounds are not particularly tight, and may perhaps be improved. Any improvement will hinge on reducing the number of transistors in a gate by sharing.

4.6 ——— Estimating Parasitic Delay

Calculating the parasitic delay of logic gates is not as easy as calculating logical effort. The principal contribution to the parasitic capacitance is the capacitance of the diffused regions of transistors connected to the output signal. The capacitance of these regions includes both area and perimeter terms and depends on their layout geometry and on process parameters. However, a crude approximation can be obtained by imagining that a transistor of width w has a diffused region of capacitance equal to wC_d associated with its source and an identical region associated with its drain. The constant C_d is a property of the fabrication process and the layout.

This model allows us to compute the parasitic delay of an inverter. The output signal is connected to two diffused regions: the one associated with the pulldown of width 1 will have capacitance C_d, and the one associated with the pullup of width γ will have capacitance γC_d. The input capacitance of the inverter is likewise proportional to the transistor widths, but with a different constant of proportionality characteristic of transistor gate capacitance. Thus the input capacitance is $(1 + \gamma)C_g$. The parasitic delay is the ratio of the parasitic capacitance to the input capacitance of the inverter, which is just $p_{inv} = C_d/C_g$.

Table 4.2 — Estimates of the parasitic delay of logic gates.

Gate type	Formula	Parasitic delay when $p_{inv} = 1.0$			
		$n = 1$	$n = 2$	$n = 3$	$n = 4$
NAND	np_{inv}		2	3	4
NOR	np_{inv}		2	3	4
Multiplexer	$2np_{inv}$		4	6	8
XOR, XNOR, parity	$n2^{n-1}p_{inv}$		4	12	
Majority	$6p_{inv}$			6	
C-element	np_{inv}		2	3	4
Latch	$2p_{inv}$	2			

The two constants of proportionality can be determined from layout geometry and process parameters (see Exercise 4-9). We shall adopt a nominal value of $p_{inv} = 1.0$, which is representative of inverter designs. This quantity can also be measured from test circuits, as shown in Section 5.1.

We can estimate the parasitic delay of logic gates from the inverter parameters. The delay will be greater than that of an inverter by the ratio of the total width of diffused regions connected to the output signal to the corresponding width of an inverter, provided the logic gate is designed to have the same output drive as the inverter. Thus we have

$$p = \left(\frac{\sum w_d}{1 + \gamma} \right) p_{inv} \tag{4.4}$$

where w_d is the width of transistors connected to the logic gate's output. For this estimate to apply, we assume that transistor layouts in the logic gates are similar to those in the inverter. Note that this estimate ignores other stray capacitances in a logic gate, such as contributions from wiring and from diffused regions that lie between transistors that are connected in series.

This approximation can be applied to an n-input NAND gate, which has one pulldown transistor of width n and n pullup transistors of width γ connected to the output signal, so $p = np_{inv}$. An n-input NOR gate likewise has $p = np_{inv}$. An n-way multiplexer has n pulldowns of width 2 and n pullups of width 2γ, so $p = 2np_{inv}$. Table 4.2 summarizes some of these results.

This estimate of parasitic delay has a serious limitation because it predicts that delay scales linearly with the number of inputs. In fact, the parasitic delay of a series stack of transistors increases quadratically with stack height because of internal diffusion and gate-source capacitances. The Elmore delay model [10] handles distributed RC networks and shows that stacks of more than about four series transistors are best broken up into multiple stages of shorter stacks. Because parasitics are so geometry dependent, the best way to find parasitic delay is to simulate circuits with extracted layout data. Fortunately, we select gate sizes using stage effort, which is independent of parasitic delay. Therefore, accurate parasitic delay estimates are unnecessary when applying the method of logical effort to find the best transistor sizes.

4.7 —— Properties of Logical Effort

The calculation of logical effort for a logic gate is a straightforward process:

- Design the logic gate, picking transistor sizes that make it as good a driver of output current as the reference inverter.

- The logical effort per input for a particular input is the ratio of the capacitance of that input to the total input capacitance of the reference inverter.

- The total logical effort of the gate is the sum of the logical efforts of all of its inputs.

Table 4.1 reveals a number of interesting properties. The effect of circuit topology on logical effort is generally more pronounced than the effect of fabrication technology. For CMOS with $\gamma = 2$, the total logical effort for two-input NAND and NOR gates is nearly, but not quite, three. If CMOS were exactly symmetric ($\gamma = 1$), the total logical effort for both NAND and NOR would be exactly three; the asymmetry of practical CMOS processes favors NAND gates over NOR gates.

In contrast to its weak dependence on γ, the logical effort of a gate depends strongly on the number of inputs. For example, the logical effort per input of an n-input NAND gate is $(n + \gamma)/(1 + \gamma)$, which clearly increases with n. An additional input to a NAND gate increases the logical effort of each of the existing inputs through no fault of its own. Thus the total logical effort of a NAND gate includes a term that increases as the square of the number of inputs; and in the worst case, logical effort may increase exponentially with the number of inputs. When many inputs must be combined, this nonlinear behavior forces the designer to choose carefully between single-stage logic gates with many inputs and multiple-stage trees of logic gates with fewer inputs per gate. Surprisingly, one logic gate escapes superlinear growth in logical effort—the multiplexer. This property makes it attractive for high fan-in selectors, which are analyzed in greater detail in Chapter 11.

The logical effort of gates covers a wide range. A two-input XOR gate has a total logical effort of eight, which is very large compared to the effort of NAND and NOR of about three. The XOR circuit is also messy to lay out because the gates of its transistors connect in a crisscross pattern. Are the large logical effort and the difficulty of layout related in some fundamental way? Whereas the output of most other logic functions changes only for certain transitions of the inputs, the XOR output changes for every input change. Is its large logical effort related in some way to this property?

The designs for logic gates we have shown in this chapter do not exhaust the possibilities. Chapter 6 considers logic gates with reduced logical effort for certain inputs that can lower the overall delay of a particular path through a network. Chapter 7 considers designs in which the rising and falling delays of logic gates differ, which saves space in CMOS and permits analysis with the method of logical effort of ratioed NMOS designs.

4.8 ——— Exercises

[20] **4-1** Modify the latch shown in Figure 4.9 so that its output is statically stable, even when the clock is LOW. How big should the transistors be? What is the logical effort of the new circuit?

[20] **4-2** In a fashion similar to Exercise 4-1, modify the dynamic C-element so that its output is static. How big should the transistors be? What is the logical effort of the new circuit?

[20] **4-3** Another way to construct a static C-element is shown in Figure 4.11. What relative transistor sizes should be used? What is the logical effort of the gate?

[20] **4-4** Figure 4.8 shows a carry propagation element that inverts the polarity of the carry signal. A different design will be required for stages that accept a complemented carry input and generate a true carry output. Design such a circuit and calculate the logical effort of each input.

[10] **4-5** In many CMOS processes, the ratio of pullup to pulldown conductance γ is greater than 2. How high does γ have to be before the logical effort of two-input NOR is twice that of NAND?

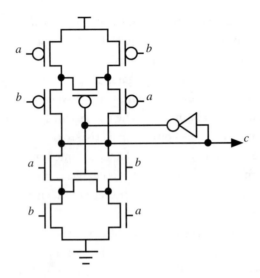

Figure 4.11—A static Muller C-element.

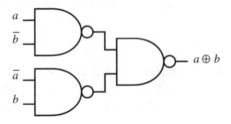

Figure 4.12—A two-stage XOR circuit.

[20]   **4-6**   The choice of transistor sizes for the inverter of Figure 4.1 was $\gamma = \mu$ to obtain equal rising and falling delays. Relax this constraint to find the value of γ as a function of μ to minimize the delay through a two-inverter pair.

[20]   **4-7**   Compare the logical effort of a two-stage XOR circuit such as the one shown in Figure 4.12 with that of the single-stage XOR of Figure 4.5. Under what circumstances is each preferable?

[25]   **4-8**   Figure 4.13 shows a design for an inverting bus driver that achieves the same effect as a tristate inverter. Compare the logical effort of the two circuits given that the ratio of NAND to NOR gate size is chosen for minimum delay. Under what circumstances is each preferable?

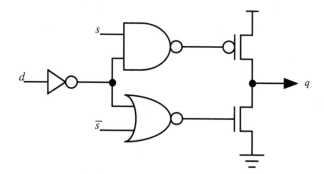

Figure 4.13 — An inverting bus driver circuit, equivalent to the function of a tristate inverter.

[25]   **4-9**   Use a simulator to find the gate and diffusion capacitances of your process. From these values, estimate p_{inv}.

g = 1.18
P = 1.36

Calibrating the Model————5

We can calculate the logical effort and parasitic delay of a logic gate from simple transistor models, as in the preceding chapter, or can obtain more accurate values by measuring the behavior of suitable test circuits. This chapter shows how to design and measure such circuits to obtain the two parameter values. The reader who wishes to skip this chapter may want to glance at Table 5.1, which summarizes the characterization of one set of test circuits.

5.1 ——Calibration Technique

We calibrate by measuring the delay of a logic gate as a function of its load— its electrical effort—and fitting a straight line to the results. Figure 5.1 shows simulated data for an inverter design. Because the logical effort of an inverter is 1, we expect from Equation 3.8 that the delay will be $d = \tau(h + p_{inv})$. The straight line that connects the points will have slope τ and will intercept the $h = 0$ axis at $d = \tau p_{inv}$. Thus the measurements yield values of $\tau = 43$ ps and $p_{inv} = 46$ ps.

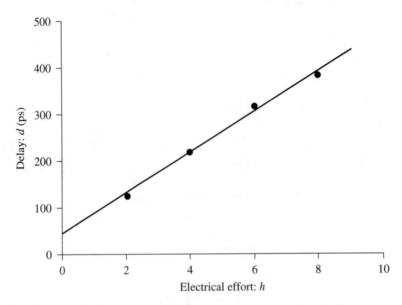

Figure 5.1 — Simulated delay of inverters driving various loads. Results from 0.6μ, 3.3v process.

The measurements are an independent verification of the linear delay model behind the method of logical effort. While only two measurements suffice to obtain values of τ and p_{inv}, more measurements increase the precision of the result and increase our confidence in the linear model. The illustration shows four data points at different values of electrical effort, fitting a straight line very well.

Figure 5.2 shows a similar set of data for a two-input NAND gate. The straight line in this case follows the equation $d = \tau(g_{2nand}h + p_{2nand})$, where the value of τ comes from the inverter characterization. This figure presents delay along the vertical axis in units of τ, using the value of τ computed from Figure 5.1. As a result, the slope of the fitted line is the logical effort of the NAND gate and the intercept is its parasitic delay. Similar simulations can calibrate an entire family of logic gates; some results are shown in Table 5.1.

Notice that the logical effort of NOR gates agrees fairly well with our model, but that the logical effort of NAND gates is lower than predicted. This can be attributed to velocity saturation, as discussed in Section 4.3.

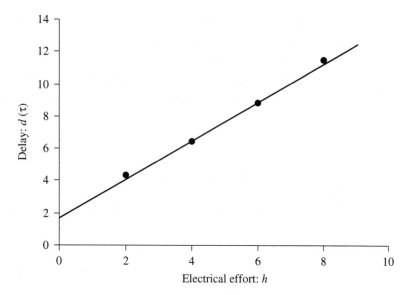

Figure 5.2 — Simulated delay of two-input NAND gate driving various loads. Results from 0.6μ, 3.3v process. The vertical axis is marked in units of τ.

Table 5.1 — Values for logical effort and parasitic delay for several kinds of logic gates for a 0.6μ, 3.3v process with $\gamma = 2$. From simulation, $\tau = 43$ ps.

Gate type	Number of inputs	Logical effort		Parasitic delay	
		From simulation	Model (Table 4.1)	From simulation	Model (Table 4.2)
Inverter	1	1.00 (def)	1.00 (def)	1.08	1.00
NAND	2	1.18	1.33	1.36	2.00
	3	1.40	1.67	2.12	3.00
	4	1.66	2.00	2.39	4.00
NOR	2	1.58	1.66	1.98	2.00
	3	2.18	2.33	3.02	3.00
	4	2.81	3.00	3.95	4.00

The parasitic delay depends on layout and on the order of input switching. These effects are discussed later in this chapter.

The values in these figures and table were obtained through simulation. The characterization scripts are available on the Logical Effort Web page. The remainder of this chapter discusses methods and pitfalls of logical effort characterization.

5.2 —— Designing Test Circuits

Designing a good test circuit is more subtle than one might initially imagine. A reasonable first attempt would be to load a gate with a capacitor, apply a step input, and measure the delay to the output crossing 50%. Such a circuit has two major problems. It does not account for the input slope dependence of delay, and it neglects the nonlinearity of MOS capacitors.

A better test circuit is shown in Figure 5.3 for a two-input NAND. The circuit has four stages. The first two stages are responsible for shaping the input slope. The third stage contains the gate being characterized. The final stage serves as a

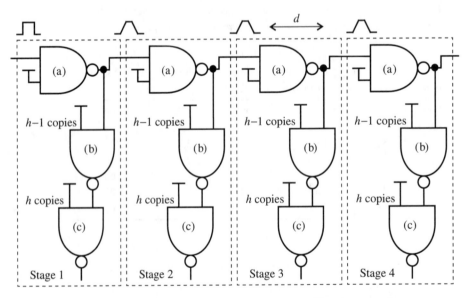

Figure 5.3 — Test circuit for two-input NAND calibration.

load on the gate. Each stage contains a primary gate (a), a load gate (b), and a load on the load (c)!

Gate (c) is necessary because of gate-drain overlap capacitance. If gate (c) were removed, the output of gate (b) would switch very rapidly. Because of the Miller effect, this would increase the effective input capacitance to gate (b). Simulation shows that this leads to an 8% overestimation of the delay of an FO4 inverter.

5.2.1 Rising, falling, and average delays

The rising and falling delays of gates usually differ. Which should we use? In Section 7.1, we show that considering only average gate delays is sufficient to minimize the average delay of a path. Therefore, we normally define the logical effort and parasitic delay of a gate to be the average of the values from the rising and falling transitions.

Occasionally it is useful to do a case analysis, considering rising and falling delays separately. The logical effort and parasitic delay for rising and falling transitions can be found from a curve fit in just the same way as for average delay. The results should still be normalized to the average delay of an inverter.

5.2.2 Choice of input

Designing test circuits with logic gates other than inverters requires deciding which input signals to use to propagate signals along the circuit. Our estimates of logical effort from Chapter 4 assumed that when transistors are in parallel, exactly one turns on, while when transistors are in series, all series transistors turn on simultaneously to give a resistance of R through each. In contrast, real circuits tend to have a single latest input that arrives after all other inputs have settled. This leads to lower effective resistance through series transistors because the transistors with early inputs are fully turned on when the late input arrives and thus provide more current. It also influences parasitic delay because internal nodes may already be charged or discharged before the latest input arrives. Which of the two or more inputs to a logic gate should we choose as the late arrival? It turns out that the inputs have distinct properties, so we could find the logical effort and parasitic delay parameters for each input separately. The unused inputs must be wired so that the gate's output will be controlled by the single input: unused NAND inputs are wired HIGH, and unused NOR inputs are wired LOW.

Table 5.2—Variation of the logical effort of NAND gate inputs for different choices of input signal. Data obtained from simulation of a 0.6μ, 3.3v process.

Number of inputs	Input number	Logical effort	Parasitic delay
2	0	1.18	1.36
	1	1.11	1.89
3	0	1.40	2.12
	1	1.32	3.06
	2	1.28	3.64
4	0	1.66	2.39
	1	1.58	3.89
	2	1.49	5.04
	3	1.48	5.59

Table 5.2 shows the variation of logical effort and parasitic delay with different choices of input signals. An input signal is identified by a number that records the largest number of transistors between the transistors controlled by the signal and the output node of the logic gate, as shown in Figure 5.4. Signal 0 connects to two transistors that have drains connected directly to the output node. Signal 1 connects to two transistors, one of which is connected to the output node, but the other is one transistor away from the output node. This numbering scheme works for NOR and NAND gates equally. Signal 0 is called the innermost signal, while signal $n - 1$ is the outermost.

The parasitic delay of a gate changes greatly with choice of input, as shown in Table 5.2. When input 0 of a NAND gate rises, all the other NMOS transistors are already on and had discharged diffusion capacitances $C_1 - C_3$ to ground. The gate has little parasitic delay because only the diffusion C_0 on the output node must switch. On the other hand, when the outer input (e.g., input 3 of a four-input NAND) rises last, all the diffusion capacitances $C_0 - C_3$ are initially charged to near V_{DD}. Discharging this capacitance diverts output current and increases the parasitic delay. Indeed, parasitic delay from the outer input scales quadratically with the number of inputs as discussed in Section 4.6. Because of parasitic delay, it is usually best to place the latest arriving signal on input 0.

Multiple-input gates also have somewhat lower logical effort than computed in Chapter 4 because only one input is switching, as we have seen in Table 5.1. The other transistors have already turned on and have a lower effective resistance

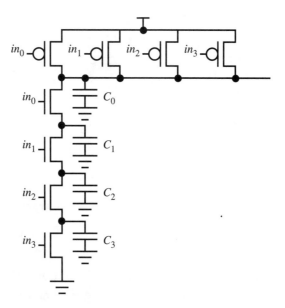

Figure 5.4 — Input numbering and parasitic capacitances of a four-input NAND.

than the switching transistor. If inputs to series transistors arrive simultaneously, the logical effort will be greater than these simulations have indicated.

Notice that the logical effort is slightly greater for inner inputs than outer inputs. This has little importance to the designer because over the range of reasonable fanouts used by well-designed circuits, the lower parasitic delay of the inner inputs is more significant than the greater logical effort, and critical signals are best assigned to inner inputs. The cause of the increased logical effort is rather subtle and is explained in the following two paragraphs for those interested in such second-order phenomena.

To understand this phenomenon, consider a stack of two series NMOS transistors discharging a load. Figure 5.5 shows the voltages on the output and middle nodes for switching inner and outer inputs. When the inner transistor switches, it is initially in saturation while the outer—that is, bottom—transistor is fully on and in linear mode. The current flowing through the outer transistor causes the middle node to rise, reducing the gate-source drive, V_{gs}, of the inner transistor and reducing the current. This negative feedback is particularly pronounced when the inner transistor is in saturation because its current depends quadratically on V_{gs}.

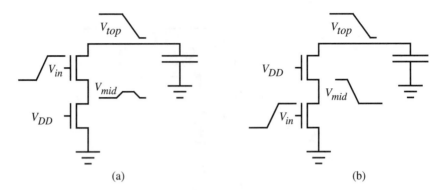

(a)   (b)

Figure 5.5 — Two series transistors discharging a load illustrating waveforms for inner (a) and outer (b) input switching.

Slower input slopes cause the inner transistor to remain in saturation for a greater portion of the switching time and thus experience more negative feedback and have a slower propagation delay. Remember that our logical effort calibration circuit from Figure 5.3 has an equal fanout at each stage and thus produces slower input slopes to gates driving a larger electrical effort. Therefore, the negative feedback effect increases with electrical effort, causing a greater slope to the delay vs. electrical effort curve that appears as greater logical effort for the inner input.

5.2.3 Parasitic capacitance

It is essential to specify accurate diffusion capacitances to simulate realistic parasitic delays. Most SPICE models fail to account for diffusion capacitance unless explicitly requested. The diffusion capacitance is specified with the AS, AD, PS, and PD parameters corresponding to the area and perimeter of the diffusion. These dimensions are shown in Figure 5.6. The diffusion perimeter measures only the length of the junction between the diffusion region and the substrate; the boundary between diffusion and channel is not counted, because the diffusion wall capacitance at the edge of the transistor gate is deliberately reduced by the fabrication process.

Diffusion area and perimeter depend on layout. Diffusion nodes that contact metal wires are larger than diffusion areas between series transistors without contacts. Good layouts share diffusion nodes wherever possible. Large cells can further reduce diffusion by folding transistors. Figure 5.7 shows the layouts of a

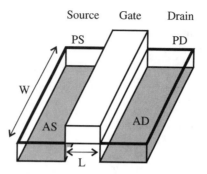

Figure 5.6 — Simplified transistor structure illustrating diffusion area and perimeter for capacitance computation.

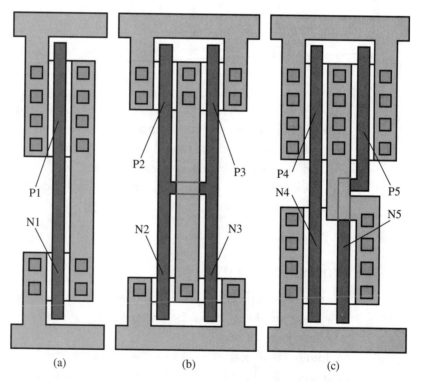

Figure 5.7 — Layout of CMOS gates for measuring diffusion capacitance: inverter (a), folded inverter (b), and NAND (c). MOSIS design rules are available at *www.isi.edu/mosis.*

Table 5.3 — Diffusion area and perimeter capacitances of transistors in Figure 5.7. Reported in units of λ^2 and λ, respectively, where λ is half of the minimum drawn channel length.

Transistor	W	AS	AD	PS	PD
N1	8	40	40	18	18
P1	16	80	80	26	26
N2	4	20	12	14	6
N3	4	20	12	14	6
P2	8	40	24	18	6
P3	8	40	24	18	6
N4	16	80	24	26	3
N5	16	24	80	3	26
P4	16	80	48	26	6
P5	16	80	48	26	6

simple inverter (a), an inverter with folded transistors (b), and a NAND gate (c). Table 5.3 lists the diffusion capacitance of each transistor.

Ideally, wire capacitance should also be included in the parasitic estimate. This can be done by extracting parasitic values from actual cell layouts. The parasitic delays reported in this chapter include realistic diffusion capacitances, but omit wire capacitance.

5.2.4 Process sensitivity

The value of τ depends on process, voltage, and temperature. Figure 5.8 shows how these parameters differ for a wide variety of processes and voltages at a nominal temperature of $70°C$.

Ideally, the logical effort of a gate would be independent of process parameters, as was found in Chapter 4. In reality, effects like velocity saturation cause logical effort to differ slightly with process and operating conditions. Table 5.4 shows this variation.

Similarly, parasitic capacitance differs with process and environment. Table 5.5 shows this variation.

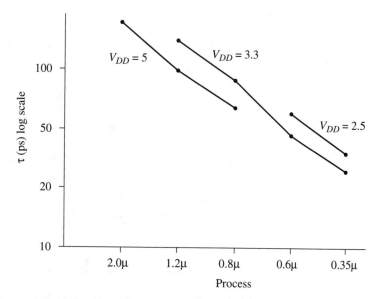

Figure 5.8 — τ for various processes and voltages. Simulated using MOSIS SPICE parameters.

Table 5.4 — Logical effort of gates for different processes and voltages. $\gamma = 2$.

Process	V_{DD}	NAND-2	NAND-3	NAND-4	NOR-2	NOR-3	NOR-4
2.0μ	5.0	1.16	1.35	1.55	1.58	2.13	2.69
1.2μ	5.0	1.20	1.41	1.65	1.50	2.00	2.47
1.2μ	3.3	1.24	1.48	1.74	1.51	2.04	2.59
0.8μ	5.0	1.15	1.32	1.53	1.51	2.00	2.55
0.8μ	3.3	1.17	1.36	1.58	1.50	2.07	2.60
0.6μ	3.3	1.18	1.40	1.66	1.58	2.18	2.81
0.6μ	2.5	1.17	1.42	1.68	1.55	2.13	2.78
0.35μ	3.3	1.17	1.37	1.57	1.54	2.03	2.61
0.35μ	2.5	1.20	1.42	1.65	1.57	2.15	2.61
Average		1.18	1.39	1.62	1.54	2.08	2.63
Theoretical		1.33	1.66	2.00	1.66	2.33	3.00

Table 5.5 — Parasitic delay of gates across process and voltage.

Process	V_{DD}	inverter	NAND-2	NAND-3	NAND-4	NOR-2	NOR-3	NOR-4
2.0μ	5.0	0.94	1.24	1.88	2.29	1.78	2.89	3.79
1.2μ	5.0	0.91	1.16	1.80	2.11	1.63	2.52	3.42
1.2μ	3.3	0.95	1.21	1.84	2.18	1.67	2.58	3.18
0.8μ	5.0	0.98	1.27	1.86	2.16	1.77	2.89	3.59
0.8μ	3.3	0.95	1.30	1.98	2.30	1.82	2.69	3.45
0.6μ	3.3	1.08	1.36	2.12	2.39	1.98	3.02	3.95
0.6μ	2.5	1.07	1.53	2.29	2.69	2.07	3.19	3.86
0.35μ	3.3	1.06	1.42	2.07	2.52	1.84	2.76	3.18
0.35μ	2.5	1.16	1.54	2.21	2.64	1.87	2.49	3.34
Average		1.01	1.34	2.01	2.36	1.83	2.78	3.53

5.3 —— Other Characterization Methods

Simulation is usually sufficient to characterize a cell library. Sometimes, accurate SPICE models for the process are unavailable. In such a case, logical effort can still be estimated from vendor data sheets or measured from test chips.

5.3.1   Data sheets

Good cell libraries come with delay-vs.-fanout information in the data sheet. Logical effort can easily be extracted by fitting a straight line to the delay-vs.-fanout curves. Care must be taken to convert fanout to electrical effort if the fanout is expressed in terms of unit inverters rather than C_{out}/C_{in}.

EXAMPLE 5.1   Compute the logical effort and parasitic delay of inverters from the LSI Logic data sheet shown in Figure 5.9.

SOLUTION   The data sheet shows various sizes of inverters from the G10-p 0.35μ 3.3v library. Gate sizes and load capacitances are measured in units of standard loads, which correspond to 15 fF. The inverters are labeled *a* through *f* in order of increasing size. A special *l* lightly loaded size is also available.

Let us define the *a*-sized inverter to have a logical effort of 1. We can obtain the logical effort and parasitic delay of other gates in the library by fitting the delay-vs.-load data to a straight line. Use the average of the rising and falling propagation delays. A spreadsheet can fit the curve as shown in Figure 5.10 for *a*-, *b*-, and *d*-sized inverters. Notice that the straight line fits the data well, validating our delay model.

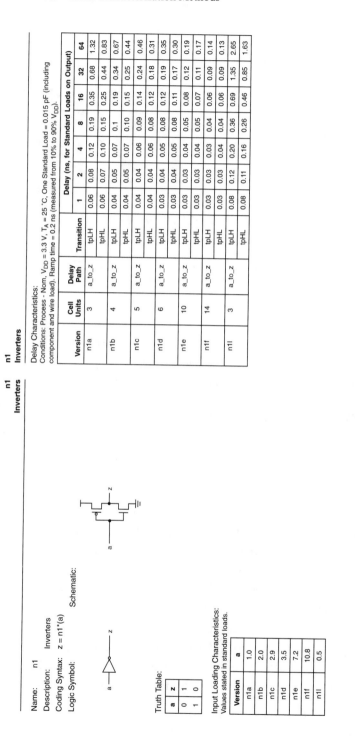

Figure 5.9 — LSI Logic data sheet (front and back) for inverters from G10-p 0.35μ 3.3v library. This form is available at *www.lsilogic.com*. (Figure shown is copyright © 1995–1998 and the G10 product name is a registered trademark of LSI Logic Corporation headquartered at 1551 McCarthy Blvd., Milpitas, CA 95035.)

Name: n1
Description: Inverters
Coding Syntax: z = n1'(a)
Logic Symbol:

Schematic:

Truth Table:

a	z
0	1
1	0

Input Loading Characteristics:
Values stated in standard loads.

Version	a
n1a	1.0
n1b	2.0
n1c	2.9
n1d	3.5
n1e	7.2
n1f	10.8
n1l	0.5

n1
Inverters

Delay Characteristics:
Conditions: Process - Nom, V_{DD} = 3.3 V, T_A = 25 °C, One Standard Load = 0.015 pF (including component and wire load). Ramp time = 0.2 ns (measured from 10% to 90% V_{DD}).

Version	Cell Units	Delay Path	Transition	Delay (ns, for Standard Loads on Output)						
				1	2	4	8	16	32	64
n1a	3	a_to_z	tpLH	0.06	0.08	0.12	0.19	0.35	0.68	1.32
			tpHL	0.06	0.07	0.10	0.15	0.25	0.44	0.83
n1b	4	a_to_z	tpLH	0.04	0.05	0.07	0.1	0.19	0.34	0.67
			tpHL	0.04	0.05	0.07	0.10	0.15	0.25	0.44
n1c	5	a_to_z	tpLH	0.04	0.04	0.06	0.09	0.14	0.24	0.46
			tpHL	0.04	0.04	0.06	0.08	0.12	0.18	0.31
n1d	6	a_to_z	tpLH	0.03	0.04	0.05	0.08	0.12	0.19	0.35
			tpHL	0.03	0.04	0.05	0.08	0.11	0.17	0.30
n1e	10	a_to_z	tpLH	0.03	0.03	0.04	0.05	0.08	0.12	0.19
			tpHL	0.03	0.03	0.04	0.05	0.07	0.11	0.17
n1f	14	a_to_z	tpLH	0.03	0.03	0.03	0.04	0.06	0.09	0.14
			tpHL	0.03	0.03	0.04	0.04	0.06	0.09	0.13
n1l	3	a_to_z	tpLH	0.08	0.12	0.20	0.36	0.69	1.35	2.65
			tpHL	0.08	0.11	0.16	0.26	0.46	0.85	1.63

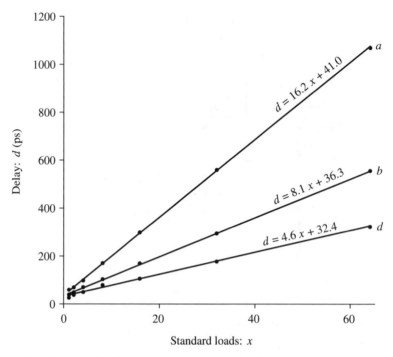

Figure 5.10 — Delay-vs.-load plots for various sizes of inverters.

We can convert the delay-vs.-load data to delay vs. electrical effort by multiplying the slope by the number of standard loads presented by the input:

$$(a) \quad d_{abs} = 16.2h + 41.0$$
$$(b) \quad d_{abs} = 16.2h + 36.3$$
$$(d) \quad d_{abs} = 16.1h + 32.4$$

The slope of the line of a gate with logical effort 1 is τ, in this case 16.2 ps. The logical effort of the other gates is found by the ratio of slopes. The parasitic delay of each gate is the parasitic delay in absolute terms divided by τ. Table 5.6 summarizes the logical effort and parasitic delay of each inverter. Observe that the logical efforts of all inverters are nearly 1.00, as they should be. The parasitic delays are rather high, perhaps including local wiring capacitance. Parasitic delay of the larger cells is lower, as should be expected because larger cells can take advantage of folded transistors and a higher transistor-to-wire length ratio to obtain lower parasitics. ∎

Exercise 5-4 examines extracting the logical effort of a NAND gate from the LSI library.

Table 5.6 — Logical efforts and parasitic delays for various sizes of inverters.

Size	g	p
a	1.00	2.53
b	1.00	2.24
d	0.99	2.00

5.3.2 Test chips

Logical effort can also be measured from fabricated chips by plotting the frequency of ring oscillators. The oscillator should contain an odd number of inverting stages. The frequency of the ring oscillator is related to the delay of the gate, as was discussed in Example 1.1. Oscillators with different fanouts provide data for the delay-vs.-electrical effort curves and thus values for logical effort and parasitic delay.

Care should be taken to load the load gates suitably to avoid excessive Miller multiplication of the load capacitance, as discussed in Section 5.2. Also, fabricated chips will include wire capacitance, which may have been neglected in simulation. Finally, the output should be tapped off from one of the load gates to avoid extra branching effort on the ring oscillator. Unfortunately, this is not possible in rings of gates with fanout of 1.

5.4 —— Calibrating Special Circuit Families

The calibration techniques explained so far work well for gates with roughly equal rise and fall times because the output of one gate is a realistic input to the next gate. Unfortunately, the techniques break down for other circuit families. For instance, a dynamic gate cannot drive another dynamic gate directly because that would violate the monotonicity rule. For gates skewed to favor a critical transition, the edge rate of the other transition is unrealistically slow and should not be used to set the input slope.

Dynamic gates have a very low switching threshold. Because one dynamic gate cannot directly drive another, there must be an inverting static gate between dynamic stages. Attempting to measure delay from input crossing 50% to output crossing 50% often leads to misleading results. If the slope of the input is slow, such a test may even report that dynamic gates have a negative delay. A better approach is to characterize the delay of the dynamic gate and subsequent static gate as a pair. Remember to use an electrical effort for the pair equal to the product of the electrical efforts of each stage. Initial estimates of logical effort can be used to determine the size of the static gate such that the stage effort of the dynamic and static gate are approximately equal.

Static gates are sometimes skewed to favor a particular transition by increasing the size of the critical transistor, as will be discussed in Section 7.2.1. For example, a HI-skew gate with a larger PMOS transistor may be used after a dynamic gate. Characterizing a chain of identical skewed gates also leads to misleading results. We would like to characterize the logical effort of the rising output of a HI-skew gate because that is the delay that would appear in a critical path. In a chain of such skewed gates, the input slope for each will come from a falling transition and will be unreasonably slow. This retards the rising output as well. To avoid this problem, characterize skewed gates as part of a unit, just as recommended for dynamic gates.

5.5 ——— Summary

This chapter has explored the accuracy of the method of logical effort through circuit simulation. The results suggest that the calculation methods described in Chapter 4 are good, but that more accurate calibrations offer somewhat greater precision and confidence.

Because the logical effort and parasitic delay of gates change only slightly with process, τ is a powerful way to characterize the speed of a process with a single number. Parasitic delay varies more than logical effort, but because effort delay usually exceeds parasitic delay, the variation is a smaller portion of the overall delay. By expressing the delay of circuits in terms of τ, or in the more widely recognized unit of fanout-of-4 (FO4) inverter delay (1 FO4 = 5τ), the designer can communicate with others in a process-independent way and can easily predict how gate performance will improve in more advanced processes.

5.6 ——— Exercises

[25] **5-1** Determine the logical effort and parasitic delay of an inverter, two-input NAND, and two-input NOR gate in your process. How well do the numbers agree with the estimates from Chapter 4 and the measurements in this chapter?

[20] **5-2** Make plots of delay vs. electrical effort for each of the three inputs of a three-input NAND gate, using values from Table 5.2. What general advice can you extract from your plot?

nd2
2-Input NAND

Name: nd2
Description: 2-Input NAND
Coding Syntax: z = nd2*(a,b)
Logic Symbol: Schematic:

Truth Table:

a	b	z
0	0	1
0	1	1
1	0	1
1	1	0

Input Loading Characteristics:
Values stated in standard loads.

Version	a	b
nd2a	0.9	0.9
nd2b	1.7	1.9
nd2c	2.6	2.8
nd2l	0.5	0.5

nd2
2-Input NAND

Delay Characteristics:
Conditions: Process - Nom, V_{DD} = 3.3 V, T_A = 25 °C, One Standard Load = 0.015 pF (including component and wire load), Ramp time = 0.2 ns (measured from 10% to 90% V_{DD}).

Version	Cell Units	Delay Path	Transition	Delay (ns, for Standard Loads)						
				1	2	4	8	16	32	64
nd2a	4	a_to_z	tpLH	0.07	0.09	0.14	0.23	0.43	0.81	1.57
			tpHL	0.07	0.09	0.14	0.22	0.38	0.70	1.33
		b_to_z	tpLH	0.07	0.10	0.14	0.23	0.43	0.81	1.57
			tpHL	0.08	0.10	0.14	0.22	0.38	0.70	1.33
nd2b	6	a_to_z	tpLH	0.05	0.06	0.09	0.14	0.23	0.42	0.81
			tpHL	0.05	0.06	0.09	0.13	0.21	0.37	0.69
		b_to_z	tpLH	0.06	0.07	0.09	0.14	0.23	0.43	0.81
			tpHL	0.06	0.07	0.09	0.13	0.21	0.37	0.69
nd2c	8	a_to_z	tpLH	0.04	0.06	0.07	0.11	0.17	0.29	0.55
			tpHL	0.05	0.06	0.08	0.11	0.16	0.27	0.48
		b_to_z	tpLH	0.05	0.06	0.08	0.11	0.17	0.29	0.56
			tpHL	0.05	0.06	0.08	0.11	0.16	0.27	0.48
nd2l	4	a_to_z	tpLH	0.10	0.15	0.24	0.45	0.86	1.68	3.30
			tpHL	0.10	0.14	0.22	0.38	0.68	1.30	2.52
		b_to_z	tpLH	0.10	0.15	0.25	0.46	0.87	1.68	3.30
			tpHL	0.10	0.14	0.21	0.37	0.68	1.29	2.51

Figure 5.11 — LSI Logic data sheet (front and back) for two-input NAND from G10-p 0.35μ 3.3v library. This form is available at *www.lsilogic.com*. (Figure shown is copyright © 1995–1998 and the G10 product name is a registered trademark of LSI Logic Corporation headquartered at 1551 McCarthy Blvd., Milpitas, CA 95035.)

[15]   **5-3**   The two inputs of an ordinary two-input NAND gate differ because one of them connects to a transistor close to the output and the other to a transistor close to a power rail. Show how to build a two-input NAND with identical delay from each input using two ordinary two-input NAND gates both driving the same output.

[20]   **5-4**   Compute the logical effort and parasitic delay from each input of the a- and c-sized two-input NAND gates from the LSI library shown in Figure 5.11. Use $\tau = 16.2$ ps.

Asymmetric Logic Gates —————— 6

Logic gates sometimes have different logical effort for different inputs. We call such gates *asymmetric*. For example, the and-or-invert gate from Section 4.4 is inherently asymmetric. The three-input XOR and majority gates from Sections 4.5.4 and 4.5.5 can appear in either symmetric or asymmetric forms, but the asymmetric forms have lower total logical effort. Finally, we can make asymmetric forms of normally symmetric gates such as NAND or NOR by sizing transistors to reduce the logical effort of one or more inputs at the expense of increasing the logical effort of the other inputs. Such asymmetric gates can speed up critical paths in a network by reducing the logical effort along the critical paths. This attractive property has a price, however: the total logical effort of the logic gate increases. This chapter discusses design issues arising from biasing a gate to favor particular inputs.

6.1 —————— Designing Asymmetric Logic Gates

Figure 6.1 shows a NAND gate designed so that the widths of the two pulldown transistors can differ: input a has width $1/(1-s)$, while input b has width

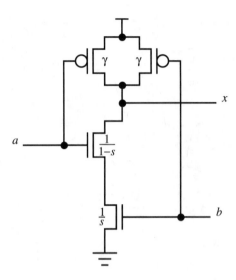

Figure 6.1—An asymmetric NAND gate.

$1/s$. The parameter s, $0 < s < 1$, called the *symmetry factor*, determines the amount by which the logic gate is asymmetric. If $s = 1/2$, the gate is symmetric, the pulldown transistors have equal sizes, and the logical effort is the same as we computed in Section 4.3. Values of s between 0 and $1/2$ favor the a input by making its pulldown transistor smaller than the pulldown transistor for b. Values of s between $1/2$ and 1 favor the b input.

Despite the flexibility to favor one of the two inputs, the gate still has the same output drive as the reference inverter with a pulldown transistor of width 1 and a pullup transistor of width γ. We can verify that the conductance of the pulldown connection is 1:

$$\frac{1}{\frac{1}{\frac{1}{(1-s)}} + \frac{1}{\frac{1}{s}}} = 1 \tag{6.1}$$

Using Equation 4.1, we can compute g_a and g_b, the logical effort per input for inputs a and b, and the total logical effort g_{tot}:

$$g_a = \frac{\frac{1}{(1-s)} + \gamma}{1 + \gamma} \tag{6.2}$$

$$g_b = \frac{\frac{1}{s} + \gamma}{1 + \gamma} \tag{6.3}$$

$$g_{tot} = \frac{\frac{1}{s(1-s)} + 2\gamma}{1 + \gamma} \qquad (6.4)$$

Choosing the least value possible for s, such as 0.01, minimizes the logical effort of input a. This design results in a pulldown transistor of width 1.01 for input a and a transistor of width 100 for input b. The logical effort of input a is then $(1.01 + \gamma)/(1 + \gamma)$, or almost exactly 1. The logical effort of input b becomes $(100 + \gamma)/(1 + \gamma)$, or about 34 if $\gamma = 2$. The total logical effort is about 35, again assuming $\gamma = 2$.

Extremely asymmetric designs, such as with $s = 0.01$, are able to achieve a logical effort for one input that almost matches that of an inverter, namely, 1. The price of this achievement is an enormous total logical effort, 35, as opposed to 8/3 for a symmetric design. Moreover, the huge size of the pulldown transistor will certainly cause layout problems, and the benefit of the reduced logical effort on input a may not be worth the enormous area of this transistor.

Less extreme asymmetry is more practical. If $s = 1/4$, the pulldown transistors have widths 4/3 and 4, and the logical effort of input a is $(4/3 + \gamma)/(1 + \gamma)$, which is 1.1 if $\gamma = 2$. The logical effort of input b is 2, and the total logical effort is 3.1, which is very little more than 8/3, the total logical effort of the symmetric design. This design achieves a logical effort for the favored input, a, that is only 10% greater than that of an inverter, without a huge increase in total logical effort.

Asymmetric gate designs require attention to stray capacitances. It is unwise, for example, to use values of $s > 1/2$ in the NAND gate design because the smaller pulldown transistor attached to input b must discharge not only the load capacitance but also the stray capacitance of the large pulldown transistor attached to input a. It is best to order transistors in series strings so that smaller transistors are near the output node. In the design shown in Figure 6.1, this means that we should use only values in the range $s \leq 1/2$, which favor the a input. Of course, the a input should be the last to change, as discussed in Section 5.2.2.

We can also approach the design of asymmetric logic gates by specifying the desired logical effort g_f of the favored input and deriving the necessary transistor sizes. This approach allows us to calculate the logical effort of the unfavored input, g_u, in terms of the logical effort of the favored input. Equation 6.5 follows

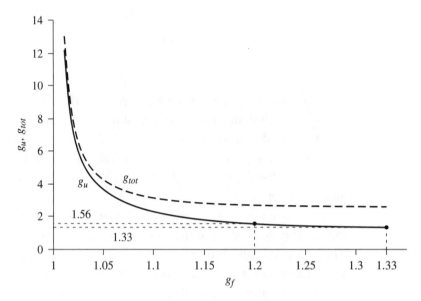

Figure 6.2 — Relationship between favored and unfavored logical efforts for a two-input NAND gate with $\gamma = 2$.

from Equations 6.2 and 6.3 for the NAND gate (see Exercise 6-1):

$$(g_f - 1)(g_u - 1) = \frac{1}{(1 + \gamma)^2} \tag{6.5}$$

Equation 6.5 shows the symmetric relationship between the favored and unfavored logical efforts: the logical effort of the unfavored input increases as the logical effort of the favored input decreases.

Figure 6.2 presents some results that summarize the effects of varying the symmetry factor of a two-input NAND gate. Recall that in a single-stage design, an effort f will result in a delay of f delay units, plus parasitic delay. To achieve a 0.13-unit reduction in the delay of the favored input (1.33 to 1.2 units), we incur a 0.23-unit increase in the delay of the unfavored input (1.33 to 1.56 units).

The same design techniques we have illustrated for a two-input NAND gate apply to other logic gates as well. Rather than catalog all these designs, we shall develop and analyze asymmetric designs as the need arises. You might wish to repeat the analysis shown here for a two-input NOR gate or for a three-input NAND gate.

6.2 —— Applications of Asymmetric Logic Gates

The principal applications of asymmetric logic gates occur where one path must be very fast. For example, in a ripple-carry adder or counter, the carry path must be fast. The best design uses an asymmetric circuit that speeds the carry even though it retards the sum output.

Paradoxically, another important use of asymmetric logic gates occurs when a signal path may be unusually slow, as in a reset signal. Figure 6.3 shows a design for a buffer amplifier whose output is forced LOW when the reset signal, $\overline{reset}$, is LOW. The buffer consists of two stages: a NAND gate and an inverter. During normal operation, when $\overline{reset}$ is HIGH, the first stage has an output drive equivalent to that of an inverter with pulldown width 6 and pullup width 12, but the capacitive load on the *in* signal is 7+12 units of width. Thus the logical effort of the *in* input is slightly larger than that of the corresponding inverter:

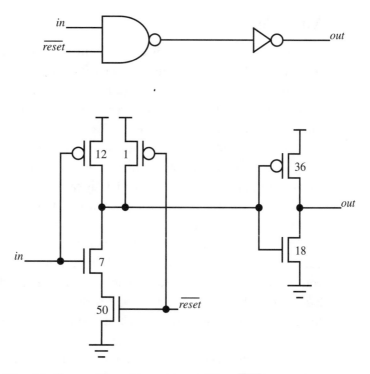

Figure 6.3 — A buffer amplifier with reset input. When $\overline{reset}$ is LOW, the output will always be LOW.

$$g = \frac{7 + 12}{6 + 12} = 1.05 \qquad (6.6)$$

This circuit takes advantage of the slow response allowed to changes on $\overline{reset}$ by using the smallest pullup transistor possible. This choice reduces the area required to lay out the gate, partially compensating for the large area pulldown transistor. Area can be further reduced by sharing the reset pulldown among multiple gates that switch at different times; this is known as a "virtual ground" technique.

The design violates the practice of designing gates that have the same drive characteristics as the reference inverter, because the pullup and pulldown drives controlled by $\overline{reset}$ differ from those of the standard inverter. In this case, the exception seems justified because we are interested only in performance when reset is not active, when the gate's output drive is nearly identical to that of the reference inverter.

6.2.1   Multiplexers

Just as the CMOS multiplexer is unique in that its logical effort per input does not grow as the number of inputs increases, asymmetric multiplexer designs have some peculiar properties. We can view an n-way multiplexer as having n "arms," each of which contains the transistors connected to one data input and one select bundle as seen in Figure 6.4. The unique properties of the multiplexer come from the independence of its individual arms; we are relatively free to design each arm independently without regard to the presence of other arms. When stray capacitance is included in delay calculations, of course, each arm of a multiplexer contributes a stray capacitance that indeed affects the other arms as described in Chapter 11.

An arm of a multiplexer may be asymmetric so as to favor the speed of the data or select signals. Favoring the select path may be appropriate when the control signals arrive late. For example, a carry select adder computes sums assuming both $carry = 0$ and $carry = 1$, then chooses the proper sum when the carry arrives. Values of $s < 1/2$ in Figure 6.4 will produce the required asymmetry.

Favoring the data input is more problematic. Choosing $1/2 < s < 1$ leads to suitable transistor sizes, but the design shown in Figure 6.4 will not tolerate much asymmetry before the stray capacitance of the larger transistors connected

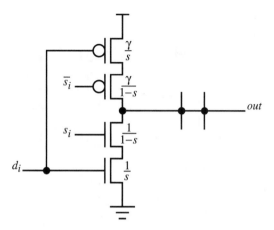

Figure 6.4 — One arm of a multiplexer. The data input is d_i and the select bundle is s_i and $\bar{s}_i$.

to select inputs slows the multiplexer and defeats the effort to reduce the load on the data input. In some cases, the data and select transistors can be interchanged in the pullup and pulldown chains to avoid loading the small transistors with large strays. This may lead to severe charge-sharing problems if many data transistors connected to the output switch dump charge from their source diffusion parasitics onto the output.

Multiplexers can be asymmetric in another way as well, by varying the conductance of different arms. Noncritical paths may use arms with lower conductance, and thus less input load. A good example of this kind of asymmetry is the static latch. Figure 6.5(a) shows a circuit diagram of a static latch, and Figure 6.5(b) shows a schematic representation in which each arm of the multiplexer is shown as a separate tristate gate. The design objective is to minimize the propagation delay through the latch when e is HIGH and $\bar{e}$ is LOW, making it transparent.

The left arm of the multiplexer is configured to favor the data input, which will experience a logical effort of $1/(1 - s)$. The transistor sizes on this arm are marked in terms of three parameters: s, the symmetry factor of the gate; a, an overall scale factor; and γ, the ratio of p- to n-type transistor widths. The right arm of the multiplexer can use minimum-size transistors because it never charges or discharges its output load, but rather supplies a trickle of current to counteract leakage.

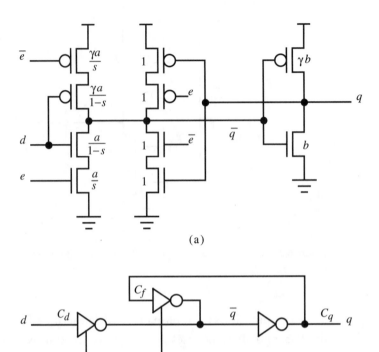

(a)

(b)

Figure 6.5 — Transistor- and gate-level schematics of a static latch, consisting of a two-way multiplexer (a) and an inverter (b). The data input is d, and the latch output is q.

Along the critical path from d to q, the logical effort of the d input to the multiplexer is $1/(1 - s)$ and the logical effort of the inverter is 1, so that the logical effort of the path is $1/(1 - s)$. The electrical effort is the ratio of the load on the inverter to the capacitance of the d input. If we define C_q to be the load capacitance, C_f to be the input capacitance of the multiplexer on the feedback path, and C_d to be the capacitance of the d input, the electrical effort is just $H = (C_q + C_f)/C_d$. Thus we have

$$F = \left(\frac{1}{1 - s}\right)\left(\frac{C_q + C_f}{C_d}\right) = \frac{C_q}{(1 - s)rC_d} \qquad (6.7)$$

where $r = C_q/(C_q + C_f)$ is the fraction of the inverter output drive available as useful output. It is clear from this equation that the effort is minimized for given input and output loads by maximizing r and $1 - s$. Not surprisingly, this means minimizing the feedback capacitance, C_f, and biasing the multiplexer in favor of the d input as much as practical.

Modifying the multiplexer to favor the data input has the side effect of increasing the logical effort of the select bundle, $e*$. This need not impact speed because favoring the data input implies that the select was noncritical. Moreover, if the multiplexer serves as a latch, the select is a clock signal whose delay can be absorbed into the clock distribution network. Nevertheless, increasing the logical effort of the $e*$ bundle increases the power consumption of its driver, and so we should avoid excessive asymmetry.

6.3 —— Summary

The theory of logical effort shows how to design logic gates with transistor sizes chosen to favor the logical effort of one input at the expense of the remaining inputs. This will have the effect of reducing the delay on the path through the favored input, while increasing the delay on paths through the other inputs. Although biasing a gate in this way raises the total logical effort of the logic gate, the technique can reduce the delay along critical paths.

The benefits of asymmetric designs are most evident when many asymmetric logic gates are connected serially along a path so as to reduce the delay along the path. Carry chains are an important application of such techniques.

6.4 —— Exercises

[15] **6-1** Derive Equation 6.5 from Equations 6.2 and 6.3.

[25] **6-2** Show how to design an asymmetric three-input NAND gate using two parameters $0 < s, t < 1$ to specify the logical effort on two of the three inputs. Derive an expression for the total logical effort in terms of s and t.

[20] **6-3** Complete the design of the static latch shown in Figure 6.5 when $C_d = 9$, $C_q = 6C_d$, assuming $\gamma = 2$. What is the delay from d to q as a function of s when the latch is transparent? Neglect parasitics.

[20] **6-4** Repeat the preceding exercise, but minimize the delay from d to $\bar{q}$, assuming the q output is not used at all. Now the load C_q is on $\bar{q}$.

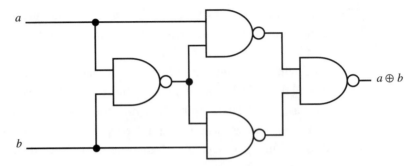

Figure 6.6—A network that computes the XOR function of two inputs.

[20] **6-5** The leftmost multiplexer arm in Figure 6.5 is by itself an inverting dynamic latch. The remaining circuits simply make the latch static. What is the "cost" in terms of logical effort for making the latch static rather than dynamic?

[20] **6-6** Suppose that the static latch of Figure 6.5 must drive a very large load, for example, $C_q = 100$, while $C_d = 3$. How would you change the design?

[25] **6-7** Which of the NAND gates in Figure 6.6 might be made asymmetric in order to yield the fastest design? Assume that both inputs a and b should be equally favored. Does the best degree of asymmetry depend on the electrical effort of the composite circuit?

Unequal Rising and ——————— 7
Falling Delays

All of our analysis of delays in CMOS logic gates has assumed that the delay of a
logic gate is the same for rising and falling output transitions. It is easy to relax
this condition and to consider rising and falling delays separately. Allowing rise
and fall times to differ permits us to analyze a greater range of designs, including
pseudo-NMOS circuits, skewed static gates, CMOS domino logic, and precharged
circuits of all kinds. It also allows us to design static CMOS gates with various
choices for the ratio of widths of PMOS to NMOS transistors.

To discuss gates with different rise and fall times, it is important to review
some transistor size definitions and introduce two new symbols for ideas we
have used but never formally defined. Remember that $\mu = \mu_p/\mu_n$ is the mobility
ratio. The P/N ratio of a gate is the ratio of the size of PMOS to the size of NMOS
transistors in the gate. Because we will use this ratio often in this chapter, we
will call it $r = P/N$. The shape factor γ is the P/N ratio of a reference inverter,
that is, the inverter defined to have a logical effort of 1. If $\gamma = \mu$, the inverter
has equal rise and fall times. This chapter is especially concerned with the case
of $\gamma \neq \mu$ in which rise and fall times are unequal.

We know that gates with series transistors require larger transistors to deliver the same current as a reference inverter. This means the P/N ratio r is not γ for NAND and NOR gates. Because we will also use this ratio often, we introduce another symbol k compensating for series transistors so that we can say a particular gate has a P/N ratio of $r = k\gamma$ when its rise and fall delays are proportional to those of the reference inverter. For a two-input NOR gate, the PMOS transistors are twice as wide as in the reference inverter, so $k = 2$. For a three-input NAND gate, the NMOS transistors are three times as wide as in the reference inverter, so $k = 1/3$.

The principal result of this chapter is that for all but the most demanding cases, we can use the techniques of logical effort without modification to determine the best transistor sizes even when rising and falling delays differ. When calculating the total delay along a path, however, we must replace τ, the delay of a reference inverter, by the average of the unequal rising and falling delays through the reference inverter.

Most often, the analysis need concern only the average of the rising and falling delays, because a signal flowing through a network of gates will alternately rise and fall as it propagates through each stage. Thus the number of rising and falling transitions differs by at most one, and the average stage delay is usually an adequate measure of the network's performance. If the speed of propagation of a particular transition is more important than that of other transitions, skewed static gates with $r \neq k\gamma$ can reduce the logical effort of that transition at the expense of larger effort on other transitions.

One of the interesting applications of this analysis is to find the best value of r, the P/N ratio of static CMOS gates. If r is too small, then the rising transition will be too slow, because the conductance of the pullup transistor will be diminished. On the other hand, if r is too large, the rising transition will be fast, but the transistor gate capacitance of the pullup transistor will be so large that the circuit driving it will slow down. The best value of r will find a compromise between these extremes. It turns out that the value of r for least total delay leads to rising and falling delays that differ.

7.1 —— Analyzing Delays

The analysis of delays when rising and falling delays differ is a variation of the analysis we used in Chapter 3 when the delays are the same. In this section, we carry out the analysis and show that the average delay is minimized using exactly the same techniques of logical effort described earlier. In all cases, rising or falling refers to the output transition, not the input transition.

We can model the delay of an individual stage of logic with one of the following two expressions, derived using techniques similar to those in Section 3.2:

$$d_u = (g_u h + p_u) \tag{7.1}$$

$$d_d = (g_d h + p_d) \tag{7.2}$$

where the delays are measured in terms of τ. Notice that the logical efforts, parasitic delays, and stage delays differ for rising transitions (u) and falling transitions (d). The efforts and parasitic delays of each transition can be extracted from a plot of delay vs. electrical effort, as discussed in Chapter 5. The electrical effort is independent of the transition direction.

In a path containing N logic gates, we use one of two equations for the path delay, depending on whether the final output of the path rises or falls. In the equations, i is the distance from the last stage, ranging from 0 for the final gate to $N - 1$ for the first gate.

$$D_u = \sum_{i \text{ odd}} (g_{di} h_i + p_{di}) + \sum_{i \text{ even}} (g_{ui} h_i + p_{ui}) \tag{7.3}$$

$$D_d = \sum_{i \text{ odd}} (g_{ui} h_i + p_{ui}) + \sum_{i \text{ even}} (g_{di} h_i + p_{di}) \tag{7.4}$$

The first equation models the delay incurred when a network produces a rising output transition. In this equation, the first sum tallies the delay of falling transitions at the output of stages whose distance from the last stage is odd, and the second tallies the delay of rising transitions in stages an even distance from the last stage, including the last stage itself. Note that every path through a network of logic gates will experience alternating rising and falling transitions, as this sum indicates. Equation 7.4 is similar to its companion, but models the network producing a falling transition: the falling edges occur in even stages, and rising ones occur in odd stages. These two equations model the two separate cases we must consider.

Usually we want the delays through a network experienced by a rising or falling input transition to be similar. The delays cannot, in general, be identical, because the two cases will experience different numbers of rising and falling delays. A reasonable goal is to minimize the average delay:

$$\overline{D} = \frac{1}{2}(D_u + D_d) = \sum \left(\left(\frac{g_{ui} + g_{di}}{2} \right) h_i + \frac{p_{ui} + p_{di}}{2} \right)$$

$$= \sum (g_i h_i + p_i) = \sum (f_i + p_i) \tag{7.5}$$

subject to the usual constraint on the total effort, $F = \prod f_i$. Notice that the logical effort g_i and parasitic delay p_i of a stage are the average of the rising and falling quantities. Once again, the observation of Section 3.3 applies, and we see that the average delay is minimized by making the total effort borne by each stage the same, so that $f_i = f = F^{1/N}$. Then we have for the average delay:

$$\overline{D} = (Nf + P) = (NF^{1/N} + P) \tag{7.6}$$

This is the same result as we obtained for equal delays, Equation 3.22. Therefore, we are justified in using the average value of rising and falling logical effort and parasitic delay to minimize the average path delay, regardless of differences between rising and falling delays. All values are normalized so that the average logical effort of the reference inverter is 1.

The maximum delay through a path, however, may be different than the delay predicted by the original theory. Maximum delay is important because it sets the cycle time of synchronous systems. To find maximum delay, we must select the worst of the delays for a rising output and for a falling output.

EXAMPLE 7.1   Size the path shown in Figure 7.1 for minimum average delay, using the logical effort and parasitic delay data from Table 7.1. What is the average and worst-case delay?

SOLUTION   Notice how the average logical effort and parasitic delays in the table are the same as we are accustomed to, but that the rising values are larger than the falling values.

We size the gates along the path for minimum average delay using average effort values. We find $G = 4/3$ and $H = 20$, so $F = 80/3$. Table 1.3 recommends $N = 3$, verifying our choice of two inverters in Figure 7.1. The effort of each stage is thus $\rho = (80/3)^{1/3} = 2.99$. Working from the output, we obtain the transistor sizes shown in Figure 7.2.

Table 7.1 — Estimated logical effort and parasitic delay of various gates designed with $\gamma = 2$ in a process with $\mu = 3$. See Exercise 7-2 for a derivation of these values.

Gate	Logical effort			Parasitic delay		
	Rising g_u	Falling g_d	Average g	Rising p_u	Falling p_d	Average p
Inverter	6/5	4/5	1	6/5	4/5	1
2-NAND	24/15	16/15	4/3	12/5	8/5	2
2-NOR	6/3	4/3	5/3	12/5	8/5	2

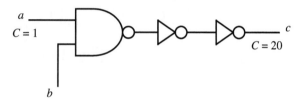

Figure 7.1 — A NAND gate driving a heavy load.

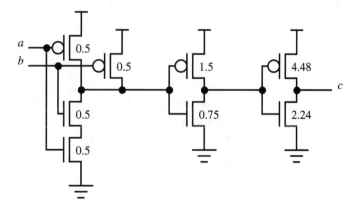

Figure 7.2 — The network of Figure 7.1, optimized for the average of rising and falling delays, assuming $\gamma = 2, \mu = 3$.

Now we can compute the delays from Equations 7.4 and 7.3:

$$D_u = (g_{u1}h_1 + p_{u1}) + (g_{d2}h_2 + p_{d2}) + (g_{u3}h_2 + p_{u3})$$

$$= \left(\frac{24}{15}\right) \times \left(\frac{2.25}{1}\right) + \frac{12}{5} + \left(\frac{4}{5}\right) \times \left(\frac{6.72}{2.25}\right) + \frac{4}{5}$$

$$+ \left(\frac{6}{5}\right) \times \left(\frac{20}{6.72}\right) + \frac{6}{5} = 13.96 \tag{7.7}$$

$$D_d = (g_{d1}h_1 + p_{d1}) + (g_{u2}h_2 + p_{u2}) + (g_{d3}h_2 + p_{d3})$$

$$= \left(\frac{16}{15}\right) \times \left(\frac{2.25}{1}\right) + \frac{8}{5} + \left(\frac{6}{5}\right) \times \left(\frac{6.72}{2.25}\right) + \frac{6}{5}$$

$$+ \left(\frac{4}{5}\right) \times \left(\frac{20}{6.72}\right) + \frac{4}{5} = 11.96 \tag{7.8}$$

The average is 12.96, which agrees with the direct calculation using Equation 7.6. ∎

7.2 —— Case Analysis

An alternative to the previous section is to consider minimizing the delay experienced by either a rising or a falling transition propagating along a path rather than minimizing the average delay. This problem frequently arises in precharged circuits where precharging sets a signal HIGH and we are interested in minimizing the propagation time of a falling transition as it travels through a network. In other words, we may want to minimize Equation 7.4 or Equation 7.3 alone, rather than the average of the two.

In such a case, we use the appropriate logical effort g_{xi} and parasitic delay p_{xi}, where x represents u or d for stages making rising or falling transitions, respectively. All of our theory of logical effort still applies. This method yields a short delay for the prescribed transition, but increases the complementary delay, as shown in the following example.

EXAMPLE 7.2 Repeat Example 7.1, but with the objective of minimizing the propagation time of a rising transition presented at the input.

SOLUTION Because the input rises, the NAND gate output will fall. The next inverter output will rise, and the final inverter output will fall. Therefore, the logical

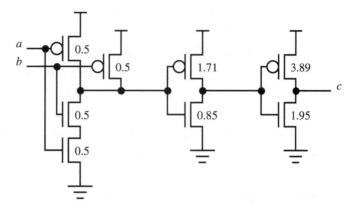

Figure 7.3—The network of Figure 7.1, optimized for the particular case of a rising transition entering on a. $\gamma = 2$, $\mu = 3$.

efforts of interest are $(16/15)$, $6/5$, and $4/5$, respectively, from Table 7.1. The logical effort of the path is $(16/15) \times (6/5) \times (4/5) = 1.02$. The electrical effort is still $H = 20/1 = 20$, so the path effort is 20.5. The stage effort is therefore $\rho = 20.5^{1/3} = 2.74$. Working from the output, the sizes are 5.84, 2.56, and 1, as shown in Figure 7.3.

Let us now analyze the delays, again using Equations 7.3 and 7.4:

$$D_u = (g_{u1}h_1 + p_{u1}) + (g_{d2}h_2 + p_{d2}) + (g_{u3}h_2 + p_{u3})$$

$$= \left(\frac{24}{15}\right) \times \left(\frac{2.56}{1}\right) + \frac{12}{5} + \left(\frac{4}{5}\right) \times \left(\frac{5.84}{2.56}\right) + \frac{4}{5}$$

$$+ \left(\frac{6}{5}\right) \times \left(\frac{20}{5.84}\right) + \frac{6}{5} = 14.43 \qquad (7.9)$$

$$D_d = (g_{d1}h_1 + p_{d1}) + (g_{u2}h_2 + p_{u2}) + (g_{d3}h_2 + p_{d3})$$

$$= \left(\frac{16}{15}\right) \times \left(\frac{2.56}{1}\right) + \frac{8}{5} + \left(\frac{6}{5}\right) \times \left(\frac{5.84}{2.56}\right) + \frac{6}{5}$$

$$+ \left(\frac{4}{5}\right) \times \left(\frac{20}{5.84}\right) + \frac{4}{5} = 11.81 \qquad (7.10)$$

Notice that the case we have optimized, $D_d = 11.81$, is indeed slightly better than the value of 11.96 given in Equation 7.8, obtained by optimizing the average delay. However, the complementary delay, 14.43, is substantially worse than the corresponding delay obtained for the previous design, 13.96. The effort delays f are all 2.74 for the critical transition, as we should expect, but are larger and unequal for the other transition.   ■

This example shows clearly that optimizing one of the two complementary delays yields slightly faster circuits at the expense of a large increase in the delay of the other transition.

7.2.1   Skewed gates

When the speed of one transition is more critical than another, it is possible to design the gate to favor that important transition. Such gates are called *skewed* gates and use a greater fraction of their input capacitance for the critical transistors. HI-*skew* gates favor rising output transitions, while LO-*skew* gates favor falling output transitions. Such gates are shown in Figure 7.4. Compare with *normal-skew* gates from Figure 4.1. Do not confuse skewed and asymmetric gates; skewed gates favor a particular transition, while asymmetric gates favor a particular input.

Skewed gates produce output current for the critical transition equal to that of a reference inverter, while producing less output current for the noncritical transition. Therefore, the input capacitance is less than for a gate that produces current equal to that of the reference inverter for both transitions. Hence, the logical effort is lower for the critical transition. The cost is greater logical effort for the noncritical transition. The logical efforts of various skewed gates are shown in Table 7.2, assuming $\gamma = \mu = 2$. Usually we are concerned only about the logical effort of the critical transition in skewed gates, not of the noncritical or average transition.

How far should a gate be skewed? In other words, how much smaller should the noncritical transistors be made? Extreme skews improve logical effort only slightly on the critical transition, but severely retard the noncritical transition. Such gates also can be difficult to lay out and may suffer hot-electron reliability problems if the noncritical edge rates become too slow. A reasonable choice makes the noncritical transistors half the size they would have been in a normal gate, as was done in Figure 7.4. Therefore, we choose that HI-skew gates use a P/N ratio $r = 2k\gamma$ and LO-skew gates use a P/N ratio $r = (1/2)k\gamma$.

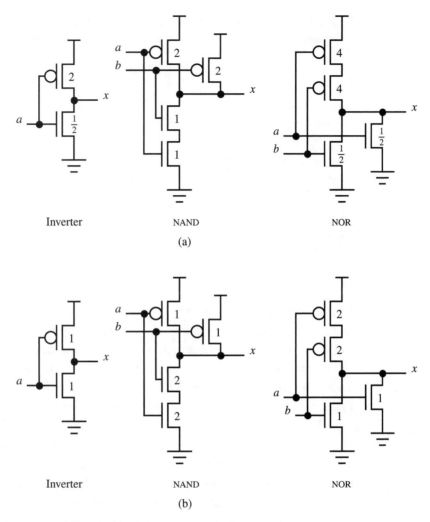

Figure 7.4 — HI-skew (a) and LO-skew (b) inverters, NAND gates, and NOR gates, assuming $\gamma = 2$.

7.2.2 Impact of γ and μ on logical effort

Before continuing, we will explore the effect of the shape factor γ and mobility ratio μ on the logical effort of gates. When $\gamma = \mu$, normal gates have equal rise and fall times. In typical CMOS processes, μ is between 2 and 3 and γ is usually chosen to be less than μ to save area and, as we shall see, improve average speed. This does not affect the average logical effort of a normal gate, but it does lead

Table 7.2 — Estimated logical effort of skewed gates with $\gamma = 2$, $\mu = \gamma$. The important effort of each gate is bold. Exercise 7-3 derives these values.

Gate	Logical effort g		
	Rising	Falling	Average
Normal-skew inverter	1	1	1
Normal-skew 2-NAND	4/3	4/3	4/3
Normal-skew 2-NOR	5/3	5/3	5/3
HI-skew inverter	**5/6**	5/3	5/4
HI-skew 2-NAND	**1**	2	3/2
HI-skew 2-NOR	**3/2**	3	9/4
LO-skew inverter	4/3	**2/3**	1
LO-skew 2-NAND	2	**1**	3/2
LO-skew 2-NOR	2	**1**	3/2

to unequal rise and fall delays and thus to larger logical efforts for rising than for falling transitions, as was seen in Table 7.1. These logical efforts can be calculated by comparing the output current to the average of that of an inverter with equal input capacitance. The analysis shows that when $\gamma < \mu$, rising efforts of gates are greater than average by a factor of $2\mu/(\mu + \gamma)$ and falling efforts are less than average by a factor of $2\gamma/(\mu + \gamma)$ than they would be for $\gamma = \mu$.

When $\gamma < \mu$, skewed gates have larger rising efforts and smaller falling efforts. This can lead to results that at first seem counterintuitive. For example, a HI-skew NOR gate with $\gamma = 2$ is shown in Figure 7.4. If the mobility of the process is $\mu = 3$, the rising effort will be 9/5, which is actually larger than the average effort of a normal-skew NOR, 5/3! Does this mean that a HI-skew NOR is worse than a regular NOR gate? The key to this puzzle is that the HI-skew gate is used only for critical rising transitions and should be compared to the rising logical effort of the normal-skew gate, which is 2 in this scenario. Therefore, the HI-skew gate is better than the normal gate for rising transitions, as expected.

Similarly, LO-skew gates may appear to have unexpectedly low falling efforts. The logical effort of dynamic gates is also measured for the falling transition and is lower than would be predicted assuming $\gamma = \mu$. Dynamic gates will be discussed further in Section 8.2.

7.3 —— Optimizing CMOS P/N Ratios

Now that we no longer insist that rising and falling delays be equal, we may ask what is the best ratio of pullup to pulldown transistor sizes in CMOS. The designs from Chapter 4 are simple to analyze because they have equal rising and falling delays. However, the wide PMOS transistors contribute a large amount of input capacitance and area. Could gates be smaller and on average faster if they use smaller PMOS transistors, thereby reducing the input capacitance and improving the falling delay at the expense of the rising delay? In this section, we will show that the P/N width ratio giving best average delay is the square root of the P/N width ratio giving equal rising and falling delays. We will also see that the minimum is very flat, so the best ratio is a weak function of process parameters.

Recall that r is the P/N ratio of a gate and that choosing $r = k\mu$ gives equal rising and falling delays. For any value of r, the falling, rising, and average gate delays are proportional to

$$d_d \propto (1 + r)$$

$$d_u \propto \frac{k\mu}{r}(1 + r)$$

$$d \propto \frac{(1 + \frac{k\mu}{r})(1 + r)}{2} \tag{7.11}$$

where the first term reflects the rising and falling resistances and the second term reflects the capacitance. Taking the derivative of Equation 7.11 with respect to r and setting it to 0 shows that minimum average delay is achieved for

$$r = \sqrt{k\mu} \tag{7.12}$$

For typical CMOS processes, $\mu = \mu_n/\mu_p$ is between 2 and 3, which implies that the best P/N ratio of an inverter is between 1.4 and 1.7.

How sensitive is delay to the P/N width ratio? Figure 7.5 plots average delay of an FO4 inverter as a function of r, the inverter's P/N ratio, for three values of μ. It assumes $p_{inv} = 1$. The vertical axis has units of τ, the delay of a fanout-of-1 inverter with $r = \mu = 1$.

Figure 7.5 shows that the delay curves are very flat near the best value of r. Indeed, values of r from 1.4 to 1.7 give FO4 inverter delays within 1% of

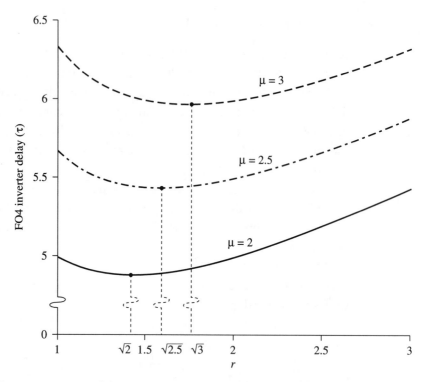

Figure 7.5 — Average delay vs. $r = P/N$ of FO4 inverters for $\mu = 2, 2.5, 3$.

minimum for any value of μ from 2 to 3. Moreover, the minimum delay at $r = \sqrt{\mu}$ is only 2–6% better than the delay at $r = \mu$. The minimum is so flat that simulation-based optimization programs often do not converge to a minimum at $r = \sqrt{\mu}$. However, the flat minimum is convenient because it means the P/N width ratio can be selected with little regard to actual process parameters. $r = 1.5$ is a convenient choice because it offers good performance and relatively easy layout. In other parts of this book, we use $r = \gamma = 2$, which is also reasonable because the delay is still low, the rise and fall times are not so different, and because 2 is a convenient number for back-of-the-envelope calculations.

The most important benefit of optimizing the P/N width ratio is not average speed, but rather reduction in area and power consumption. Remember, however, that rising and falling delays may differ substantially. For short paths, this may cause the worst-case delay to be significantly longer than the average

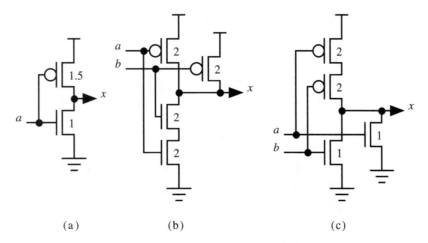

(a) (b) (c)

Figure 7.6—Inverter (a), NAND (b), and NOR (c) gates sized for improved area and average delay using a P/N width ratio of $r = \sqrt{k\mu}$, assuming $\mu = 2$. Compare these to Figure 4.1.

delay. Also, certain circuits such as clock drivers need equal rise and fall times and should use $r = \mu$.

Other gates should use a P/N ratio of about $r = \sqrt{k\mu}$. Typical values are $r = 1$ for a two-input NAND, 1.5 for an inverter or multiplexer, and 2 for a two-input NOR, as shown in Figure 7.6. Compare these designs with those of Figure 4.1. The area and power savings are especially large for NOR gates. Remember that γ is the P/N ratio r of the reference inverter. Normally, other gates have a P/N ratio of $r = k\gamma$. We see, however, that in the case of sizing for best average delay this is no longer true.

7.4 —— Summary

This chapter shows how to apply the theory of logical effort to designs using logic gates that introduce different delays for rising and falling outputs. We assign different rising and falling logical efforts, normalized such that the average logical effort of an inverter is 1. There are two ways to design paths with unequal rise and fall delays:

- Assume that each logic stage has the average of the rising and falling delays (Section 7.1). This method applies the techniques of logical effort without alteration. The maximum delay through a network may be slightly greater than the average delay.

- Use case analysis to minimize the delay of the particular transition whose propagation through the network must be fast (Section 7.2). The propagation delay of this transition can be reduced only at the expense of retarding the complementary transition. Skewed logic gates can be used to favor a critical transition even more.

The analysis of delays also leads to a calculation for the best value of r, the ratio of pullup transistor width to pulldown transistor width. While $r = \mu$ yields equal rising and falling delays for an inverter, $r = \sqrt{\mu}$ yields designs whose average delay is slightly less. Using $r = 1.5$ yields inverter designs within 1% of least delay over a wide range of processes and saves area and power relative to a circuit with equal rising and falling delays. The different rising and falling delays lead to slightly different logical efforts for gates. For simplicity, it is good enough to use the values of logical effort calculated in Chapter 4. However, more accurate effort values found from simulation or direct measurement may be used instead.

The analysis presented in this chapter must be used cautiously. The accuracy of our simple delay model of MOS logic gates is poor for modeling delay when arriving input signals have different rising and falling transition times. The accuracy would be improved by using a more accurate delay model, such as the one proposed by Horowitz [3], which considers the rise time of input transitions explicitly to predict the delay of a logic gate.

7.5 ——— Exercises

[15]   **7-1** Sketch HI-skew and LO-skew three-input NAND and NOR gates. What are logical efforts of each gate on its critical transition?

[20]   **7-2** Derive the rising, falling, and average logical efforts of the gates with unequal γ and μ in Table 7.1.

[20]   **7-3** Derive the rising, falling, and average logical efforts of skewed gates presented in Table 7.2.

[20]   **7-4** Derive the delay-vs.-γ information shown in Figure 7.5.

[15]   **7-5** Prove Equation 7.12.

Circuit Families —————————————— **8**

So far, we have applied logical effort primarily to analyze static CMOS circuits. High-performance integrated circuits often use other circuit families to achieve better speed at the expense of power consumption, noise margins, or design effort. This chapter computes the logical effort of gates in different circuit families and shows how to optimize such circuits. We begin by examining pseudo-NMOS logic and the closely related symmetric NOR gates. Then we delve into the design of domino circuits. Finally, we analyze transmission gate circuits by combining the transmission gates and driver into a single complex gate.

The method of logical effort does not apply to arbitrary transistor networks, but only to *logic gates*. A logic gate has one or more inputs and one output, subject to the following restrictions:

- The gate of each transistor connects to an input, a power supply, or the output; and

- Inputs connect only to transistor gates.

The first condition rules out multiple logic gates masquerading as one, and the second keeps inputs from attaching to transistor sources or drains, as in transmission gates without explicit drivers.

Logical effort analysis of these families will continue to use as a reference the inverter from the static logic family (shown in Figure 4.1) even though the target circuit family may use different "inverter" designs. Retaining a common reference will allow us to analyze networks that include gates from different circuit families. By contrast, if each family defined logical effort relative to the family's inverter, mixed networks would require awkward conversions from one family's logical effort to that of another. To determine the best number of stages in a path, we will have to analyze a case where the stages to be added may not be static inverters, but rather the "inverter" associated with the logic family. One consequence of using a common reference is that we will encounter gates whose logical effort is less than one, which means they are more efficient voltage-controlled amplifiers than static inverters. In fact, we will find circuit families that have lower logical effort than static CMOS.

8.1 —— Pseudo-NMOS Circuits

Static CMOS gates are slowed because an input must drive both NMOS and PMOS transistors. In any transition, either the pullup or pulldown network is activated, meaning the input capacitance of the inactive network loads the input. Moreover, PMOS transistors have poor mobility and must be wider than NMOS transistors to achieve comparable rising and falling delays, further increasing input capacitance. Pseudo-NMOS and dynamic gates offer improved speed by removing the PMOS transistor load from the input. This section analyzes pseudo-NMOS gates, while Section 8.2 explores dynamic logic.

Pseudo-NMOS gates resemble static gates, but replace the slow PMOS pullup stack with a single grounded PMOS transistor that acts as a pullup resistor. The effective pullup resistance should be large enough that the NMOS transistors can pull the output to near ground, yet low enough to pull the output HIGH quickly. Margin must be provided for manufacturing variations in the relative PMOS and NMOS mobilities. Figure 8.1 shows several pseudo-NMOS gates ratioed such that the pulldown transistors are about four times as strong as the pullup.

The analysis presented in Section 7.1 applies to pseudo-NMOS designs. The logical effort follows from considering the output current and input capacitance compared to the reference inverter from Figure 4.1. Sized as shown in Figure 8.1,

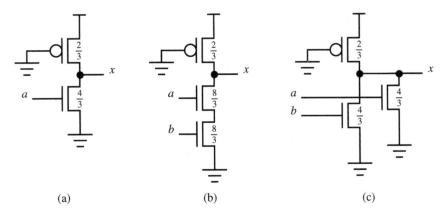

Figure 8.1 — Pseudo-NMOS inverter (a), NAND (b), and NOR (c) gates, assuming $\mu = 2$ and a 4:1 pulldown-to-pullup strength ratio.

the PMOS transistors produce 1/3 of the current of the reference inverter, and the NMOS transistor stacks produce 4/3 of the current of the reference inverter. For falling transitions, the output current is the pulldown current minus the pullup current that is fighting the pulldown, $4/3 - 1/3 = 1$. For rising transitions, the output current is just the pullup current, 1/3.

The inverter and NOR gate have an input capacitance of 4/3. The falling logical effort is the input capacitance divided by that of an inverter with the same output current, or $g_d = (4/3)/3 = 4/9$. The rising logical effort is three times greater, $g_u = 4/3$, because the current produced on a rising transition is only one-third that of a falling transition. The average logical effort is $g = (4/9 + 4/3)/2 = 8/9$. This is independent of the number of inputs, explaining why pseudo-NMOS is a way to build fast, wide NOR gates. Table 8.1 shows the rising, falling, and average logical efforts of other pseudo-NMOS gates, assuming $\mu = 2$ and a 4:1 pulldown-to-pullup strength ratio. Comparing this with Table 4.1 shows that pseudo-NMOS multiplexers are slightly better than CMOS multiplexers and that pseudo-NMOS NAND gates are worse than CMOS NAND gates. Since pseudo-NMOS logic consumes power even when not switching, it is best used for critical NOR functions, where it shows greatest advantage.

Similar analysis can compute the logical effort of other logic technologies, such as classic NMOS and bipolar and GaAs. The logical efforts should be normalized so that an inverter in the particular technology has an average logical effort of 1.

Table 8.1 — Logical efforts of pseudo-NMOS gates.

| Gate type | Logical effort g | | |
	Rising	Falling	Average
2-NAND	8/3	8/9	16/9
3-NAND	4	4/3	8/3
4-NAND	16/3	16/9	32/9
n-NOR	4/3	4/9	8/9
n-mux	8/3	8/9	16/9

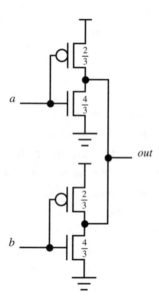

Figure 8.2 — Johnson's symmetric two-input NOR.

8.1.1   Symmetric NOR gates

Johnson [4] proposed a novel structure for a two-input NOR, shown in Figure 8.2. The gate consists of two inverters with shorted outputs, ratioed such that an inverter pulling down can overpower an inverter pulling up. This ratio is exactly the same as is used for pseudo-NMOS gates. The difference is that when the output should rise, both inverters pull up in parallel, providing more current than is available from a regular pseudo-NMOS pullup.

The input capacitance of each input is 2. The worst-case pulldown current is equal to that of a unit inverter, as we had found in the analysis of pseudo-NMOS

NOR gates. The pullup current comes from two PMOS transistors in parallel and is thus 2/3 that of a unit inverter. Therefore, the logical effort is 2/3 for a falling output and 1 for a rising output. The average effort is $g = 5/6$, which is better than that of a pseudo-NMOS NOR and far superior to that of a static CMOS NOR!

Johnson also shows that symmetric structures can be used for wider NOR functions and even for NAND gates. Exercises 8-3 and 8-4 examine the design and logical effort of such structures.

8.2 —— Domino Circuits

Pseudo-NMOS gates eliminate the bulky PMOS transistors loading the inputs, but pay the price of quiescent power dissipation and contention between the pullup and pulldown transistors. Dynamic gates offer even better logical effort and lower power consumption by using a clocked *precharge* transistor instead of a pullup that is always conducting. The dynamic gate is *precharged* HIGH, and then may *evaluate* LOW through an NMOS stack.

Unfortunately, if one dynamic inverter directly drives another, a race can corrupt the result. When the clock rises, both outputs have been precharged HIGH. The HIGH input to the first gate causes its output to fall, but the second gate's output also falls in response to its initial HIGH input. The circuit therefore produces an incorrect result because the second output will never rise during evaluation, as shown in Figure 8.3. *Domino* circuits solve this problem by using inverting static gates between dynamic gates so that the input to each dynamic gate is initially LOW. The falling dynamic output and rising static output ripple

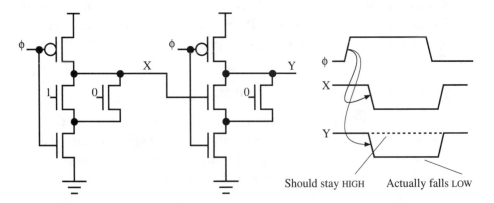

Figure 8.3 — Dynamic gates cannot be cascaded directly.

through a chain of gates like a chain of toppling dominos. Typically, domino logic runs 1.5 to 2 times faster than static CMOS logic [2] because dynamic gates present much lower input capacitance for the same output current and have a lower switching threshold, and because the inverting static gate can be skewed to favor the critical monotonically rising evaluation edges.

Figure 8.4 shows some domino gates. Each *domino* gate consists of a dynamic gate followed by an inverting static gate. A domino "gate" actually refers to two stages, rather than a single gate—unfortunate, but accepted in the literature. The static gate is often but not always an inverter. Because the dynamic gate's output falls monotonically during evaluation, the static gate should be a HI-skew gate that favors its rising output, as discussed in Section 7.2.1. We mark such gates with "H" as shown in Figure 8.4. We have calculated the logical effort of HI-skew gates in Table 7.2 and will compute the logical effort of dynamic gates in the next section. The logical effort of a domino gate is then the product of the logical effort of the dynamic gate and of the HI-skew gate. *Remember that a domino gate counts as two stages when choosing the best number of stages.*

A dynamic gate may be designed with or without a clocked evaluation transistor; the extra transistor slows the gate but eliminates any path between power and ground during precharge when the inputs are still high. Some dynamic gates include weak PMOS transistors called *keepers* so that the dynamic output will remain driven if the clock stops high.

Domino designers face a number of questions when selecting a circuit topology. How many stages are best? Should the static gates be inverters, or should they perform logic? How big should precharge transistors and keepers be? What is the benefit of removing the clocked evaluation transistors? We will show that domino logic should use a stage effort of 2–2.75, rather than 4, which we found for static logic. Therefore, paths tend to use more stages, and it is rarely beneficial to perform logic with the inverting static gates.

8.2.1   Logical effort of dynamic gates

The logical effort for dynamic gates can be computed just as for static gates. Figure 8.5 shows several dynamic gates with NMOS stacks sized for current equal to that of a unit inverter. Precharge is normally not a critical operation, so only the pulldown current affects logical effort. The logical efforts are shown in Table 8.2.

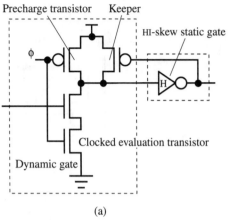

(a)

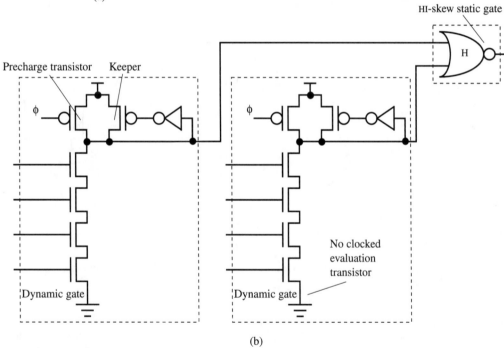

(b)

Figure 8.4—Domino buffer (a) and eight-input AND (b) gates.

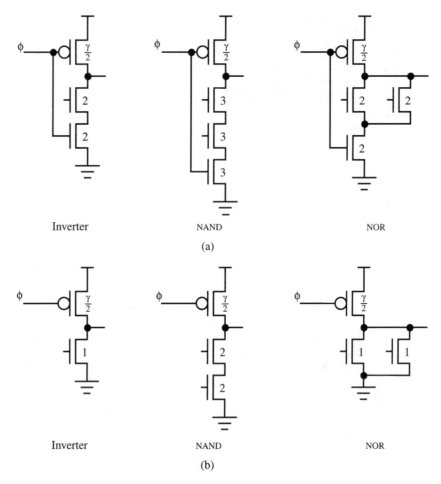

Figure 8.5 — Dynamic gates with (a) and without (b) clocked evaluation transistors.

Logical effort partially explains why dynamic gates are faster than static gates. In static gates, much of the input capacitance is wasted on slow PMOS transistors that are not even used during a falling transition. Therefore, a dynamic inverter enjoys a logical effort only 1/3 that of a static inverter because all of the input capacitance is dedicated to the critical falling transition.

Our simple model for estimating logical effort fails to capture two other reasons that dynamic gates are fast. One is the lower switching threshold of the gate: the dynamic gate output will begin switching as soon as inputs rise to V_t,

Table 8.2 — Logical effort per input of dynamic gates.

Gate type	Clocked evaluation transistor?	Formula	$n = 2$	$n = 3$	$n = 4$
Inverter	Yes	2/3			
	No	1/3			
NAND	Yes	$(n + 1)/3$	1	4/3	5/3
	No	$n/3$	2/3	1	4/3
NOR	Yes	2/3	2/3	2/3	2/3
	No	1/3	1/3	1/3	1/3
Multiplexer	Yes	1	1	1	1
	No	2/3	2/3	2/3	2/3

rather than all the way to $V_{DD}/2$. Another is the fact that velocity saturation makes the resistance of long NMOS stacks lower than our resistive model predicts. Therefore, simulations show that dynamic gates have even lower logical effort than Table 8.2 predicts.

Notice that dynamic NOR gates have less logical effort than NAND gates and indeed have effort independent of the number of inputs. This is reversed from static CMOS gates and motivates designers to use wide NOR gates where possible.

8.2.2 Stage effort of domino circuits

In Section 3.4, we found that the best stage effort ρ is about 4 for static CMOS paths. This result depends on the fact that extra amplification could be provided by a string of inverters with logical effort 1. Domino paths are slightly different because extra amplification can be provided by domino buffers with logical effort less than 1. Adding more buffers actually reduces F, the path effort! Therefore, we would expect that domino paths would benefit from using more stages, or equivalently, that the best stage effort ρ is lower for domino paths. In this section, we will compute this best stage effort.

Our arguments parallel those in Section 3.4. We begin with a path that has n_1 stages and path effort F. We contemplate adding n_2 additional stages to obtain a path with a total of $N = n_1 + n_2$ stages. This time, however, the gates we add are not static inverters. Instead, we may add domino buffers, which count as two stages. In general, the additional stages have logical effort g and parasitic delay p. The extra gates therefore change the path effort. The minimum delay of the path is

$$\hat{D} = N \left(Fg^{N-n_1} \right)^{1/N} + \left(\sum_{i=1}^{n_1} p_i \right) + (N - n_1)p \tag{8.1}$$

We can differentiate and solve for $\hat{N}$, which gives minimum delay (see Exercise 8-5). When parasitics are nonzero, it proves more convenient to compute the best stage effort $\rho(g, p)$, which depends on the logical effort and parasitic delay of the extra stages. The mathematics is hideous, but the conclusion is remarkably elegant:

$$\rho(g, p) = g\rho\left(1, \frac{p}{g} \right) \tag{8.2}$$

where $\rho(1, p_{inv})$ is the best stage effort for a given parasitic inverter delay, determined by Equation 3.25 and plotted in Figure 3.4. This result depends only on the characteristics of the stages being added, rather than on any properties of the original path.

Let us apply this result to domino circuits, where the extra stages are domino buffers. We must first find g and p per stage of the buffer. Because the buffer is made of two stages, the average logical effort per stage is the square root of the logical effort of the two stages. The average parasitic delay per stage is half of the parasitic delay of the two stages.

The logical effort of a domino buffer with a clocked evaluation transistor, like the one in Figure 8.4, is $(2/3) \times (5/6) = 10/18$ using the information from Tables 8.2 and 7.2. By counting diffusion capacitance on the output node, let us estimate the parasitic delays to be $(5/6)p_{inv}$ for the HI-skew static inverter, and p_{inv} for the dynamic inverter with series evaluation transistor, for a two-stage parasitic delay of $5/6 + 1 = (11/6)p_{inv}$. Hence, the average logical effort per stage is $g = \sqrt{10/18} = 0.75$, and the average parasitic delay per stage is $p = (11/6)p_{inv}/2 = 0.92p_{inv}$. If $p_{inv} = 1$, the best stage effort is $\rho(0.75, 0.92) = 0.75\rho(1, 0.92/0.75) = 2.76$. The same reasoning applies to dynamic inverters with no clocked evaluation transistors having average $g = 0.52$ and $p = 2/3$ per stage, yielding a best stage effort of 2.0.

In summary, domino paths with clocked evaluation transistors should target a stage effort around 2.75, rather than the effort of 4 used for static paths. If the stage effort is higher, the path may be improved by using more stages. If the stage effort is lower, the path may be improved by combining logic into more complex gates. Similarly, domino paths with no clocked evaluation transistors should target a stage effort of 2.0. Because it is impractical to leave out all of the clocked evaluation transistors, many domino paths mix clocked and unclocked dynamic gates and should target an effort between 2 and 2.75. As with static logic, the delay is a weak function of path effort near the best effort, and so the designer has freedom to stray from the best effort without severe performance penalty. The following examples will help build intuition about the similarities and differences of static and domino path designs.

EXAMPLE 8.1   Design a string of inverters to drive a load of 256 units if the input capacitance is 1 unit. Show both static and domino designs.

SOLUTION   The static design has a path effort of $F = 256$. Therefore, it should have about $\log_\rho F = 4$ stages assuming $\rho = 4$. Each of the four stages has a stage effort of $f = 256^{1/4} = 4$.

The domino design path effort depends on the number of stages. A $2n$ stage path built from n domino buffers has a path effort of $F = 256(10/18)^n$ because we know the logical effort of a domino buffer is $10/18$. We can find the best number of stages by solving $f = F^{1/(2n)} = \rho$, where $\rho = 2.75$ for domino paths. This recommends $2n = 4.25$ stages, so again we choose a four-stage design. The stage effort is $f = \left(256(10/18)^2\right)^{1/4} = 2.98$, close to our target $\rho = 2.75$.

These two designs are shown in Figure 8.6. The gate sizes are selected for equal stage effort. Notice that this causes unequal electrical efforts in the domino design because the dynamic and HI-skew inverters have different logical efforts. The electrical effort per pair of stages is 16 in both cases. This shows that in a buffer chain, the best average electrical effort per stage is independent of the circuit family and should be about 4, depending on parasitics. The best stage effort, however, is lower for domino than static circuits because the domino gates have lower logical effort. The next example will investigate a path that includes logic as well as buffers.   ∎

EXAMPLE 8.2   Design an amplifier for the 16-input OR gate shown in Figure 8.7. Show both static and domino amplifier designs.

SOLUTION   Observe that the OR gate is built from four four-input NOR gates driving a four-input NAND. As we will see in Chapter 11, it may be better to break the

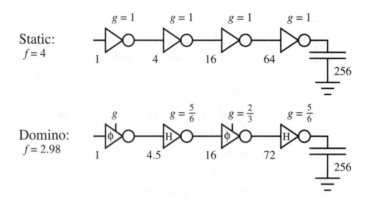

Figure 8.6 — Static and domino buffer designs.

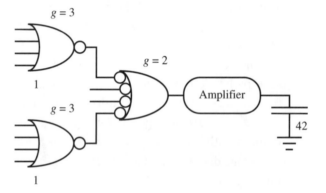

Figure 8.7 — 16-input OR gate driving a large load.

gate into more stages of gates with fewer inputs, but for this example we will keep the given structure and add inverters.

For the static design, the path effort is $F = 42 \times 3 \times 2 = 252$, so we should use a four-stage design with a stage effort of about 4.

For the domino design, we retain the OR gate, and simply add n domino buffers. The path effort decreases with the number of buffers in the amplifier. Table 8.3 shows the path and stage efforts of a variety of designs. The best stage effort is $\rho = 2.75$, so the one- and two-amplifier designs are reasonable. Let us choose the design with a single domino amplifier because fewer gates lead to lower area and power.

Table 8.3 — Path and stage efforts of 16-input OR gate with n domino buffers.

n	F	f
0	252	15.9
1	140	3.43
2	77	2.06
3	42	1.60

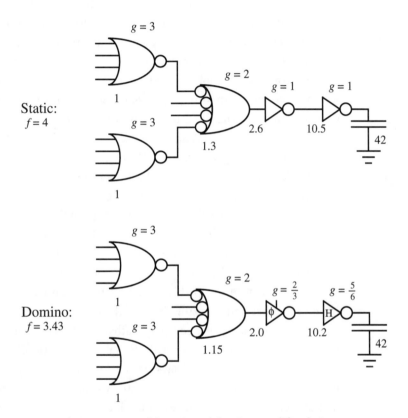

Figure 8.8 — 16-input OR gates with static and domino amplifier designs.

Figure 8.8 shows both designs with gate sizes. Notice that a greater portion of the electrical effort is borne by the amplifier in the domino case than the static case because, compared to the OR gate, the domino buffer is a better amplifier than the static buffer. ∎

8.2.3   Building logic in static gates

We have seen that the HI-skew static gate following a dynamic gate can be either an inverter or a more complex function. When, if ever, is it beneficial to build logic into the HI-skew static gate rather than use an inverter? At first the static inverters may seem wasteful because they have propagation delay and perform no logic. Remember, however, that a principal lesson of logical effort is that a path has a best number of stages set by its path effort and that using fewer stages actually makes the path slower rather than faster. In this section, we will show that it is rarely beneficial to replace inverters with more complex gates. The argument is somewhat complex and tangential to the rest of the chapter, so you may skip it unless you are particularly interested in domino design.

For a concrete example, consider the two ways of building an eight-input domino AND gate shown in Figure 8.9. One design (a) consists of {dynamic 4-NAND, inverter, dynamic 2-NAND, inverter}. Another design (b) is {dynamic 4-NAND, HI-skew 2-NOR}. Which is better? The logical effort of the path is always larger when HI-skew gates are used. However, the HI-skew gate could reduce the parasitic delay if it reduces the total number of stages. If the stage effort of the first design is very small, the path may become faster by using fewer stages. But if the stage effort is large, the first design is best. In this section, we will quantify "small" and "large" to develop guidelines on the use of logic in static gates.

We can use our results from the previous section to address this question. The topology should be chosen to obtain a stage effort $\rho = \rho(g, p)$. What do g and p mean in this equation? In the previous section, they were the logical effort and parasitic delay of the extra inverters being added to the path. In general when we compare paths of different lengths, they describe the extra "stuff" in the longer path. By taking the ratio of logical efforts and the difference in parasitic delays of the longer and shorter paths, we capture the extra "stuff" in the longer path. We then partition this extra among the number of additional stages in the longer path to find a mean logical effort and parasitic delay, which are g and p. In summary, when we compare two paths with n_1 and $n_1 + n_2$ stages with logical efforts and parasitic delays g_1, p_1, g_2, and p_2, respectively, $g = (g_2/g_1)^{1/n_2}$ and $p = (p_2 - p_1)/n_2$. For stage effort below $\rho(g, p)$, the shorter path is better, meaning it is advantageous to use logic in the static stage. For stage efforts above ρ, the longer path is better. The following example will clarify this calculation.

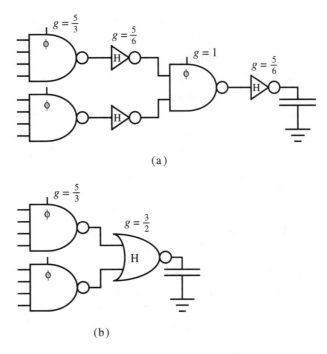

(a)

(b)

Figure 8.9 — Two designs for eight-input domino AND gates: {dynamic 4-NAND, inverter, dynamic 2-NAND, inverter} (a) and {dynamic 4-NAND, HI-skew 2-NOR} (b).

EXAMPLE 8.3 Which of the designs in Figure 8.9 is best if the path has electrical effort of 1? if the path has electrical effort of 5?

SOLUTION We could solve this problem by computing the delays of each design and directly comparing speed. Instead, we will use the stage effort criteria derived in this section. The change in logical effort from design (b) to design (a) is $\frac{(5/6) \times (1) \times (5/6)}{3/2} = 0.46$. This occurs over two extra stages, so the logical effort per stage is $g = \sqrt{0.46} = 0.68$. We could work out the parasitic delay exactly, but we recall that over a range of parasitics, using $\rho(1, p) = 4$ gives good results. We will use this approximation to find $\rho(0.68, p/0.68) = 0.68\rho(1, p) \approx 0.68 \times 4 = 2.72$. If the stage effort is below 2.7, design (b) is best. If the stage effort is above 2.7, design (a) is best.

   Design (b) has a logical effort of $(5/3) \times (3/2) = 2.5$ and thus a path effort of $2.5H$ and stage effort of $\sqrt{2.5H}$. If $H = 1$, the stage effort is 1.6 and design (b) is best. If $H = 5$, the stage effort is 3.5 and design (a) is best. ∎

This seems like too much work for a simple example in which comparing delays is easy. The advantage of the method is the insight it gives: we should build logic into static gates only when the stage effort is below about 2.7, indicating that the path has too many stages. Moreover, it is best first to reduce the number of stages by using more complex dynamic gates. Simple calculations show that the logical effort of a dynamic gate with up to four series transistors followed by a HI-skew inverter generally is lower than the logical effort of the same function built from a smaller dynamic gate followed by a static gate. An exception is very wide dynamic NOR gates and multiplexers, which may be faster when divided into narrower chunks feeding a HI-skew NAND gate to reduce parasitic delay.

In summary it is rarely beneficial to build logic into the static stages of domino gates. If a domino path has stage effort below about 2.7, the path can be improved by reducing the number of stages. The designer should first use more complex dynamic gates with up to 4 series transistors. If the stage effort is still below 2.7, only then should the designer consider replacing some of the static inverters with more complex static gates.

8.2.4   Designing dynamic gates

In addition to the logic transistors, dynamic gates have transistors to control precharge and evaluation and to prevent the output from floating. How big should each transistor be?

The size of the precharge transistor influences precharge time. A reasonable choice is to size it as if the dynamic gate were a LO-skew gate; hence the PMOS transistor can source half the current of the pulldown stack. Figure 8.5 uses such sizes.

The designer has several choices regarding the evaluation transistor. If the circuit inputs can be designed so that there is no path to ground during precharge, the clocked evaluation transistor can safely be omitted. Even if there is a path to ground during part of precharge, the transistor can be removed if some extra power consumption is tolerable and the precharge transistor is strong enough to pull the output acceptably HIGH in the time available.

When a clocked evaluation transistor is necessary, how big should it be? One reasonable choice is to make the clocked evaluation transistor equal in size to the logic transistors in the dynamic gate. For higher speed, the clocked device can be

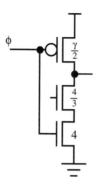

Figure 8.10 — Dynamic inverter with double-sized clocked evaluation transistor.

made larger, just as an unbalanced gate can favor the critical inputs at the expense of the noncritical ones. For example, Figure 8.10 shows a dynamic inverter with a clocked pulldown twice as large as in Figure 8.5. Because the input transistor is smaller, the total pulldown resistance matches that of a normal inverter. The logical effort is thus only 4/9, much better than the effort of 2/3 with a normal pulldown size and nearly as good as 1/3 for a dynamic inverter with no clocked pulldown. The main cost of large clocked transistors is the extra clock power. Therefore, a small amount of unbalancing such as 1.5 or 2× is best.

Some dynamic gates use keepers to prevent the output from floating high during evaluation, as shown in Figure 8.11. The keepers also slightly improve the noise margin on the input of the dynamic gate. They have little effect on the noise margin at the output because they are usually too small to respond rapidly. The drawback of keepers is that they initially fight a falling output and retard the dynamic gate. How big should keepers be?

The keeper current subtracts from the pulldown stack current during evaluation. If the ratio of keeper current to pulldown stack current is r, the logical effort of the dynamic gate increases by $1/(1 - r)$. Therefore, a reasonable rule of thumb is to size keepers at $r = 1/4$ to $1/10$ of the strength of the pulldown stack. For small dynamic gates, this implies that keepers must be weaker than minimum-sized devices. Increasing the channel length of the keepers will weaken them, but will also add to the capacitive loading on the inverter. A better approach is to split the keeper into two series transistors, as shown in Figure 8.12. Such an approach minimizes the load on the inverter while reducing keeper current.

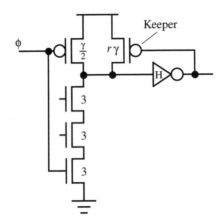

Figure 8.11 — Keeper on a dynamic gate.

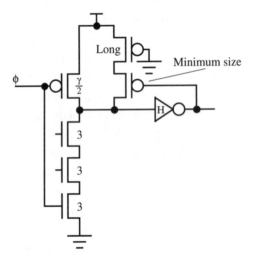

Figure 8.12 — Weak keeper split into two parts.

8.3 ——— Transmission Gates

Many transmission gate circuits can be analyzed with the method of logical effort by incorporating the transmission gate into the logic gate that drives it. Figure 8.13 shows an inverter driving a transmission gate, and then shows the same circuit redrawn. The second circuit is essentially a leg of a multiplexer; see also Figure 4.4.

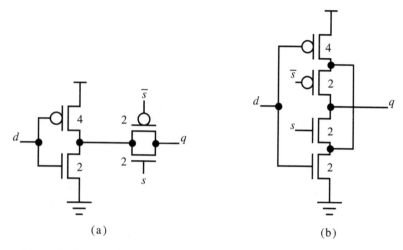

Figure 8.13 — An inverter driving a transmission gate (a), and the same circuit redrawn as a single logic gate for the purposes of logical effort analysis (b).

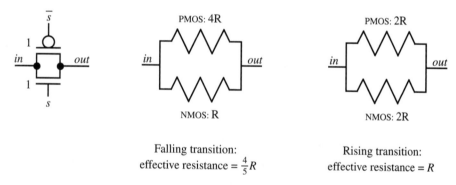

Figure 8.14 — A transmission gate with unit NMOS and PMOS transistors, and its equivalent model for rising and falling transitions.

The PMOS and NMOS transistors in the transmission gate can be equal in width because both transistors operate in parallel while driving the output. Remember that NMOS transistors are good for pulling an output down but poor at pulling an output up. PMOS transistors have the opposite capability. Figure 8.14 shows the transmission gate modeled as two parallel resistors representing the two transistors. It assumes the PMOS transistor has half the mobility of the NMOS transistor and that when a transistor pulls in its poor direction, it has twice as much resistance as when it pulls in its good direction. The figure shows that the effective pulldown and pullup resistance of the transmission gate are nearly equal even though the PMOS and NMOS transistors are the same width. For simplicity, we ignore the slightly lower falling transition resistance and model the transmission gate as having resistance R, the same as an ideal NMOS transistor that could pull up or down equally well. A larger PMOS transistor would slightly improve current drive on rising outputs, but would add significant diffusion capacitance, which slows both transitions and would increase the loading on the select input.

Given this model, the circuit in Figure 8.13 has drive equal to that of an inverter for both rising and falling transitions. The logical effort is 2 for input d and only 4/3 for $s*$, the bundle consisting of s and its complement $\bar{s}$. This improvement in logical effort on $s*$ relative to a normal tristate inverter comes at the expense of increased diffusion capacitance, leaving no great advantage for transmission gate tristates over normal tristates.

In general, transmission gate circuits are sized with equal PMOS and NMOS transistors and compared to an inverter with equal output current. As long as a delay equation such as Equation 3.8 describes the delay of a circuit, the method of logical effort applies. However, the parasitic capacitance increases rapidly with series transmission gates, so practical circuits are normally limited to about two series transmission gates.

A common fallacy when characterizing circuits with transmission gates is to measure the delay from the input to the output of the transmission gate. This makes transmission gate logic seem very fast, especially if the input were driven with a voltage source. As logical effort shows, because the transmission gate retards its driver, the only meaningful way to characterize a transmission gate circuit is in conjunction with the logic gate that drives it.

8.4 —— Summary

This chapter used ideas of best stage effort, unbalanced gates, and unequal rise and fall delays to analyze circuit families other than static CMOS. Quantifying the logical effort of these circuit families enables us to understand better their advantages over static CMOS and to choose the most effective topologies.

We first examined ratioed circuits, such as pseudo-NMOS gates, by computing separate rising and falling logical efforts. The analysis shows that Johnson's symmetric NOR is a particularly efficient way to implement the NOR function at the expense of extra power dissipation.

We then turned to domino circuits and found a remarkable result for the best stage effort of a path when considering additional stages, given in Equation 8.2. The equation tells us that the best stage effort for dynamic circuits is in the range of 2–2.75, depending on the use of clocked evaluation transistors. The equation also tells us when it is beneficial to break a path into more stages of simpler gates. We conclude that a path should incorporate logic into static gates only when the dynamic gates are already complex and the stage effort is still less than 2.7.

Finally, we explored transmission gate circuits. The logical effort of transmission gate circuits can be found by redrawing the driver and transmission gates as a single complex gate. Neglecting the driver is a common pitfall that makes transmission gates appear faster than they actually are.

8.5 —— Exercises

[20] **8-1** Derive the logical efforts of pseudo-NMOS gates shown in Table 8.1.

[20] **8-2** Design an eight-input AND gate with an electrical effort of 12 using pseudo-NMOS logic. If the parasitic delay of an n-input pseudo-NMOS NOR gate is $(4n + 2)/9$, what is the path delay? How does it compare to the results from Section 2.1?

[25] **8-3** Design a three-input symmetric NOR gate. Size the inverters so that the pulldown is four times as strong as the net worst-case pullup. What is the average logical effort? How does it compare to a pseudo-NMOS NOR? to static CMOS?

[20] **8-4** Design a two-input symmetric NAND gate. Size the inverters so that the pullup is four times as strong as the pulldown. What is the average logical effort? How does it compare to static CMOS?

[30] **8-5** Prove Equation 8.2.

[25] **8-6** Design a 4–16 decoder like the one in Section 2.2, using domino logic. You may assume you have true and complement address inputs available.

[25] **8-7** A 4:1 multiplexer might use two levels of transmission gates. Design such a structure and compute its logical effort when the inputs are driven by inverters.

Forks of Amplifiers ———————— 9

The most difficult problems in applying the method of logical effort stem from branching. When a logic signal divides within a network and flows along multiple paths, we must decide how to allocate the available current. How much should each path load the common signal? In general, paths that have higher logical or electrical effort should receive a greater share of the signal's drive. When a logic signal has significant parasitic capacitance—for example, when it drives a long wire—it branches: because some of the signal's current charges the parasitic load, less drive is available to the logic path.

Optimizing networks that branch usually involves adjusting branching effort along paths to equalize the delays in several paths through the network. Determining the branching factors adds a new element of difficulty to our design method that can be quite tricky to handle. One of the complications is that different paths through a network often have different numbers of stages. Branching can sometimes be straightforward, depending on the design problem. For example, branching is simple in the synchronous arbitration problem of Section 2.3.

This chapter covers the simple but common case of branching: generating the true and complement forms of a logic signal. We call such circuits *forks*, after the general appearance of their circuit diagrams. Forks are interesting not only for their own utility, but also as a further exercise in applying the method of logical effort. Many CMOS circuits require forks to produce such true and complement signals. For example, an arm of the multiplexer circuit of Figure 4.4 switches on when one of its control lines, s_i, goes HIGH, and the other, $\overline{s_i}$, goes LOW. The XOR circuit shown in Figure 4.5 also requires true and complement forms of its two input signals. We often use the notation $x.H$ and $x.L$ to indicate true and complement forms of a signal x, respectively. The signal $x.H$ is HIGH and $x.L$ is LOW when x is TRUE; $x.H$ is LOW and $x.L$ is HIGH when x is FALSE.

9.1 —— The Fork Circuit Form

An *amplifier fork*, or simply a *fork*, consists of two strings of inverters that share a common input, as shown in Figure 9.1. One of the strings contains an odd number of inverters, and the other contains an even number. True and complement signals of this kind, particularly for driving multiplexers, are often required at relatively high power levels. For example, to multiplex an entire 64-bit word onto a bus would require true and complement signals that can drive all 64 multiplexers. As we have already learned, least delay in driving such large loads will be obtained by including the proper number of amplifying inverters in the drive path. The figure illustrates a notation we use when the exact number of inverters in each path is not known: an inverter symbol with a star inside it represents a string of an odd number of inverters, while a triangle symbol with an embedded star but without the small circle at its output stands for an even number of inverters. We have chosen to name forks by the number of inverters in each string. A 3–2 fork, for example, has three amplifiers in one string and two in the other. Figure 9.2 shows a 2–1 fork and a 3–2 fork.

It is useful to think of pairs of amplifier strings as a fork only when the true and complement output signals must emerge at the same time. The driver for the address lines in Figure 2.3 has this property; delays in either leg of the fork can result in increased overall delay. We therefore wish to design forks so that the delay in each leg is the same.

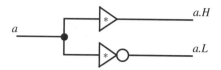

Figure 9.1 — General form of an amplifier fork. One leg inverts the input signal, and one does not.

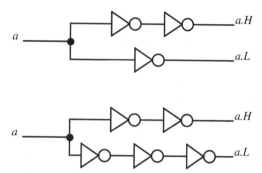

Figure 9.2 — A 2–1 fork and a 3–2 fork, both of which produce the same logic signals.

In this chapter we shall assume that the load driven by each leg of the fork is the same. A fork that drives an XOR gate such as that of Figure 4.5 has this property; both a and $\bar{a}$, for example, drive the same load. A multiplexer like the one in Figure 4.4, however, presents unequal loads, because the pullup transistor driven by $\bar{s}$ is wider than the pulldown transistor driven by s. We shall defer to Chapter 10 consideration of circuits with multiple outputs driving different load capacitance.

The design of a fork starts out with a known load on the output legs and known total input capacitance. As shown in Figure 9.3, we shall call the two output capacitances C_a and C_b. We will call the combined total load driven $C_{out} = C_a + C_b$. The total input capacitance for the fork we shall call $C_{in} = C_{in_a} + C_{in_b}$, and can thereby describe the electrical effort for the fork as a whole to be $H = C_{out}/C_{in}$. This electrical effort of the fork may differ from the electrical efforts of the individual legs, C_a/C_{in_a} and C_b/C_{in_b}.

The input current to an optimized fork may divide unequally to drive its two legs. Even if the load capacitances on the two legs of the fork are equal, it is not in general true that the input capacitances to the two legs of the fork

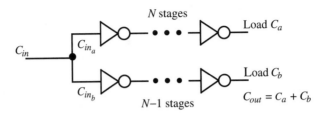

Figure 9.3—A general fork, showing notation for load capacitances.

should be equal. Because the legs have different numbers of amplifiers but must operate with the same delay, their electrical efforts may differ. The leg that can support the larger electrical effort, usually the leg with more amplifiers, will require less input current than the other leg, and can therefore have a smaller input capacitance. If we call the electrical efforts of the two legs H_a and H_b, using the notation of Figure 9.3, then $H_a = C_a/C_{in_a}$ and $H_b = C_b/C_{in_b}$. Even if $C_a = C_b$, H_a may not equal H_b, and C_{in_a} and C_{in_b} may also differ.

The design of a fork is a balancing act. Either leg of the fork can be made faster by reducing its electrical effort, which is done by giving it wider transistors for its initial amplifier. Doing so, however, takes input current away from the other leg of the fork and will inevitably make it slower. A fixed value of C_{in} provides, in effect, only a certain total width of transistor material to distribute between the first stages of the two legs; putting wider transistors in one leg requires putting narrower transistors in the other leg. The task of designing a minimum delay fork is really the task of allocating the available transistor width set by C_{in} to the input stages of the two legs.

EXAMPLE 9.1 Design a 2–1 fork with input capacitance $C_{in} = 10$ and total output capacitance $C_{out} = 200$. What is the total delay of the fork?

SOLUTION Using the notation of Figure 9.3, we have $C_{in} = 10$ and $C_a = C_b = 100$. Let's use the symbol β to denote the fraction of input capacitance allocated to the two-inverter leg, that is, $C_{in_a} = \beta C_{in}$. The remainder is allocated to the one-inverter leg, that is, $C_{in_b} = (1 - \beta)C_{in}$. We want to find the value of β that will equalize delays in the two legs. Applying Equation 1.17 to both legs, we have

$$2\left(\frac{100}{10\beta}\right)^{1/2} + 2p_{inv} = \left(\frac{100}{10(1 - \beta)}\right) + p_{inv} \qquad (9.1)$$

We solve this equation numerically to find that $\beta = 0.258$, so $C_{in_a} = 10\beta = 2.6$ and $C_{in_b} = 10(1 - \beta) = 7.4$. The second inverter in the two-inverter leg has input capacitance $C_{a2} = 2.6 \times \sqrt{100/2.6} = 16.1$. The delay in the one-inverter leg is $C_b/C_{in_b} + p_{inv} = 100/7.4 + 1 = 14.5$. The delay in the two-inverter leg is $C_{a2}/C_{in_a} + C_a/C_{a2} + 2p_{inv} = 16.1/2.6 + 100/16.1 + 2 = 14.5$. Thus, the two legs have equal delay as expected. ∎

EXAMPLE 9.2 Design a 3–2 fork with the same input and output capacitances as in the previous example.

SOLUTION Again using β to determine the fraction of input capacitance allocated to the longer leg, we have

$$3 \left(\frac{100}{10\beta} \right)^{1/3} + 3p_{inv} = 2 \left(\frac{100}{10(1 - \beta)} \right)^{1/2} + 2p_{inv} \tag{9.2}$$

This equation solves to $\beta = 0.513$, with a delay of 11.1. Note that this delay is less than the delay we computed for the 2–1 fork with the same input and output capacitances. ∎

These two examples show that obtaining the least delay requires choosing the right number of stages in the fork. This result is not surprising. In fact, we should have anticipated that the first design could be improved because the effort of the one-inverter leg is 13.5, very far from the best ρ. This result suggests that we should develop a method to determine the best number of stages to use in a fork. The next section turns to this problem.

9.2 — How Many Stages Should a Fork Use?

An optimized fork must have legs that differ in length by at most one stage. We can see that this is true by examining in detail the relationship between total delay and electrical effort that was discussed in Chapter 1. Figure 9.4 shows schematically a plot of delay vs. electrical effort for amplifiers with $N - 1$, N, and $N + 1$ stages. The thick curve represents the fastest possible amplifier for any given electrical effort, and so no amplifier design may lie below it. For different electrical efforts, different numbers of stages are required to obtain this optimum design, as the figure shows.

The task of designing a fork is specified by giving an electrical effort that the combined activities of its two legs are to support. In Figure 9.4 such an electrical effort is represented by the vertical line. One possible design for the fork requires

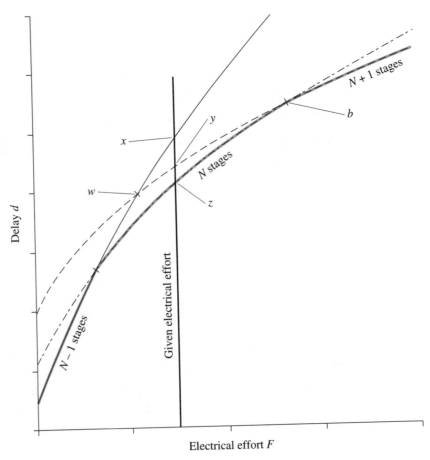

Figure 9.4—A plot of delay vs. electrical effort for reasoning about forks.

each leg to support exactly this electrical effort. Since the two legs of the fork must produce true and complement signals, their lengths must differ by an odd number of inverters. Thus if one leg has N stages, its delay can be reduced to the point labeled z in the figure, but the other leg must have either $N - 1$ or $N + 1$ stages, and its delay can be reduced only to the points labeled x and y, respectively. For the particular electrical effort we have chosen, point y is faster than point x. Thus we have a fork with two legs that support equal electrical effort but have unequal delay.

We can improve such a fork by raising the electrical effort of one leg and reducing the electrical effort of the other in such a way as to continue supporting the required total electrical effort. In effect we slide to the right from point z, thus increasing its delay, and the left from point y, thus decreasing its delay. We do this by reallocating transistor width from the transistors of the first amplifier in one leg to the transistors of the first amplifier in the other leg. Our intent, of course, is to decrease the delay of the slower leg as much as we can, which will be until the two legs are equal in delay.

You might think that there are two possible discontinuities in the process of reallocating the input transistor width. From point z moving to the right we may reach point b before the equal delay condition is met, or from point y moving to the left we may reach point w before the equal delay condition is met. Z could not possibly reach point b, however, because the delay at point y is already less than that at point b. If point y reaches point w before the equal delay condition is met, we should change it from $N + 1$ to $N - 1$ stages and continue along the $N - 1$ stage curve until we reach the equal delay condition. It is not hard to see that for any placement of the given electrical effort line, this optimization procedure will result in a fork with legs that differ in length by a single amplifier.

One leg of a fork will always have exactly the same number of stages as would an optimum amplifier supporting an equal electrical effort. This is easy to see from Figure 9.4. If the given electrical effort line crosses through the dark optimum curve in the segment where N stages are best, one arm will have N stages. The other arm will have either $N + 1$ or $N - 1$ stages. Thus one simple way to design nearly optimal forks is to choose the number of stages for one leg from Table 1.3, and then use one more or one fewer stage for the other leg. The electrical effort for the fork as a whole, $H = C_{out}/C_{in}$, can be used as a guide, since the electrical efforts of each leg will turn out to be nearly that value. Applying this technique to Example 9.1, $H = 20$ would have correctly suggested a 3–2 fork as the best design.

A more precise guide for choosing the number of stages in a fork appears in Table 9.1. For any given electrical effort, the table shows what kind of fork to use. Remember that the electrical effort of the fork is the total load of all the legs divided by the total input capacitance. The break points in Table 9.1 lie between the break points in Table 1.3. It is easy to see that this must be so. Table 1.3 lists certain electrical efforts, namely, 5.83, 22.3, 82.2, and so on, for which strings of amplifiers N and $N - 1$ long give identical delays. Therefore, for an electrical effort of 22.3, for example, a 3–2 fork is best, because both strings of three amplifiers and strings of two amplifiers have the same delay for this electrical effort. For an electrical effort of 82.2, a 4–3 fork is best for a similar reason. In these special cases, moreover, the input capacitance to the legs will

Table 9.1 — Break points for forks assuming $p_{inv} = 1.0$.

Electrical effort		Fork structure
From	To	
	9.68	2–1
9.68	38.7	3–2
38.7	146	4–3
146	538	5–4
538	1970	6–5
1970	7150	7–6

also be identical. For some electrical effort between 22.3 and 82.2, a 4–3 fork and a 3–2 fork will give identical results. This is the break point recorded in Table 9.1.

It is easy to see how Table 9.1 was computed. Consider the break point where a 3–2 fork and a 4–3 fork provide identical results. At this break point the two forks exhibit identical delays. The three-amplifier legs in each fork must be identical. Moreover, the amount of input current left over from the three-amplifier leg in each fork must also be the same, and thus the input currents of the two-amplifier leg in one fork and the four-amplifier leg in the other fork must also be the same. Thus at the break point between 3–2 and 4–3 forks, the electrical effort of the two-amplifier leg and of the four-amplifier leg must be the same, and they are operating with identical delays. In terms of Figure 9.4, they must both be operating at point w. This reasoning leads directly to equations with solutions that give the electrical effort of optimal forks at these break points (see Exercise 9-1).

EXAMPLE 9.3 Design a path to drive the enable signals on a bank of 64 tristate bus drivers. The first stage of the path can present an input capacitance of 12 unit-sized transistors, and the tristate drivers are each 6 times unit size. A unit-sized tristate is shown in Figure 9.5.

SOLUTION The load on each of the true and complement enable signals is $64 \times 6 \times 2 = 768$ unit-sized transistors. Therefore the electrical effort of the entire bundle is $(768 + 768)/12 = 128$. From Table 9.1, we find that a 4–3 fork is best. Now we must divide the input capacitance between the two legs. If the four-inverter leg gets a fraction β, then we have

$$4 \left(\frac{768}{12\beta} \right)^{1/4} + 4p_{inv} = 3 \left(\frac{768}{12(1 - \beta)} \right)^{1/3} + 3p_{inv} \qquad (9.3)$$

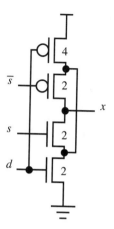

Figure 9.5 — A unit-sized tristate inverter.

This equation solves to $\beta = 0.46$. Therefore, the input capacitance on the 4-fork is $12 \times 0.46 = 5.5$, and the input capacitance on the 3-fork must be $12 - 4.8 = 6.5$. Hence, the electrical effort of the 4-fork is $768/5.5 = 140$, and the electrical effort of the 3-fork is $768/6.5 = 118$. Notice how the electrical effort of the entire bundle, 128, is unevenly allocated to the legs to improve the delay of the slower leg at the expense of the faster until the two have equal delay of 17.7. The stage effort of the 4-leg is $140^{1/4} = 3.44$, and the stage effort of the 3-leg is $118^{1/3} = 4.90$. Therefore, the capacitances of each gate can be computed, as shown in Figure 9.6. ∎

If very large amplification is required, forks with large numbers of amplifiers in each leg may be best. We may well ask whether to prefer an 11–10 fork to a string of eight amplifiers followed by a 3–2 fork. In fact, there is little to be gained by using forks with more than 3–2 amplifiers; this is quantified in Exercise 9-2. On the other hand, long strings of amplifiers will no doubt contain very large transistors that will be laid out in sections anyway. Thus the layout penalty of a long fork may be small.

Ironically, the most difficult case occurs when very *small* amplification is required. It is almost never advisable to use a 1–0 fork such as the one shown in Figure 9.7, because the delays in the two paths cannot be equalized: the delay of the zero-stage path is guaranteed to be less than that of the one-stage path. Exercise 9-3 examines the performance penalty of 1–0 forks. Rather than use a 1–0 fork, it is better to use a 2–1 fork and, if necessary, remove a stage somewhere

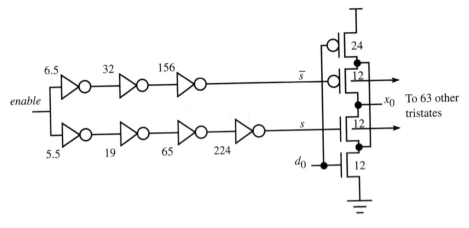

Figure 9.6 — The tristate enable path, properly sized.

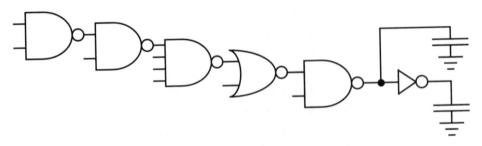

Figure 9.7 — A path ending with a 1–0 fork.

else in the network. Alternatively, the stage immediately preceding the fork can be duplicated in each of the fork's paths, in effect moving the branch point from after this gate to before this gate.

9.3 —— Summary

The forks we have designed in this chapter are a special case of more complex circuits with branches that operate in parallel. While the general cases are more difficult to solve, two of the techniques shown in this chapter apply to more complex branching problems covered in the next chapter:

- The path effort of a network, measured as the total load capacitance of all its outputs divided by its input capacitance, sets the correct number of stages to use.

- Once a network topology is selected, it's a simple matter to write equations that describe the delay in each path and solve them for the branching factor β that equalizes delays in multiple paths.

In the case of amplifier forks driving equal loads, we have shown that the number of stages in the two paths should be nearly the same. In the next chapter, we will find that this is still true even when the paths drive unequal loads or differ in logical effort.

9.4 —— Exercises

[25] **9-1** Set up equations for computing the entries in Table 9.1. Solve them and verify that your answers match those of the table. (You'll want to write a computer program or use a spreadsheet to find the solutions.)

[30] **9-2** Suppose that for $H > 38.7$, rather than building a pure fork, we use a string of inverters driving a 3–2 fork. How far does this strategy depart from the optimum fork designs?

[25] **9-3** Propose an improvement to the design of Figure 9.7 that uses a 2–1 fork. If each of the load capacitances is 400 times as large as the input capacitance, what are the delays of the original and improved designs?

[20] **9-4** Consider the two designs in Figure 9.8. The first uses a 1–0 fork, while the other avoids this structure. Compare the delays of the two designs over a range of plausible electrical efforts. Is the first design ever preferred?

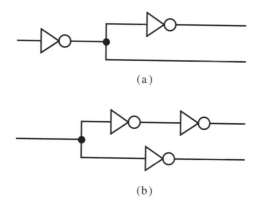

(a)

(b)

Figure 9.8 — Comparing designs with (a) and avoiding (b) 1–0 forks illustrates inherent problems.

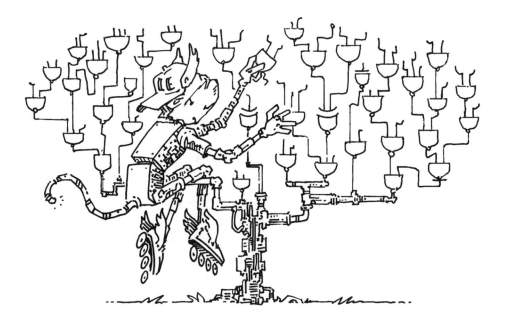

Branches and Interconnect——10

Logical effort is easy to use on circuits with easily computed branching efforts. For example, circuits with a single output or a regular structure are easy to design. Real circuits often involve more complex branching and fixed wire loads. There is often no closed-form expression for the best design of such circuits, but this chapter develops approximations and iterative methods that lead to good designs in most cases.

Designing networks that branch requires not only finding the best topology for the network, but also deciding how to allocate the available drive at a branch so that delays in all paths are equalized. The previous chapter covered the special case of "forks of amplifiers" that generate true and complement forms of an input signal. In this chapter, we build on the previous results to handle more general cases. We shall consider circuits with two or more legs, where each leg may contain a different number of stages, each leg may perform a different logic function, and each leg may drive a different load. As you might guess, we can combine the logical and electrical efforts associated with each leg to obtain a composite effort on which to base our computations.

The simplicity of the forks considered in the previous chapter makes it possible to choose their topology from a table on the basis of the overall electrical effort imposed on the fork. In this chapter we will consider a more complex and varied set of circuits. We will use the theory of logical effort to write equations that relate the size of individual logic elements to their delay. By balancing the delay in the various legs of the circuit, we will be able to reduce the delay in the worst path.

The first section analyzes a series of examples in order to develop some intuitive arguments about branching networks. These examples are generalizations of forks of amplifiers. Next, we turn to an exclusive-or network that involves not only branching but also recombination of signals within the network. Interconnect presents new problems because the capacitance of the wire does not scale with gate size. However, circuits with interconnect can be analyzed on a case-by-case basis. We close the chapter with an outline of a general design procedure for dealing with branching networks.

Although it is possible to formulate network design problems as a set of delay equations and solve for a minimum, the method of logical effort often provides simple insights that yield good designs without a lot of numerical work. If necessary, these initial designs can be adjusted through more detailed timing analysis.

10.1 —— Circuits That Branch at a Single Input

This section analyzes a series of increasingly complex circuits that branch. We will start with simple circuits that branch immediately at a single input, and postpone to later circuits with logic functions preceding a branch point. Such circuits are very similar to the forks of Chapter 9, except that we shall now consider also unequal loading on the outputs and unequal logical effort in the legs.

10.1.1   Branch paths with equal lengths

The first example, a two-path fork shown in Figure 10.1, will serve as a vehicle to remind us that logical effort can make certain branching decisions very easy. The variables C_1 and C_2 are the input capacitance of the first inverters in each path, as shown. We can assume, without loss of generality, that the total input capacitance is 1, and simply scale all capacitances appropriately. Including the

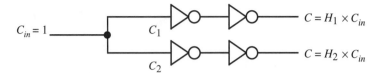

Figure 10.1 — A 2–2 fork with unequal effort.

branching at the input, the loads driven by the two paths are $H_1 \times C_{in}$ and $H_2 \times C_{in}$, so the total electrical effort of the circuit is $H_1 + H_2$. Writing the delay equations for each path and setting them equal quickly tells us that

$$\frac{H_1}{C_1} = \frac{H_2}{C_2} \tag{10.1}$$

This equation holds for paths of any length, provided there are the same number of stages in each path and that the parasitic delay of each path is equal. It shows that the input drive should be allocated in proportion to the load and therefore the electrical effort borne by the path. Once we have determined how to allocate the input capacitance, we can calculate transistor sizes for each path independently.

What happens if the paths include logic, rather than simply inverters? The method of logical effort teaches us that logical effort and electrical effort are interchangeable. So if path 1 had a total logical effort of G_1 and path 2 a total logical effort of G_2, then Equation 10.1 becomes simply

$$\frac{F_1}{C_1} = \frac{F_2}{C_2} \tag{10.2}$$

where $F_i = G_i H_i$ for each path. In other words, the input capacitance should be allocated in proportion to the total effort borne by each path.

Even more important, the entire configuration of Figure 10.1 is equivalent to a single string of two inverters with output capacitance $F_1 + F_2$. The key point is that *the equivalent configuration has no branch;* we capture the effect of the branch by summing the efforts of the two paths. This property allows us to analyze branching networks with equal lengths by working backward from the outputs, replacing branching paths with their single-path equivalents. The branching effort of the leg is

$$B = \frac{F_{leg} + F_{others}}{F_{leg}} \tag{10.3}$$

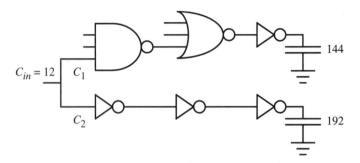

Figure 10.2 — A path with different logical and electrical efforts on each leg.

The path effort $F = G_{leg}BH_{leg}$ and stage effort $f = F^{1/N}$ can then be calculated. The stage effort is the same for all legs of the branch. This is a powerful technique for designing networks with branches, as illustrated in the following example.

EXAMPLE 10.1   Size the circuit in Figure 10.2 for minimum delay.

SOLUTION   The electrical effort of the top leg is $H_1 = 144/12 = 12$, and the electrical effort of the bottom leg is $H_2 = 192/12 = 16$. At first it might appear that the electrical efforts are $144/C_1$ and $192/C_2$, but instead this increased effort will be captured by the branching effort of each leg.

The logical effort of the top leg is $G_1 = 5/3 \times 7/3 \times 1 = 3.89$, and the logical effort of the bottom leg is $G_2 = 1 \times 1 \times 1 = 1$. Thus, the path effort of the top leg is $F_1 = G_1H_1 = 46.7$, and the path effort of the bottom leg is $F_2 = G_2H_2 = 16$. The overall path effort is $F_1 + F_2 = 62.7$.

First consider sizing the top leg. From the perspective of the top leg, the circuit has a branching effort of $B = (F_1 + F_2)/F_1 = 1.34$. Thus, we can design the circuit as if it had only one leg with $F = G_1BH_1 = 62.7$. The stage effort is $f = 62.7^{1/3} = 3.97$. Starting at the output and working backward, we find gate input capacitances of 36, 31, and 9 for the inverter, NOR, and NAND, respectively.

The bottom leg is now easy to size because we know the stage effort must be the same, 3.97. Working backward, we find input capacitances of 48, 12, and 3, respectively. The total input capacitance of the path is $3 + 9 = 12$, meeting the original specification. Also, the input capacitance is divided between the legs in a 3:1 ratio, just as path effort is in a $46.7:16 \approx 3:1$ ratio.

The delay of the top leg, including parasitics, is $3(3.97) + 3 + 3 + 1 = 18.91$. The delay of the bottom leg is $3(3.97) + 1 + 1 + 1 = 14.91$. Although we had attempted to size each leg for equal delay, the different parasitics result in different delays. To equalize delay, a larger portion of the input capacitance must be dedicated to the top leg with more parasitics. Even when this is done, however, the delay of each path is 18.28, representing only a 3% speedup. ∎

This example illustrates a general problem: unequal parasitics damage Equation 10.1. Sometimes the difference in parasitic delays is small, and our previous analysis is very nearly correct. Even if the difference is large, as it was in the example, the overall improvement from devoting more input capacitance to the slower leg is often small.

If differences in parasitic delay are too great, we can use our analysis to find an initial design, but to get the best design, we will need to adjust the branching allocation. Usually, this is simply a matter of making accurate delay calculations for each path, and modifying the branching allocation slightly. In effect, we are finding a value of C_1 for which

$$D = N \left(\frac{F_1}{C_1}\right)^{1/N} + P_1 = N \left(\frac{F_2}{1 - C_1}\right)^{1/N} + P_2 \qquad (10.4)$$

Because parasitic delay adds considerable complexity to the algebra for analyzing branching circuits, we will omit the effects of parasitic delay in the other examples in this chapter. In all cases, assuming zero parasitic delay leads to a pretty good design that can then be refined by more accurate delay calculations and adjustments. A spreadsheet program is a handy tool for making such calculations.

10.1.2   Branch paths with unequal lengths

The amplifier forks we studied in Chapter 9 are simple networks that have branch paths of unequal lengths. We will revisit their analysis here to introduce the problem of designing arbitrary branching networks. As a first example, consider the simple case of a 2–1 fork with unequal loading, as shown in Figure 10.3. We use similar conventions as in Figure 10.1 for denoting inverter input capacitances, but to remind us that our analysis accommodates different logical effort in each path, we have labeled each path's load with the effort, F_i. If we want the delay in each path to be D, the inverter in the first path will have delay D and

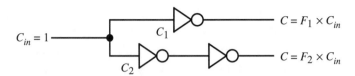

Figure 10.3—A 2–1 fork with unequal effort.

each inverter in the second path will have delay $D/2$. Recalling Equation 1.17, when $P = 0$, we have $F = (D/N)^N$ for each path:

$$\frac{F_1}{C_1} = D$$

$$\frac{F_2}{C_2} = \left(\frac{D}{2}\right)^2 \tag{10.5}$$

Setting $C_1 + C_2 = 1$ yields a quadratic equation:

$$D^2 - F_1 D - 4F_2 = 0 \tag{10.6}$$

that can be solved for D to obtain

$$D = \frac{F_1 + \sqrt{F_1^2 + 16F_2}}{2} \tag{10.7}$$

We can verify some known configurations, for example, $F_1 = 0$ implies $C_1 = 0$, and $F_2 = 0$ implies $C_2 = 0$. In the special case when $F_1 = F_2 = 2$, we find that the input current divides equally between the two legs, and $D = 4$.

The analysis generalizes easily to a fork with three paths as shown in Figure 10.4. For each path i, we have, by analogy to Equation 10.5:

$$\frac{F_i}{C_i} = \left(\frac{D}{i}\right)^i \tag{10.8}$$

Not surprisingly, solving yields a cubic equation in D:

$$D^3 - F_1 D^2 - 4F_2 D - 27F_3 = 0 \tag{10.9}$$

As expected, when $F_3 = 0$, this reduces to Equation 10.6.

Now it is time to step back and consider what we have done. First of all, assuming that all three legs of the fork of Figure 10.4 must operate with the same delay, is there any point to having one leg with a single stage and another

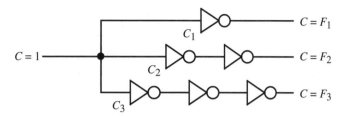

Figure 10.4 — A 3–2–1 fork with unequal effort.

with three? There is not, for the same reason that it is pointless to make the two legs of a simple fork differ in length by more than one. For any value of F_1, F_2, and F_3, we could improve the performance of the circuit of Figure 10.4 by removing one leg. If the delay is short, because F_1, F_2, and F_3 are small compared to $C = 1$, then a simple 2–1 fork will have less maximum delay, and we should eliminate two amplifiers from the three-amplifier leg, in effect collapsing it into the first leg. If the delay is long, because F_1, F_2, and F_3 are large compared to $C = 1$, then a 3–2 fork will have less maximum delay, and we should add two amplifiers to the one-amplifier leg, thus combining it with the three-amplifier leg.

Of course, our example involves only inverters, and we want to consider cases where each leg contains a logic function as well. When there are logic functions involved, we might argue that the particular logic functions require the given number of stages. That may be a valid argument for preserving the three-stage leg, because there may be logic functions that can be done with less logical effort in three stages than in a single stage. Thus if the delay is short, because F_1, F_2, and F_3 are small compared to 1 and the logical efforts of the legs are also small, we may nevertheless require the three-stage leg. On the other hand, if the delay is long, because F_1, F_2, and F_3 are large compared to 1 or large logical efforts are involved, we could improve the design by augmenting the single-stage leg with a pair of inverters. We will think it unusual, therefore, to find a least-delay circuit whose legs differ in length by more than one. An important exception arises when the problem is constrained by minimum drawn device widths.

This reasoning suggests that for purposes of branch analysis, we can always collapse N-way branches ($N > 2$) into two-way branches by combining paths. This simplifies the equations for allocating input capacitance: we will have at most two equations like Equation 10.8. Moreover, because logical and electrical effort are interchangeable, all these branching problems are equivalent to designing amplifier forks, covered in Chapter 9. Note, however, that when we model parasitic delay properly, collapsing paths of equal length but different parasitic delay may introduce errors.

In summary, circuits with a single input and multiple outputs can be analyzed as forks, except that the effective load capacitance on each output must be increased by the logical effort of the leg driving it. Because the minimum delay circuits will generally have paths of nearly the same length, a good approximation to their performance comes from assuming that all paths are the same length, summing the path efforts, and analyzing the entire network as a single path. We learned in Section 3.5 that the performance of strings of amplifiers or strings of logic is relatively insensitive to small changes in their length. A good first approximation, therefore, lumps all the effort of the network for choosing a suitable path length.

10.2 —— Branches after Logic

We are now ready to consider circuits with logic functions preceding a branch point. One common form of circuit contains a logic element followed by a 2–1 fork, as shown in Figure 10.5. Such circuits have a "fan-in" part followed by a "fanout" part joined by a single connection that is the obvious place to break the circuit for analysis. The delay in each of the inverters in the lower leg of the fork is d_a. The delay in the logic element with logical effort g is d_g. We have used separate variables for these two delays because there is no reason to believe that they will be equal. In fact, we expect that in designs for least overall delay, d_g will have a value somewhere between d_a and $2d_a$; the longer leg of the fork will use inverters operating faster than the logic element, and the shorter leg of the fork will use an inverter operating slower than the logic element.

Analyzing this case as we did the forks, we write equations for effort:

$$\frac{H_1}{C_1} = 2d_a$$

$$\frac{H_2}{C_2} = d_a^2$$

$$g(C_1 + C_2) = d_g$$

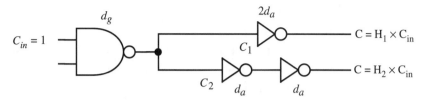

Figure 10.5—Branching after logic.

Using the first two equations to eliminate C_1 and C_2 from the third, and writing an equation for D, we have

$$D = d_g + 2d_a = g\left(\frac{H_1}{2d_a} + \frac{H_2}{d_a^2}\right) + 2d_a \qquad (10.10)$$

Taking the partial derivative of D with respect to d_a and setting the result to zero, to find a minimum, yields

$$d_a^3 - \frac{gH_1}{4}d_a - gH_2 = 0 \qquad (10.11)$$

Now let us choose sample values to match closely the special case of a 2–1 fork with stage delay of 2. The logical effort of the NAND gate is 4/3, and $H_1 = H_2 = 3$, so the total effort is 8, considering the outputs as a bundled pair, which would give a stage delay of 2 in a pure three-stage design. If both sides of the fork had two stages, a per-stage delay of 2 would be best, and the overall delay would be 6. One side of the fork, however, has only one stage instead of two. We might think that because of the similarity of a single inverter with stage delay of 4 to a pair with stage delays of 2 each, substituting the single inverter for two to make the fork would leave the stage delay unchanged. This is simply not so, as the numbers show. Solving Equation 10.11 for the sample values, we find $d_a = 1.796$ and $d_g = 2.35$. In other words, a slightly faster circuit can be obtained by using more time in the logic element and less in the fork, with an overall delay of 5.94 instead of 6. This is not entirely unreasonable because the single-amplifier leg of the fork is not as good at driving heavy loads as is the two-amplifier side. Nevertheless, in keeping with the relative insensitivity of delay to the number of stages, the improvement of 1% may not be worth the effort of calculating how to get it.

Now let us choose sample values with an overall effort of 20, namely, $g = 5/3$, and $H_1 = H_2 = 6$. Here three stages are more obviously required. If both sides of the fork had two stages, we would have a pure three-stage design with a stage delay of 2.71 and an overall delay of 8.14. Solving Equation 10.11, and $d_a = 2.54$ and $d_g = 3.52$, and the best we can do is $D = 8.60$, reflecting the fact that there is only one amplifier in one side of the fork. As we expected, $d_g = 3.52$ lies between $d_a = 2.54$ and $2d_a = 5.08$.

In some circuits several stages of logic or amplification precede a single branch point that leads to a fork. For such circuits, least delay will be obtained with a stage delay in the early circuitry that lies between the stage delay of the longer leg of the fork and the stage delay of the shorter leg of the fork. As the number of stages grows larger, the influence of one stage more or less on the overall delay becomes less, as we learned in Section 3.5, and thus nearly minimal delays can be obtained by treating the outputs as a bundle. If more accurate results are desired, it is easy to write equations similar to those in the figures for any particular case. The solution of such equations leads to the fastest design.

10.3 —— Circuits That Branch and Recombine

Some circuits fail to fit either of the forms we have so far considered; they both branch and recombine. Such circuits can be analyzed in the same way as we have done with the previous examples. The simple delay model provides expressions for the input capacitance of each logic gate. To optimize we can differentiate these expressions.

An interesting example of such a circuit is the form of xor shown in Figure 10.6. While this circuit has only one output, its early stages branch and recombine in a way that requires an analysis similar to others in this chapter. The topology of this circuit involves some paths with three stages and some paths with two stages. The output of the first stage recombines with direct inputs at the second stage. Our interest in this example lies in learning how to analyze it and in understanding the resulting delays.

We will solve this example three times. First, we shall assume that all delays are equal and obtain the circuit with least delay that meets that condition. Second, we shall permit the delay in the first stage, c, to differ from that of the other two stages, d, and again obtain the circuit with least delay. We are interested in whether minimum delay in this second situation requires c to be longer or shorter than d, and whether the circuit where c and d differ will be faster or slower than when they must be the same. Third, as a thought experiment, we shall add mythical noninverting amplifiers to the circuit, as indicated by the

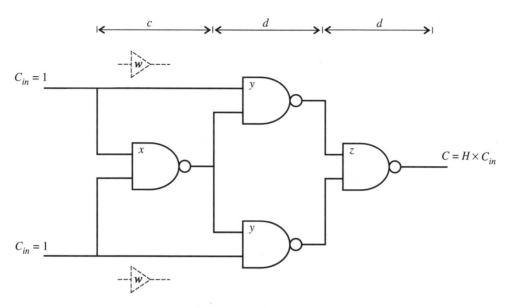

Figure 10.6—The four-NAND XOR illustrating branching and recombining.

dotted symbols in the figure. Although such amplifiers are not realizable, it will be instructive to study the changes that they would cause to circuit performance by providing three stages in each path.

As shown in the figure, the circuit consists of four NAND gates, which we shall treat as having a logical effort of 4/3 per input; in order not to write 4/3 over and over, we shall use the symbol g for it. In order to have a particular electrical effort to work with, we shall assume that the output loading, H, is the same as the combined input capacitance, 2. We will also take advantage of symmetries in the circuit to deal only with capacitances labeled x, y, and z. Now we can write three delay equations, one for each stage of the circuit, and one equation constraining the branch:

$$c = g\left(\frac{2y}{x}\right)$$

$$d = g\left(\frac{z}{y}\right)$$

$$d = g\left(\frac{H}{z}\right)$$

$$x + y = 1$$

Eliminating x, y, z, we find an equation for c in terms of d. In the special case where we insist $c = d$, we can solve to obtain $d = 2.67$, so $D = c + 2d = 8$. To obtain the lowest delay possible, we write an equation for $D = c + 2d$, substitute the expression for c, take the partial derivative of D with respect to d, and set it to zero. We obtain a fourth-order equation in d, which we solve to find $d = 2.98$, implying $c = 1.78$, for an overall delay of $D = 7.74$. This is an improvement over the value $D = 8$ obtained with $c = d$. Notice that the delay is distributed unequally to the three stages; the first stage operates with less delay, and the remaining two with more delay than when all three delays were forced to be equal. This is because NAND x must operate faster than usual to approximate the zero delay through the zero-stage path from the input to gates y.

Notice that the first stage operates in parallel with the direct connection from the inputs to the second stage. Since the direct connection is not an amplifier, it pays to provide more amplification in later stages by making them operate relatively more slowly.

We have assumed in these calculations that the delay, d, in the second and third stages should be equal. Why is this a reasonable assumption? Proving that it is so may be an interesting exercise for the reader.

As a final exercise, let us put in the mythical noninverting amplifiers with a logical effort of 1 in the positions shown as dotted symbols in Figure 10.6. This case is easy to solve, because we want the delays in all three stages to be equal. We can easily write expressions for the input capacitances of the two paths:

$$w = \frac{g^2 H}{d^3}$$

$$x = \frac{2g^3 H}{d^3}$$

Note how the path effort—namely, the product of the branching, logical, and electrical effort—enters into these expressions. Setting $w + x = 1$ and solving, we find $d = 2.35$ and $D = 7.06$, an improvement over both of the other cases we have considered. Clearly, there is a delay cost from failure to amplify the direct input signals while the first stage of logic operates. The lesson to be learned from this example is to seize every opportunity to buffer less-critical signals because such amplification in one path can make available more source current for other paths and thus improve overall performance. Carried to an extreme, we should buffer faster paths until all paths complete simultaneously. Paths that are too fast retard in others by taking current away from them.

10.4 —— Interconnect

Interconnect introduces particular problems for designing with logical effort because it has fixed capacitance. The branching effort at a wire driving a gate load is $(C_{gate} + C_{wire})/C_{gate}$. This branching effort changes whenever transistor sizes in the network change because the wiring capacitance fails to change in proportion to the transistor size changes. Therefore, our handy rule that delay is minimized when the effort of each stage is equal breaks down; the gate driving the wire may use higher effort, while the gate at the end of the wire will use lower effort. This problem leads us to approximate the branching effort or to solve complex equations for the exact optimum. This section addresses approximations for circuits with interconnect. The necessity to make such approximations is one of the most dissatisfying limitations of logical effort.

When doing designs that account for wiring capacitance, it is helpful to relate the total capacitance of a wire to the input capacitance of logic gates. The gate capacitance of a minimum-length transistor is approximately 2 fF/μm and has remained so over many process generations because both length and dielectric thickness scale by about the same amount. The wire capacitance of minimum-pitch interconnect is approximately 0.2 fF/μm and also remains constant when wire thickness, wire pitch, and dielectric thickness scale uniformly. Therefore, a handy rule of thumb is that wire capacitance per unit distance is 1/10 that of gate capacitance. Of course this does not apply for wider wires and depends somewhat on the details of your process. It is very useful to know the ratio for your process to one significant figure so that you can quickly convert wire capacitances into equivalent gate widths.

10.4.1 Short wires

Within a functional block, most wires are short and gate delay is dominated by gate capacitance. Moreover, actual wire lengths are very difficult to estimate until layout is complete. What effect do such short wires have on gate sizing?

Short wires can be treated as additional parasitic capacitance. Given the average length of a wire and the average size of a gate, we can compute the average ratio of parasitic diffusion capacitance to parasitic wire capacitance. The total parasitic capacitance is the sum of these two components. A best stage effort ρ can be computed from this total parasitic capacitance; this effort usually is slightly over four for paths with reasonably short wires.

This result makes intuitive sense. As wire parasitics increase relative to gate capacitance, it is wise to use fewer stages with greater stage effort to minimize the number of wires to drive. Fortunately, we found in Section 3.5 that the path delay is good for stage efforts anywhere near ρ. Designing with a target stage effort of four is sufficient for most problems.

10.4.2   Long wires

Wires between functional blocks can be hundreds or thousands of times larger than most transistors within the functional blocks. We consider a wire to be long when its capacitance is large compared to the gate capacitance it drives.

A logic path containing a long wire can therefore be split into two parts. The first part drives the wire. The second part receives its input from the wire. The size of the receiving gate makes little difference to the delay of the first path because the gate capacitance is small compared to the wire capacitance. In other words, the branching effort is a weak function of the receiving gate size. However, the size directly affects the electrical effort and thus the delay of the second path, so it should be made as large as possible, limited by area and power considerations.

The first part of the logic path typically ends with an inverter chain to drive the large wire capacitance. The final inverter can be very large, consuming significant area and power. Therefore, choosing a stage effort of closer to eight for this stage reduces the cost and only slightly increases delay. Because it is expensive in time and area to build the inverter chains that drive long wires, it is best to clump logic as much as possible so a path passes through few long wires. For example, the arbitration circuit of Section 2.3 was greatly improved by computing the function at a central location rather than daisy-chaining the logic across multiple long wires.

When wires are very long, the resistance of the wire becomes important. Because both wire resistance and capacitance are proportional to wire length, wire delay scales quadratically with wire length. Therefore, it is beneficial to break long wires into sections, each driven by an inverter or buffer called a *repeater.* Wires with proper repeaters have delay that is only a linear function of length [1]. When using repeaters, the designer must plan where the repeaters will be located on the chip floorplan.

10.4.3 Medium wires

The most difficult sizing problems occur when interconnect capacitance is comparable to the gate load capacitance. Such medium-length wires introduce branching efforts that are a strong function of the sizes of the gates they drive.

A brute force solution to sizing paths with medium wires is to write the delay equation as a function of the sizes of all the gates along the path and of the wire capacitance. This leads to a polynomial function that can be differentiated with respect to the gate sizes and solved numerically for the best sizes.

Such a solution is usually more work than is worthwhile. For most circuits, reasonable results follow from maintaining a stage effort of about four through the path. Choosing the best number of stages is complicated by the fact that the branching effort caused by the wires is initially unknown. This leads to a few simple iterations, described in the next section.

10.5 —— A Design Approach

The examples of this chapter all illustrate common themes in the design of branching networks. The analytical treatment is intended to give insight into design trade-offs. In practice, however, designers are unlikely to take partial derivatives and solve *Nth*-order polynomial equations just to achieve a few percentage points of improvement in delay. Instead, a practical design approach uses the insight about branching networks to select a reasonable topology and make an initial guess of stage efforts. Then the designer iterates on paths that are unacceptably slow until either the path meets specification or it becomes clear that a better topology is required.

Moreover, real circuits frequently contain fixed capacitances. For example, interconnect capacitances are independent of the gate sizes, as discussed in Section 10.4. There is a minimum size each transistor may be drawn, which limits how small a load can be presented by a noncritical leg of a circuit. Finally, some outputs may be required at different times, and so devoting a larger portion of the input capacitance to critical outputs can speed them at the expense of noncritical outputs.

When fixed capacitances are small compared to other capacitances on the node, ignore them. When fixed capacitances are large compared to other capacitances, the fixed capacitance dominates delay. If other gates loading the node are not fast enough, increase them in size to reduce their own delay while only slightly increasing the total capacitance on the node. The most difficult case is when fixed capacitances are comparable to gate capacitances. In such a case, the designer may have to iterate to achieve acceptable results.

Here we will try to summarize some of these techniques by suggesting a design procedure.

1. Draw a network.

2. Buffer noncritical paths with minimum-sized gates to minimize their load on the important paths. Try to make all critical paths have similar numbers of stages.

3. Estimate the total effort along each path, for example, by working backward from the outputs, combining efforts at each branch point.

4. Verify that the number of stages for the network is appropriate for the total effort that the network bears.

5. Assign a branching ratio to each branch; work backward from the outputs, considering each branch you reach. Estimate a branching ratio based on the ratio of the effort required by each path leaving the branch. You may choose not to optimize certain paths that bear very little effort or whose speeds are not critical for your purpose.

6. Compute accurate delays for your design, including the effects of parasitic delay. Adjust the branching ratios to minimize these delays. You can write algebraic equations, but it is usually easier to use repeated evaluations of the delay equations for the competing paths, observing the effects of small adjustments. If a path is too slow, allocate more drive to that path by using a greater fraction of the input capacitance.

Although the general problem of optimizing a network requires a complex optimization algorithm, this procedure works well for most cases.

10.6 —— Exercises

[35] **10-1** Modify Equation 10.5 to account for parasitic delay in the inverters, and find a polynomial equation for D. If Equation 10.7 is used as an approximation to determine D, how much does the resulting design differ from the optimum over reasonable values of F_1, F_2, and P?

[20] **10-2** In Section 10.3, we assume that the delay, d, of the second and third stages are equal. Why is this a good assumption?

[50] **10-3** Develop better heuristics for selecting topologies and choosing gate sizes in the presence of capacitive interconnect.

Wide Structures —————— **11**

One of the applications of logical effort is the analysis of wide structures, such as decoders or high fan-in gates and multiplexers, to find the topological structure that offers the best performance. This chapter presents four examples. The first is the design of an n-input AND structure. Then we design an n-input Muller C-element, in which the n-input AND structure can be used. Third, we present alternative designs for decoders that form 2^n selection outputs from an n-bit address. Finally, we analyze high fan-in multiplexers and show that it is best to partition wide multiplexers into trees of four-input multiplexers.

11.1 —— An n-input AND Structure

It is sometimes necessary to combine a large number of inputs in an AND function—for example, to detect that the output of an ALU is zero, or that a large number of conditions are all true. Let us find a circuit structure that minimizes the logical effort of that function.

11.1.1   Minimum logical effort

The simplest way to build an n-input AND function is to use an n-input NAND gate followed by an inverter. In Section 4.5.1, we found that the logical effort per input of this structure is

$$g = \frac{n + \gamma}{1 + \gamma} \tag{11.1}$$

Although this is a simple solution, its logical effort grows rapidly as the number of inputs increases. An n-input NOR gate could also be used, with an inverter on each input, to compute the AND function. But since the logical effort of an n-input NOR gate is always greater than that of an n-input NAND gate, this structure is not an improvement.

To avoid the linear growth of logical effort, we can build a tree of NAND and NOR gates to compute the AND function. Figure 11.1 shows such a tree: it has a NOR gate at the root, alternating levels of NAND and NOR gates, and an even number of levels. Observe that the number of inputs to gates at different levels in the tree may differ. In the figure, most levels have two-input gates, but the gates at the leaves of the tree use three-input gates. In some cases, the gates at certain levels in the tree may have only one input—that is, they will be inverters. Figure 11.2 shows an example in which the root NOR gate is an inverter.

The tree of Figure 11.1 has a logical effort per input of 6.17 (for $\gamma = 2$), while an equivalent 24-input NAND gate and inverter would have a logical effort per input of 8.67. Of course, a 24-input NAND gate is also impractical because parasitic delay grows quadratically with stack height. The tree in Figure 11.1 does not yield the lowest logical effort for 24 inputs: as we shall shortly see, a tree with eight levels and a logical effort per input of 3.95 is best.

A simple procedure can find the tree structure with the least logical effort. The design process searches recursively through all plausible tree structures with the right number of inputs. When designing a tree for n inputs, we first calculate the logical effort of using a single n-input gate at the current level, perhaps using inverters on its inputs to make the number of levels in the tree even. Then we consider trees with a b-input gate at the root, and subtrees that have $\lceil n/b \rceil$ inputs, where b ranges from 1 to n. The determination of the best subtree design is achieved by a recursive call on the same tree-design procedure. Care is required in the control of recursion to be sure that we don't explore endlessly deep trees that use one-input gates at every level.

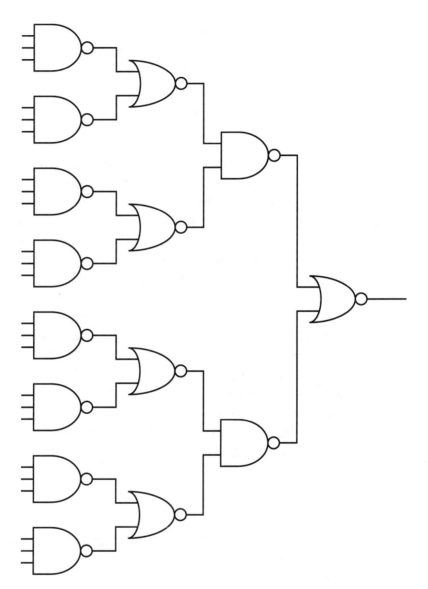

Figure 11.1 — A 3, 2, 2, 2 AND tree composed of alternating levels of NAND and NOR gates.

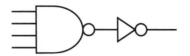

Figure 11.2—A degenerate case of the tree, in which the NOR gate has only one input; in other words, it is an inverter.

Logical effort offers several hints about the nature of the solution. Because the logical effort of NOR gates exceeds that of NAND gates, we expect the NOR gates in the tree to have fewer inputs than the NAND gates. In fact, to obtain minimum logical effort, all the NOR gates in the tree will have only one input— they will be inverters! Rather than inserting a NOR gate, the design procedure will find it advantageous to use a NAND gate at the next lower level in the tree.

Table 11.1 shows designs for trees with up to 64 inputs. Notice that the trees are very skinny, using only inverters and two- and three-input NAND gates. Observe too that *no* NOR gates with multiple inputs are used. This table shows the minimum effort design for the 24-input problem. Note that it is a tree eight levels deep.

The results of these designs can be used to formulate a lower bound on the logical effort of an n-input AND tree. The tree will contain only two-input NAND gates, alternating with inverters, with as many levels as necessary to accommodate n inputs. Thus if l is the number of levels of NAND gates, $2^l = n$, or $l = \log_2 n$. The logical effort per input of an n-input AND tree is

$$G_{and}(n) = \left(\frac{2+\gamma}{1+\gamma}\right)^{\log_2 n} = n^{\log_2((2+\gamma)/(1+\gamma))} \qquad (11.2)$$

When $\gamma = 2$, this simplifies to $G_{and} = n^{0.415}$. Note that the logical effort of AND trees grows much more slowly than the linear growth of a single NAND gate (Equation 11.1).

11.1.2   Minimum delay

While these skinny trees offer the least logical effort, they are not always the best choice in a given situation. It may happen that the path effort is so small that the best design requires fewer stages than are called for in the tree. For example, if $n = 6$ and the electrical effort $H = 1$, the design with the least delay is a three-

Table 11.1—AND tree designs that minimize logical effort, for $\gamma = 2$. The tree structure gives the number of inputs of the gates at each level of the tree, starting with the NAND gate at the leaves and ending with the one-input NOR gate (inverter) at the root.

n	$G_{and}(n)$	Tree structure	Number of stages
1	1.0	1, 1	2
2	1.333	2, 1	2
3	1.667	3, 1	2
4	1.778	2, 1, 2, 1	4
5–6	2.222	3, 1, 2, 1	4
7–8	2.370	2, 1, 2, 1, 2, 1	6
9	2.778	3, 1, 3, 1	4
10–12	2.963	3, 1, 2, 1, 2, 1	6
13–16	3.160	2, 1, 2, 1, 2, 1, 2, 1	8
17–18	3.704	3, 1, 3, 1, 2, 1	6
19–24	3.951	3, 1, 2, 1, 2, 1, 2, 1	8
25–32	4.214	2, 1, 2, 1, 2, 1, 2, 1, 2, 1	10
33–36	4.938	3, 1, 3, 1, 2, 1, 2, 1	8
37–48	5.267	3, 1, 2, 1, 2, 1, 2, 1, 2, 1	10
49–64	5.619	2, 1, 2, 1, 2, 1, 2, 1, 2, 1, 2, 1	12

input NAND gate followed by a two-input NOR. Only when the electrical effort is large will the skinny trees be fastest.

We can modify the design procedure to determine the fastest structure for a given electrical effort. Again, we use a procedure that evaluates all branching factors and recursively evaluates the required subtrees. When the procedure encounters a leaf node, it knows the logical effort of the proposed structure, so the path effort $F = GH$ can be calculated, and the delay can then be determined including effects of parasitic delay along the path. We find the best tree by minimizing this delay rather than minimizing the logical effort. Such a program is available on the Logical Effort Web page (see the section titled About the Web Site in the Preface).

Table 11.2 shows some results for the electrical efforts of $H = 1$, $H = 5$, and $H = 200$. The trees with low effort are bushier than those that minimize logical effort because the limited total effort will make designs with too many stages slow. The trees with high effort, on the other hand, use one of the skinny

Table 11.2 — AND tree designs that minimize delay, for $\gamma = 2$, when the total electrical effort is specified. Note that these trees are different than those in Table 11.1 because the electrical effort influences the number of stages to use.

n	$H = 1$		$H = 5$		$H = 200$	
	Delay	Tree	Delay	Tree	Delay	Tree
2	5.3	2, 1	8.2	2, 1	21.2	2, 1, 1, 1
3	6.6	3, 1	9.8	3, 1	23.1	3, 1, 1, 1
4	7.0	2, 2	10.7	2, 2	23.4	2, 1, 2, 1
5–6	8.3	3, 2	12.5	3, 2	25.4	3, 1, 2, 1
7–8	9.7	4, 2	14.2	4, 2	25.8	2, 1, 2, 1, 2, 1
16	12.9	4, 4	16.9	2, 2, 2, 2	28.2	2, 2, 2, 1, 2, 1
32	16.6	4, 2, 2, 2	19.9	4, 2, 2, 2	30.9	2, 2, 2, 2, 2, 1
64	19.3	4, 2, 4, 2	22.9	4, 2, 4, 2	33.6	2, 2, 2, 2, 2, 2
128	22.5	4, 4, 4, 2	26.5	4, 2, 2, 2, 2, 2	36.7	2, 2, 2, 2, 2, 2, 2, 1

designs from Table 11.1, possibly followed by additional inverters to yield the best number of stages. For example, when $n = 2$, the least logical effort tree has logical effort of 4/3. Thus, the path with electrical effort of 200 has total effort 800/3. Table 3.1 shows a five-stage design would be fastest, but the number of stages must be even. Four stages turns out to be better than six, so two additional inverters are used after the two-stage minimum logical effort tree.

11.1.3 Other wide functions

DeMorgan's law helps us transform AND trees to compute OR, NAND, or NOR functions. In all cases, the trees have alternating layers of NAND and NOR gates. To perform the OR function, the order of NAND and NOR gates in the AND tree is reversed. Similar trees having an odd number of stages, obtained by appending an inverter to the tree, implement the complementary functions NAND and NOR. Hence, the minimum logical effort of all four functions is the same. The minimum delay trees can be found in much the same way that we computed Table 11.2.

11.2 —— An n-input Muller C-element

Muller C-elements are used in asynchronous circuit designs to detect when a group of processes have completed. The C-element's output becomes HIGH only

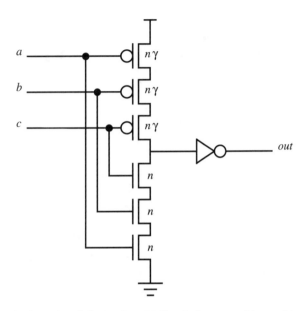

Figure 11.3 — The "simple-C" design for a Muller C-element, with $n = 3$ inputs.

after all of its inputs become HIGH, and its output becomes LOW only after all of its inputs become LOW. For other combinations of input values, the output of the C-element retains its previous state.

11.2.1   Minimum logical effort

Figure 11.3 shows the simplest way to build an *n*-input C-element, which we shall call a "simple-C." It consists of a dynamic "C-arm" with series pullup and pulldown transistors, followed by an inverter. The logical effort per input of this gate is just n (see Section 4.5.8). Variations of this dynamic circuit make it static by adding some form of feedback. Although the feedback will increase the logical effort slightly, we will ignore this effect.

Figure 11.4 shows another way to build a C-element using AND trees to detect when the inputs are all HIGH and when they are all LOW. We shall call this design an "AND-C." If we seek a design with the least logical effort, then the design of the two AND trees will be identical, and each will have the same logical effort. It might seem that the calculation of the logical effort for the entire C-element would require deciding on the fraction of input current that is directed into each AND tree. However, we can appeal to the results on bundles and observe

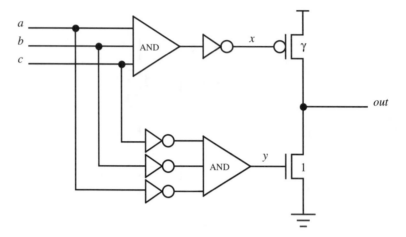

Figure 11.4—The "AND-C" design for a Muller C-element, using AND trees to determine when all inputs are HIGH or LOW.

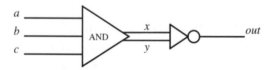

Figure 11.5—A different drawing of Figure 11.4, showing the bundle of two signals computed by the AND trees.

that both top and bottom paths experience the same logical effort in the AND trees, and so signals x and y can be treated as a bundle, as shown in Figure 11.5. This bundle drives a circuit that is identical to an inverter, which has a logical effort of 1. So we see that the minimum logical effort of an n-input C-element is equal to the logical effort of an n-input AND tree. The design of these trees was addressed in the previous section.

If we study Table 11.1, we can see that the AND-C design has lower logical effort than the simple-C design for any number of inputs. The column labeled G_{and} in this table gives the logical effort of the n-input AND tree, which is the logical effort of the n-input AND-C design. In comparison, the logical effort of an n-input simple-C design is n.

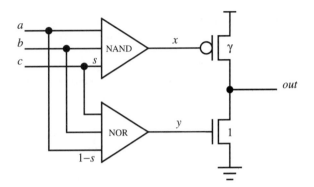

Figure 11.6 — More precise version of Figure 11.4, showing NAND and NOR functions driving the output stage.

11.2.2   Minimum delay

As with AND trees, the structure with the lowest logical effort does not always offer the least delay, because it may have an improper number of stages. Obtaining the design with the least delay requires knowing the overall electrical effort that the C-element must bear.

The analysis of the simple-C circuit follows the familiar form used in all our logical effort calculations. If the electrical effort of the *n*-input gate is H, the total effort is nH, which is used to determine the best number of stages, N. Then the delay is $D = N(nH)^{1/N}$. The circuit can be modified to have the right number of stages by adding inverters or by building a tree of C-arms.

The analysis of the AND-C circuit depends on a slightly better design, shown in Figure 11.6. NAND and NOR functions, rather than the AND function and inverters shown in Figure 11.4, compute the x and y signals. These designs are logically equivalent and have the same minimum logical effort. However, when we consider limited electrical effort, the improved design allows two-stage solutions, while the design in Figure 11.4 must have at least four stages, because the AND tree has at least two.

As an initial design, we can assume that the NAND and NOR trees have equal logical efforts. Therefore, we should choose $s = \gamma/(1 + \gamma)$ to divide the input capacitance between the legs of the fork in proportion to the load each leg drives. Of course, the logical effort and parasitic delay of the NOR tree is somewhat larger. Therefore, speed could be improved somewhat by iteratively adjusting s

Table 11.3 — Comparison of minimum-delay designs for Muller C-elements, for $\gamma = 2$, when the total electrical effort is specified.

		Simple-C		AND-C		
n	H	Delay	Stages	Delay	NAND tree	NOR tree
2	1	5.8	2	5.6	2	2
	5	9.3	2	8.8	2	1, 2, 1
3	1	7.5	2	7.1	3	3
	5	11.7	2	10.8	3, 1, 1	1, 3, 1
4	1	8.0	2	8.5	4	4
	5	12.9	2	12.7	2, 1, 2	2, 2, 1
6	1	9.9	2	12.2	3, 1, 2	2, 3, 1
	5	16.4	4	14.7	3, 1, 2	2, 3, 1
8	1	11.7	2	12.5	2, 2, 2	2, 2, 2
	5	17.1	4	15.3	2, 2, 2	2, 2, 2
16	1	16.0	2	15.1	4, 2, 2	2, 4, 2
	5	20.0	4	18.2	4, 2, 2	2, 4, 2
32	1	19.5	4	18.1	4, 2, 4	4, 4, 2
	5	25.2	6	21.6	4, 2, 4	2, 2, 2, 2, 2
64	1	23.3	4	21.2	4, 4, 4	4, 4, 4
	5	28.9	6	24.9	4, 2, 2, 2, 2	2, 4, 2, 2, 2

until delays of the two legs are equal. The improvement is small and generally not worth the bother.

Table 11.3 compares designs for the simple-C and AND-C designs, when the electrical effort that must be borne by the circuit is $H = 1$ and $H = 5$. Notice that the AND-C design is almost always faster than the simple-C design, even for small numbers of inputs. The exceptions occur for designs with low electrical efforts where the AND-C requires too many stages.

Nevertheless, a closer look at Table 11.3 shows that the relative advantage of the AND-C design is small. This may seem surprising because the minimal logical effort of the AND-C design scales as $n^{0.415}$, while the minimal logical effort of the simple-C design scales as n. To understand why, consider the various components of delay. Equation 3.28 can be rewritten with $\rho = 4$ as

$$D \approx 4 \left(\log_4 G + \log_4 H \right) + P \tag{11.3}$$

This shows that logical effort is only one of three components of delay. The AND-C design can reduce the logical effort delay component by a factor of

$$\frac{\log n}{\log n^{0.415}} \approx 2 \tag{11.4}$$

by using a minimal effort tree. However, the parasitic delays are comparable to the logical effort delay, and so the reduced logical effort delay is a smaller fraction of total delay. Moreover, when electrical effort is small, the trees are bushy and do not achieve minimal logical effort; they may also have stage efforts well below optimal. When electrical effort is large, the electrical effort delay term is large, also making the savings in logical effort delay a smaller fraction of the total delay. The conclusion is that for both large and small electrical efforts, the overall speedup of the AND-C design is much less than we would expect by considering logical effort alone.

11.3 —— Decoders

Efficient decoders are important for addressing memories and microprocessor register files, where speed is critical. Decoding structures tend to have large total effort because the fanout of address bits to all decoders and the fanout of the decoder output to the transistors in the memory word are both large. In this section, we analyze three decoder designs from the perspective of logical effort.

The considerations that affect decoder design are many, and minimizing logical effort may not be paramount. Layout considerations are important, because often the decoder must fit on the same layout pitch as the memory cells it addresses. Overall decoder size and power are important; a design that minimizes logical effort may require too much power or too many transistors to be practical. Finally, many decoder structures use precharging to reduce logical effort; we will not analyze such designs here.

11.3.1   Simple decoder

The simplest form of decoder appears in Figure 11.7: each output is computed by an AND tree, wired to the true or complement form of n address bits. Each address bit is wired to 2^n decoders, half in true form and half in complement form. The path effort from an address bit to the output is therefore

$$F = 2^n G_{and}(n)H \tag{11.5}$$

where $G_{and}(n)$ is the logical effort of an n-input AND tree. By way of example, consider a 64-entry file of 32-bit registers, so $n = 6$. If the load on each address

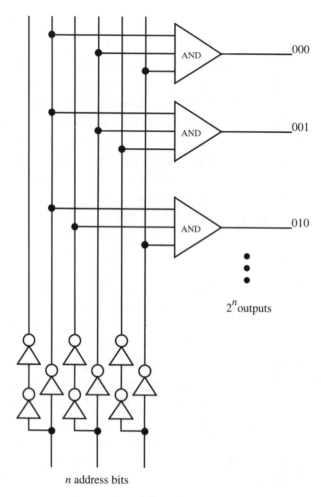

2^n outputs

n address bits

Figure 11.7—A decoder generating 2^n outputs from an n-bit address.

bit is 8 times the capacitance of a register cell, $H = 32/8 = 4$. A lower bound on G_{and} from Equation 11.2 is 2.10, yielding a total effort of 538. This is a large total effort that calls for a five-stage AND tree design with minimum logical effort.

11.3.2   Predecoding

Figure 11.8 illustrates the idea of predecoding. The n address bits form p groups of q each. Each group is decoded to yield 2^q predecode values. Then a second layer of p-input AND trees combines the predecoded signals to generate 2^n final

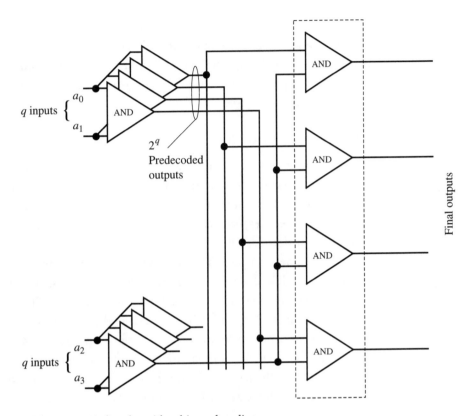

Figure 11.8—A decoder with q-bit predecoding.

signals. Let us compute the total effort on the longest path through the decoder. Each address bit fans out to 2^q decoders in the first layer, so there will be a branching effort of 2^q. The decoder will introduce a logical effort of $G_{and}(q)$, the logical effort of an AND tree with q inputs. Then there will be a fanout to 2^{n-q} AND gates in the second layer, each with logical effort $G_{and}(p)$. The path effort from an address bit to the output is

$$F = 2^q G_{and}(q) 2^{n-q} G_{and}(p) H = 2^n G_{and}(p) G_{and}(q) H \qquad (11.6)$$

We can compare this result with Equation 11.5, given $n = pq$. If we try a few values, we find that predecoding has the same logical effort as the simple structure. This result has an intuitive explanation: the predecoder structure is really a reorganization of an AND tree that moves the fanout from the address inputs to internal points in the tree.

Do not conclude from this analysis that predecoding offers no benefits. It requires fewer transistors than other designs, and leads to more compact structures than the skinny trees of the previous section. Predecoding represents an intermediate point between using a single n-input gate as a decoder and using a minimum-effort AND tree.

11.3.3   Lyon-Schediwy decoder

Lyon and Schediwy [6] have invented a decoder that reduces the logical effort by taking advantage of the fact that most outputs will be LOW. A NOR gate is a good way to pull an output LOW, but usually has poor logical effort because large series-connected PMOS transistors must pull the output HIGH. Because only one output of a decoder will be HIGH, it is possible to share the PMOS transistors across all of the decoder gates! This is shown in Figure 11.9 for a 3:8 decoder. The decoder can be viewed as eight three-input NOR gates that share PMOS pullups.

Rather than making the pullups all the same size, we shall make the transistors higher in the tree wider. The lowest-level pullup transistors will have width w, the next pullup transistors will have width $2w$, then $4w$, and so on. This scheme has the effect of loading the input lines equally, so they will all have equal logical effort. Other sizing schemes might reduce the logical effort of certain inputs and increase the logical effort of others. If we compute the conductance of the n series pullup transistors sized in this way, and equate it to the conductance of a PMOS transistor of width γ from the reference inverter, we find

$$w = \gamma \left(\frac{1 - \frac{1}{2^n}}{1 - \frac{1}{2}} \right) \approx 2\gamma \tag{11.7}$$

Now that we have designed the decoder to have the same output drive as the reference inverter, the logical effort per input is just the input capacitance of each input, divided by $1 + \gamma$, the input capacitance of the reference inverter. Observe that each input is connected to 2^{n-1} pulldown transistors, each of width 1, and to a total pullup width of $2^{n-1}w$. So the logical effort per input is

$$G(n) = 2^{n-1} \left(\frac{1 + \gamma \left(\frac{1 - \frac{1}{2^n}}{1 - \frac{1}{2}} \right)}{1 + \gamma} \right) \tag{11.8}$$

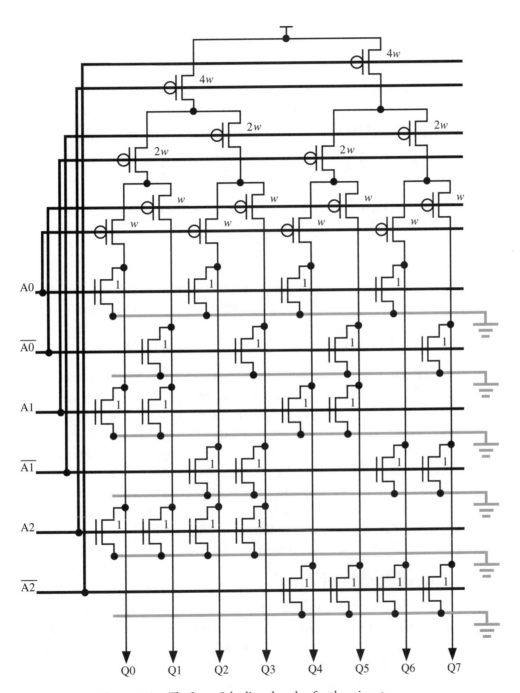

Figure 11.9 — The Lyon-Schediwy decoder, for three inputs.

and the path effort is

$$F = G(n)H \tag{11.9}$$

Compare this equation to Equation 11.5: the fanout of address bits to all parts of the decoder is incorporated into Equation 11.8. For $\gamma = 2$, the Lyon-Schediwy decoder has path effort

$$F = G(n)H = 2^n \left(\frac{5 - 2^{2-n}}{6} \right) H \leq 2^n \left(\frac{5}{6} \right) H \tag{11.10}$$

The corresponding expression for the AND tree, using Equation 11.5 and the lower bound from Equation 11.2, is

$$F = 2^n n^{0.415} H \tag{11.11}$$

The second factors in the two equations are the only differences, so we see that the Lyon-Schediwy decoder always has lower effort than the AND tree.

11.4 —— Multiplexers

CMOS multiplexers are interesting structures because the logical effort of a multiplexer is independent of the number of inputs. This suggests that multiplexers could have a large number of inputs without speed penalty. Common sense tells us otherwise. One problem is that decoding select signals for wide multiplexers requires large effort, though this does not impact delay from data inputs. When stray capacitance is considered, we discover that multiplexers should not be very broad at all. In fact, over a broad range of assumptions, the best multiplexer has four inputs. To select one of a large number of signals, we will see that it is best to build a tree of four-input multiplexers. Nevertheless, it is sometimes beneficial to use multiplexers with up to eight inputs.

11.4.1 How wide should a multiplexer be?

A multiplexer that selects one of r inputs has r independent *arms*. Figure 11.10 shows the form of each arm and defines several important capacitances. C_{out} is the load capacitance driven by the multiplexer. C_{in} is the capacitance of the data input transistor gates. C_s is the stray capacitance, principally from drain diffusions, contributed by each arm of the multiplexer. Notice that the circuit has the selection signals s and $\bar{s}$ near the output so that unselected multiplexers

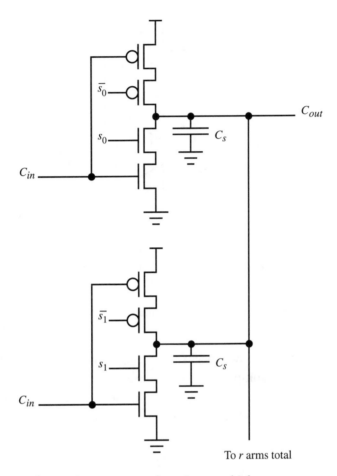

Figure 11.10—The transistor structure of an r-input multiplexer.

present the least stray capacitance to their common output. Our model of stray capacitance (see Table 1.2) estimates a parasitic delay of $2rp_{inv}$ for an r-way multiplexer.

Figure 11.11 shows a branching structure of multiplexers that together select one of n inputs. The branching structure consists of n_m layers of multiplexing, each with an r-way branch. The branching structure is followed by n_a stages of amplifiers. Let C_{out} be the load capacitance driven by the amplifier string and C_{in} be the input capacitance of one of the n inputs. Thus the electrical effort per input is $H = C_{out}/C_{in}$.

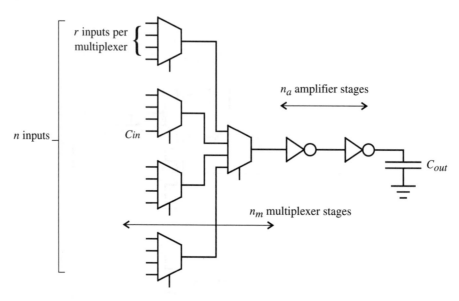

Figure 11.11 — A tree of r-way multiplexers to select one of N inputs.

We can now begin to develop some expressions that describe properties of the multiplexer tree. We have $n = r^{n_m}$, or alternatively, $r = n^{1/n_m}$ or $n_m = (\ln n)/(\ln r)$. We will define the electrical effort of a multiplexer stage as h_m and the electrical effort of an amplifier stage as h_a. Using these values, we can compute

$$d_m = 2h_m + 2rp_{inv} \tag{11.12}$$

$$d_a = h_a + p_{inv} \tag{11.13}$$

$$D = 2n_m(h_m + rp_{inv}) + n_a(h_a + p_{inv}) \tag{11.14}$$

where d_m is the delay of a multiplexer stage, d_a is the delay of an amplifier stage, and D is the total delay.

Note how the logical effort per input of a multiplexer, 2, enters into the first equation. We want to minimize the delay D subject to a constraint on total electrical effort:

$$H = h_m^{n_m} h_a^{n_a} \tag{11.15}$$

The theory of logical effort teaches us that for the best speed, the effort borne by all stages should be equal, which suggests that $2h_m = h_a$. Although all stages have equal effort, they will not introduce equal delay, because the delay through a stage is the sum of effort delay and parasitic delay. But once again, the principal lesson of the theory of logical effort—to equalize the effort borne by each stage—results in the lowest overall delay, regardless of parasitic delay. However, the parasitic delays will influence the best number of stages.

Let us now turn to the selection of the best number of logic stages. The structure of the multiplexer tree requires that there be n_m multiplexer stages, but we can vary n_a, the number of amplifier stages, to achieve the minimum delay. Taking notice that $2h_m = h_a$ and $r = n^{1/n_m}$, we obtain from Equation 11.14:

$$D = (n_m + n_a)\left(2^{n_m}H\right)^{1/(n_m+n_a)} + 2n_m n^{1/n_m} p_{inv} + n_a p_{inv} \qquad (11.16)$$

The first term is the familiar $NF^{1/N}$ effort delay in a network; the second term is the parasitic delay of the multiplexer stages; and the third is the parasitic delay of the amplifier stages. We can find the fastest network by computing the values of n_m and n_a that minimize D. From the best value of n_m we can obtain the best multiplexer width $r = n^{1/n_m}$.

Before starting to minimize the delay, let us try to anticipate the result. Suppose that the overall electrical effort is H. We observe that the logical effort of the n_m multiplexer stages in cascade will be 2^{n_m}, so the total effort will be $F = 2^{n_m}H$. If the best effort borne by each stage is ρ, the best number of stages is $n_m + n_a = (\ln F)/(\ln \rho)$. Solving for n_a, we obtain

$$n_a = n_m\left(\frac{\ln 2}{\ln \rho} - 1\right) + \frac{\ln H}{\ln \rho} \qquad (11.17)$$

This equation shows that as the electrical effort grows, the number of stages increases. But it also shows that there will be cases where no amplifiers are required, that is, $n_a = 0$. For example, if $H = 1$, then $n_a = 0$ because it is always true that $\rho \geq 2$ (see Equation 3.25). For values of H not much greater than one, the number of amplifiers will still be zero.

This result has an intuitive explanation. The logical effort of a multiplexer stage, 2, is less than the best step-up ratio, ρ, which is always $e = 2.718 \ldots$ or greater. Thus a multiplexer stage has some "gain." If the electrical effort per stage is less than $\rho/2$, no additional amplifier stages are necessary. For sufficiently large electrical effort, of course, extra amplifiers are required.

Let us now find the best value of n_m, and therefore the best width for a multiplexer, $r = n^{1/n_m}$. Minimizing Equation 11.16 is quite complex, because there are two independent variables, n_m and n_a, and because the equation is itself complex. In the simple case that $H = 1$, we have observed that $n_a = 0$. In this case, we obtain

$$D_{H=1} = 2n_m(1 + p_{inv}n^{1/n_m}) = 2\left(\frac{\ln n}{\ln r}\right)(1 + rp_{inv}) \qquad (11.18)$$

Taking the partial derivative with respect to r and setting it to zero, we find

$$1 + \frac{1}{rp_{inv}} - \ln r = 0 \qquad (11.19)$$

This striking equation lets us calculate r, the width of a multiplexer, given only some information about the stray capacitance of the multiplexer design. The best width is independent of the total number of inputs, n.

Figure 11.12 plots r for different values of p_{inv}, computed using Equation 11.19. In practice, to make decoding manageable, we will require r to be a power of two. With this constraint, it is clear from the figure that for reasonable contributions of stray capacitance, multiplexers should have four inputs.

To be sure of this result, we should analyze Equation 11.14 for electrical efforts other than one. This analysis leads to slightly smaller values for r than those predicted by Equation 11.19, as will be seen in Exercise 11-2, but the best width for a practical multiplexer is still four!

11.4.2 Medium-width multiplexers

The analysis in the last section offers advice on designing very wide multiplexers as trees of four-input multiplexers. But what if a multiplexer has 6 inputs? 10 inputs? Is it better to build a partial tree of a four-input multiplexer followed by a two- or three-input multiplexer, or to use a single six- or ten-input multiplexer? Such medium-width multiplexers are common in superscalar execution unit bypass paths.

The answer depends on the electrical effort borne by the path as well as the number of inputs. At higher electrical efforts, a two-stage design is helpful to drive the load as well as to reduce parasitic capacitance. Therefore, we consider three topologies for medium-width multiplexers:

- an n-input multiplexer

- an n-input multiplexer followed by an inverter

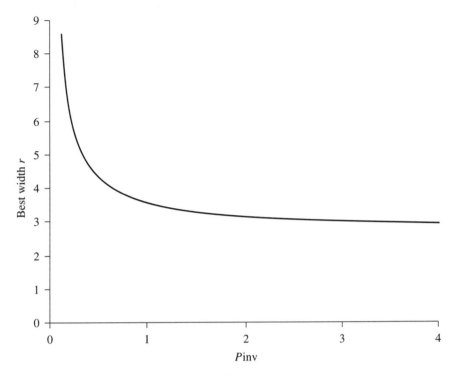

Figure 11.12 — Best multiplexer width, as a function of stray capacitance p_{inv}.

- a four-input multiplexer followed by an $\lceil n/4 \rceil$ multiplexer

The best design can be determined by comparing the delay equations of the three choices. Figure 11.13 shows the ranges of n and H for which each design is best. The choice between the first and second designs of adding an inverter depends on the electrical effort: larger electrical efforts are best driven by more stages. The third design is better than the first driving large electrical efforts, but not as good as the second. Therefore, the number of inputs at which the multiplexer is best divided into a tree varies with the electrical effort. At electrical efforts above 12, it is worth considering three stage designs as well.

The plot shows that it is useful to have multiplexers with up to 6 or 7 inputs in a library. This cutoff depends on the parasitic capacitance; if the capacitance were cut by two, multiplexers with 8–10 inputs become useful.

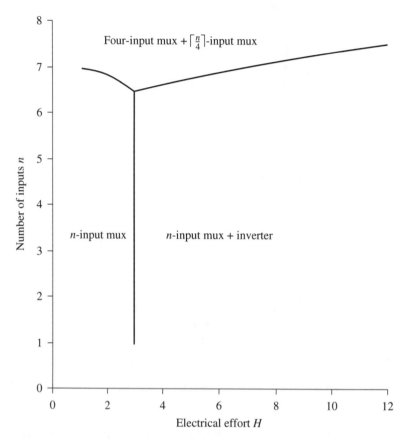

Figure 11.13 — Best multiplexer design given n and H, assuming $p_{inv} = 1$.

11.5 —— Summary

This chapter surveyed a number of tree-structured designs. The logical effort of a tree structure grows more slowly with the number of inputs than does the logical effort of a single gate that computes the same function. We made two observations from the design of the tree structures in this chapter:

- Trees that minimize logical effort are deep and have low branching factor, that is, the number of inputs to gates is two or three. Moreover, NOR gates never appear in these trees, because a NAND gate and inverter computes the same function with less logical effort.

- It is not always advisable to use the tree with the lowest logical effort, because the tree may have too many stages for best speed. Bushier trees with larger logical effort and fewer stages may result in less delay.

We have applied the tree structures to the design of C-elements and decoders. We have seen, however, that logical effort is but one component of the delay and that often electrical effort and parasitics dominate total delay. Thus, the delay advantage of tree-based C-elements is lower than a simple logical effort analysis would predict. Similarly, wide multiplexers are best divided into trees of four-input multiplexers to reduce the parasitic delay, despite the increase in logical effort.

11.6 —— Exercises

[25] **11-1** The Lyon-Schediwy decoder is presented in its NOR form. Show the NAND form, and compute its logical effort per input. Which form has less logical effort?

[30] **11-2** Determine the best multiplexer width for values of $H > 1$, as suggested at the end of Section 11.4. Your results will depend on n. Make plots of the best value of r as a function of p_{inv} for $n = 16$, $H = 4, 16, 64$. How does r vary with H?

[25] **11-3** Make a plot similar to Figure 11.13 if $p_{inv} = 0.5$.

Conclusions ——————————— **12**

12.1 —— The Theory of Logical Effort

The theory of logical effort seeks to answer ubiquitous questions of circuit designers. What is the fastest way to compute my logic function? How many stages of logic should I use? How should I size each gate? What circuit family and topology should I select?

Many designers know Mead and Conway's result [7] that strings of inverters with no parasitics have minimum delay with a uniform step-up ratio of e. How does this apply to more complex logic functions? What happens when realistic parasitics are considered?

The theory of logical effort stems from a simple model that the delay of a gate has two parts: an intrinsic delay driving internal parasitics, and an effort delay driving a capacitive load. The effort depends on the ratio of the load size to gate size and also on the complexity of the gate. We call the first term *electrical effort*, defined as

$$h = \frac{C_{out}}{C_{in}} \tag{12.1}$$

We characterize the complexity of the gate by a number called *logical effort*. Logical effort g is the ratio of the input capacitance of a gate to the input capacitance of an inverter that can produce equal current; in other words, it describes how much bigger than an inverter a gate must be to drive loads as well as the inverter can. By this definition, an inverter has logical effort of 1.

The delay through a single logic gate can now be written as

$$d = gh + p \tag{12.2}$$

where p is the intrinsic delay. The results are in units of τ, the delay of an inverter driving another identical inverter with no parasitics. The first term gh is called f, the stage effort or effort delay.

One can estimate logical effort by sketching gates sized for output drive equal to that of an inverter, or may extract logical effort from simulated delay vs. fanout curves. The logical effort depends on γ, the ratio of PMOS to NMOS transistor sizes in an inverter. Using $\gamma = 2$ is representative of CMOS processes and is convenient for calculation. Table 12.1 lists the logical efforts of various gates in different circuit styles.

A similar calculation finds the delay through a path. The path's logical effort G is the product of the logical efforts of gates along the path. The path's electrical

Table 12.1 — Typical logical effort per input for gates built with various circuit families, with $\gamma = 2$.

Gate type	Static CMOS	HI-skew	LO-skew	Dynamic	Pseudo-NMOS
Inverter	1	5/6	2/3	2/3	8/9
2-NAND	4/3	1	1	1	16/9
3-NAND	5/3	7/6	4/3	4/3	8/3
4-NAND	2	4/3	5/3	5/3	32/9
2-NOR	5/3	3/2	1	2/3	8/9
3-NOR	7/3	13/6	4/3	2/3	8/9
4-NOR	3	17/6	5/3	2/3	8/9
n-mux	2	5/3	4/3	1	16/9
2-XOR	4	10/3	8/3	2	32/9

effort H is the path's load capacitance divided by its input capacitance. The path's branching effort B accounts for internal fanout. The product of these three terms is the path effort F which must be the product of the stage efforts of each stage. Finally, the path's intrinsic delay P is the sum of intrinsic delays of gates along the path. We found that delay of a particular path is minimized when the stage efforts are equal:

$$\hat{f} = g_i h_i = F^{1/N} \tag{12.3}$$

We now know how to compute the sizes of gates along a given path to minimize delay, taking into account the varying complexity of gates. But how did we know the path itself was a good design? A good path uses the right number of stages and selects gates for each stage with low logical effort and parasitic delay. The path effort and the best stage effort set the best number of stages. For gates with no parasitics, the best stage effort is $e \approx 2.7$. For gates with realistic parasitics, the best stage effort is larger because it is better to use fewer stages and reduce parasitic delay of paths. Stage effort of 4 is an excellent choice over a range of assumptions. The designer has significant freedom to deviate from this best stage effort, however. Stage efforts from 2.4 to 6 give delays within 15% of minimum. The best number of stages is thus about

$$N \approx \log_4 F \tag{12.4}$$

The designer not only should select a reasonable number of stages, but also should employ gates with low logical efforts. For example, NAND gates are better than NOR gates in static CMOS. Multiple stages of gates with few inputs have less logical effort than a single gate with many inputs. Indeed, considering parasitics and logical effort, fast gates generally have no more than four series transistors. Path design may involve iteration because the path's logical effort depends on its topology, but the best number of stages cannot be known accurately without knowing the logical effort.

Logical effort also explains and quantifies the benefits of various circuit families. For example, domino circuits are faster than static because they have lower logical effort. Pseudo-NMOS wide NOR structures are also fast because of low logical effort. When static CMOS is insufficient to meet delay requirements, consider other circuit families.

12.2 —— Insights from Logical Effort

The theory of logical effort is most valuable for the insights it lends into several aspects of circuit design. While the same results might emerge from long design experience or from many circuit simulations, they emerge quite readily from logical effort. We list the following among the interesting results:

1. The idea of a numeric "logical effort" that characterizes the delay characteristics of a logic gate or a path through a network is very powerful. It allows us to compare alternative circuit topologies and to show that some topologies are uniformly better than others.

2. Circuits are fastest when the effort delay of each stage is the same. Moreover, we should select the number of stages to make this effort about four. CAD tools can automatically check a design and flag nodes with poorly chosen efforts.

3. Fortunately, path delay is very insensitive to modest deviations from the optimum. Stage efforts of 2.4–6 give designs within 15% of least delay. Therefore, the designer has freedom to adjust the number of stages. Sizing calculations can be done "on the back of an envelope" or in the designer's head to one or two significant figures. The final results will be very close to minimum delay for the topology, so there is little benefit to tweaking transistor sizes in a circuit simulator.

4. The delay of a well-designed path is about $4(\log_4 G + \log_4 H) + P \approx \log_4 F$ fanout-of-four (FO4) delays. Each quadrupling of the load driven by the path adds about the delay of an FO4 inverter. Control signals that must drive a 64-bit datapath therefore incur an amplification delay of about 3 FO4 inverters.

5. The logical effort of each input of a gate increases through no fault of its own as the number of inputs grows. This vividly illustrates the cost of gates with many inputs. Logical effort can compare designs that are bushy and shallow with those that are narrow and deep.

6. Considering both logical effort and parasitic capacitance, we find a practical limit of about four series transistors in logic gates and four inputs to multiplexers. Beyond this width, it is best to split gates into multiple stages of skinnier gates.

7. When one input arrives significantly later than the others, unbalancing the gate by increasing the size of the transistors on the early input will speed the delay from the late input.

8. The average delay of a gate is minimized by choosing a P/N width ratio equal to the square root of the ratio that gives equal rising and falling delays. This also improves the area and power consumption of the gate. Other width ratios in the vicinity of this value give excellent results, so an inverter P/N width ratio of 1.5 works well for virtually all processes.

9. When the delay of the rising or the falling transition is most important, the critical delay can be improved by skewing the gate. This is done by reducing the size of the noncritical transistors by a factor of about two.

10. Logical effort quantifies the benefits of different circuit families. It shows that pseudo-NMOS is good for wide NOR structures. Johnson's symmetric NOR gate is even better. Domino logic is faster than static logic because it uses dynamic gates with low logical effort and also uses skewed static gates that favor the critical transition. The best stage effort for domino logic is about 2–3 because domino buffers provide more amplification than static inverters.

11. Circuits that branch should generally have path lengths differing by no more than one gate between the branches. Input capacitance is divided among the legs in proportion to the effort of each leg. It is much better to use 1–2 forks or 2–3 forks than 0–1 forks because the capacitance can be balanced between the legs.

It may be that logical effort is a useful measure of computational complexity. What is the minimum logical effort required to add two N-bit numbers? to multiply them? A model of the cost of computation based on logical effort far more accurately portrays the time and space required to complete a calculation than does a simple count of logic gates, perhaps with restricted numbers of inputs. Extending complexity results to logical effort might lend new insights into the limits of computation. The point is not that you should become preoccupied with reducing logical effort, but rather that logical effort is a uniform basis on which to assess the performance impact of different circuit choices.

12.3 —— A Design Procedure

We can apply the method of logical effort with a simple design procedure shown in Figure 12.1. When there is little branching, the path effort is easy to compute and no iteration is necessary. In such a case, the procedure described in Section 1.5 is simple and fast. When there is more complex branching and wire capacitance, the procedure in this section helps refine an initial guess at path effort into a good design with a few iterations.

The design procedure must begin with a *block specification* describing the function of the path, the input and output capacitances, and the maximum tolerable delay. A common mistake of beginning circuit designers is to specify only the function and the output capacitance. Unless a specification includes an input capacitance limit, the block can be made arbitrarily fast by increasing the sizes of gates. This inevitably causes a previous block to slow down. Similarly, if no delay specification is given, the designer has no way of knowing when the design is "good enough." While feasibility studies may explore the fastest possible implementations, real designs waste area, power, and design time if they are made faster than necessary.

Given the block spec, the designer can select a topology. Critical paths may use domino circuits or other special families for extra speed, but when in doubt it is best to start with static CMOS. The best number of stages emerges from preliminary logical effort calculations, but may be revised later. Label each gate with its logical effort.

Next, the designer should consider interconnect because the flight time across long wires is independent of the driver size. Each wire should be labeled with its length, metal layer (e.g., metal4), and width and spacing. Wires can default to minimum width and spacing unless they prove to be critical. From these parameters, the designer can compute the wire resistance R, capacitance C, and distributed delay, $RC/2$. If this delay is small enough, perhaps less than a gate delay, the wire is acceptable. If the delay is too large, the designer may increase the width or spacing or insert repeaters. Once the wire design is complete, the wire can be treated as a lumped capacitance for logical effort purposes.

It is now time to pick sizes for the gates. If there are no long wires or branching, the stage effort should be equal for each gate. If there are significant

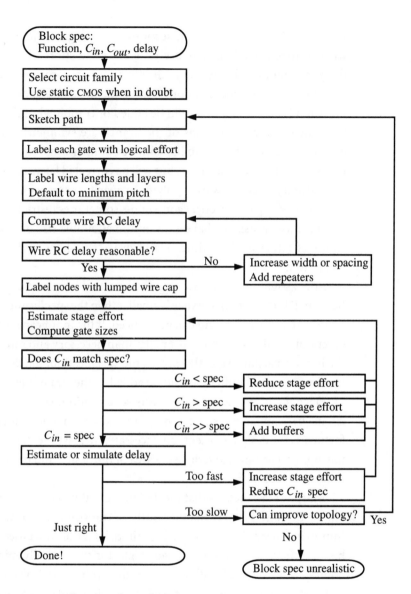

Figure 12.1 — A flowchart for path design.

wires, the design is analyzed in sections consisting of gates between the major wires; different sections may use different stage efforts. For each section, the designer should estimate the path effort and thus compute the stage effort. The stage effort should be about 4 for static logic and about 2.75 for domino logic; if it is far off, stages should be added or combined. If the path has simple branching where all portions of the branch are symmetric, the path effort is easy to determine. If the path has complex branches and medium-length wires, the estimate may be inaccurate, but will be corrected later. The designer starts at the end and works backward, applying a capacitance transformation to compute the size of each gate. Practical constraints sometimes restrict the choice of sizes. For instance, transistors have a minimum allowable size or a library may limit choice of gate sizes. Sometimes a large driver should be undersized to save area and power.

After assigning gate sizes, compare the actual input capacitance to the specification. If the input capacitance is smaller than the specification, the stage effort is larger than necessary and can be reduced. If the input capacitance exceeds the specification, the stage effort is smaller than necessary and must be increased. If the input capacitance greatly exceeds the specification, the design probably has too few stages and buffers should be added to the end of the path.

Once the input capacitance meets specification, compute the delay of the circuit by simulation, static timing analysis, or hand estimation. If you are fortunate, the design is faster than necessary. Increase the stage effort and reduce the input capacitance to reduce the area of the design and present a smaller load to the previous path.

Murphy's law dictates that the design is usually too slow. A common mistake among beginners is to tweak the widths of transistors in the path in the hope of improving speed. This is doomed to failure if logical effort was correctly applied because the gate widths are already right for theoretically minimum delay, as accurately as the model allows. Often the problem is "solved" by upsizing all of the devices in the path, but such a solution violates the input capacitance specification and pushes the problem to the previous path. Moreover, it leads to designs with overly large gates. A better approach is to rethink the overall topology. Perhaps it is possible to use faster circuit families or rearrange gates to favor late inputs. If a better topology is found, repeat the sizing process. If the topology and sizes are thoroughly optimized, the block spec is infeasible and the specification must be modified. Sometimes logical effort allows us to reject a specification as unrealistic with very little design work.

With practice, this design procedure is easy to use and works for a wide range of circuit problems. It is intended only as a general guide; the designer should also trust his or her own intuition and special knowledge of the problem.

12.4 —— Other Approaches to Path Design

Designers have been selecting topologies and sizing gates for years without the method of logical effort. This section describes some alternate approaches and discusses the strengths and weaknesses of each, relative to logical effort.

12.4.1   Simulate and tweak

Junior circuit designers with no instruction on sizing techniques tend to use the *simulate and tweak* method. This method begins with a randomly selected topology that implements the logic function. The engineer simulates the circuit and, finding that it is too slow, tries increasing the size of gates. This only pushes the problem from one gate to another. After extensive simulation, the engineer concludes that the topology is still too slow and tries compressing the function into fewer stages with the hope of reducing the number of gate delays by reducing the number of gates. If the stage effort was too large in the first topology, this only makes delay worse. After sufficient experience, the engineer begins to develop heuristics for path selection and design. Nevertheless, the design method involves tedious and time-consuming simulation and spoils the joy of circuit design.

Fortunate engineers read this book, get instruction from veteran designers, or realize themselves that simulate and tweak is a bad method and derive better techniques.

12.4.2   Equal fanout

A better technique is to use equal fanout per stage and to target a fanout of about four. This method is an intuitive extension of the result that inverter chains with fanouts of four are fastest. The term *fanout* is used in place of *electrical effort*. Equal fanout design is sufficient for circuits like decoders in which the logical effort tends to be low, but is suboptimal for paths with large logical effort because it results in stage efforts well above four.

12.4.3   Equal delay

Another improved design technique is *delay allocation* or equal delay per stage. This is also provably nonoptimal because it equalizes the sum of the effort and parasitic delays rather than just the effort delays. Nevertheless, because path delay is a weak function of exact sizes, equal delay sizing tends to give good results unless parasitic delays are very large. An optimal delay per stage can be found for a particular process. Given a delay specification, this dictates the number of stages that should be used. Equal delay sizing has many practical advantages. Designers usually are given specifications in picoseconds, which directly relate to the number of stages they should employ. CAD tools also report delays in picoseconds, so circuits can be optimized by adjusting sizes until the delays are equal. This is easier than adjusting sizes until efforts are equal because efforts cannot be determined directly from simulation or static timing analysis.

Besides nonoptimal results, equal delay sizing has other theoretical drawbacks. It gives less insight about circuits and about the cost of fanout. It also produces process-dependent delay results, expressed in picoseconds. Therefore, intuition developed in one process is more difficult to scale to the next generation of process.

Both equal delay sizing and logical effort have a place in the designer's toolbox. Logical effort is most useful for reasoning about circuits and doing simple calculations to determine topology. Equal delay sizing is convenient when finding a low-cost circuit to meet a delay specification and when tuning a circuit based on simulation or static timing analysis.

12.4.4   Numerical optimization

There are many tools available that harness the speed of computers to optimize circuit sizes numerically. Visweswariah [9] surveys the principles and challenges of numerical circuit optimization. Because these tools can obtain optimal results and can use more accurate models than the simple RC delay model, why are manual techniques relevant?

The greatest value of logical effort is the insight it provides. While a numerical optimizer can tweak a given path for maximum speed, it does not explain why the path is fast nor whether the topology was a good one in the first place. Moreover, numerical methods are prone to get stuck in local optima and are unlikely to produce meaningful results unless the user knows approximately what results to expect. Synthesis tools make some effort to explore topologies, but still cannot match experienced designers on critical paths. Moreover, designers have in their heads many constraints on the design, such as performance, floorplan, wiring, and interfaces with other circuits. Merely specifying all of these constraints to an optimization tool may take longer than selecting reasonable sizes by hand. Finally, accurate circuit optimization is fundamentally a nonlinear problem that tends to have runtime and convergence problems when applied to real designs.

12.5 —— Shortcomings of Logical Effort

Logical effort is based on a very simple premise: equalize the effort delay of each stage. The simplicity of this method is its greatest strength, but it also results in a number of limitations:

- The RC delay model is overly simplistic. In particular, it fails to capture the effects of velocity saturation and of variable rise times [3]. Fortunately, rise times tend to be about equal in well-designed circuits with equal effort delay and, fortunately, velocity saturation can be handled by characterizing the logical effort of gates through simulation.

- Logical effort explains how to design a path for maximum speed, but does not easily show how to design a path for minimum area or power under a fixed-delay constraint.

- Logical effort calculations can be difficult for paths that branch and have a different number of stages or different parasitic delays on each branch. Usually the logical effort calculations for such circuits require iteration. Iteration is also required when fixed-wire capacitances are comparable to gate capacitance.

- Many real circuits are too complex to optimize by hand. For example, problems in Chapter 11 were solved with spreadsheets or with simple scripts. Given that numerical optimization is sometimes necessary, perhaps the optimizer should use a more accurate delay equation.

12.6 —— Parting Words

One of the joys of circuit design is the challenge of designing ever more powerful chips. High-speed processors push circuit design to the limit. Low-power circuits are also created by operating high-speed designs at the lowest feasible voltage. Every circuit designer constantly confronts the question of how to choose fast circuit topologies and how to size transistors for greatest speed. As a result, every good designer has developed a set of heuristics that lead to fast circuits. Logical effort should not displace this insight but should supplement it by providing a simple and powerful framework to reason about delay in circuits and by providing a common language for designers to communicate their ideas.

Even more importantly, we hope this monograph will help new circuit designers to develop their own intuition quickly. We too experienced the frustration of endless simulation and tweaking of gate sizes before we developed logical effort. We hope we have provided a useful teaching tool.

The only way to become skilled with logical effort is to use it. At first, you will find it slow and cumbersome. With practice, however, you will develop proficiency and soon discover logical effort to be a productive way to design fast circuits.

Cast of Characters

The notation used in this monograph obeys certain conventions whenever possible:

- Parameters of the fabrication process and design parameters that are likely to be the same for all logic gates are given by Greek letters.

- Logic gate inputs and outputs are single, lowercase letters, in the set *a*, *b*, *c* whenever possible. Subscripts are often used to indicate different stages of logic along a path in a network.

- Quantities used in equations for modeling transistor properties are chosen to match existing conventions.

The principal notational symbols are as follows.

d	The delay in a single stage of a logic network, or "stage delay." Often subscripted to identify a single stage of a network.
D	The total delay along a path through a logic network.
$\hat{D}$	The total delay along a path through a logic network when the design of the network is optimized to obtain least delay.
g	The logical effort per input or bundle of a logic gate. Often subscripted to denote the particular input or bundle, or to identify a single stage of a network. We chose the letter g to represent logical

effort because it is the first letter in the word "logical" that is not easily confused with other symbols—l with one and o with zero.

g_{tot} The total logical effort of a single logic gate. Often subscripted to identify a single stage of a network.

G The path logical effort borne by one or more paths through a logic network. When subscripted with characters, denotes the logical effort between two points in a network: G_{ab} is the logical effort along the path from a to b.

h The electrical effort borne by a single stage: $h = C_{out}/C_{in}$. This is the ratio of a logic gate's load capacitance to the input capacitance of a single input. Often subscripted to identify a single stage of a network. We chose the letter h so that the formula $f = gh$ reads in alphabetical order.

H The path electrical effort borne by one or more paths through a logic network. When subscripted with characters, denotes the electrical effort between two points in a network: H_{ab} is the electrical effort along the path from a to b.

b The branching effort borne at the output of a single logic gate. Often subscripted to identify a stage of a network.

B The path branching effort borne by one or more paths through a network. Note that branching effort at the last stage in a network is not counted, because the electrical effort reflects the effort of branching in the last stage.

f The effort, electrical and logical, borne by a single stage: $f = gh$. Often subscripted to identify a single stage of a network. Sometimes called the *effort delay*, because it is the contribution to delay in a single logic gate that is induced by the effort the gate bears. We chose the letter f to represent the word "effort," the letter e being too easily confused with the constant 2.718.

$\hat{f}$ The optimum value of f to minimize delay along a path with a given number of stages.

ρ The optimum value of $\hat{f}$ when the number of stages in a path is chosen to minimize delay.

F	The path effort—electrical, branching, and logical—borne by one or more paths through a logic network: $F = GBH$. When subscripted with characters, denotes the path effort between two points in a network: F_{ab} is the path effort along the path from a to b.
p	The parasitic delay of a logic gate.
p_{inv}	The parasitic delay of an inverter.
P	The parasitic delay along a path of a network.
N	The number of stages along a logic path.
R	Resistance. R_w is the resistance per unit length of a metal wire.
C	Capacitance. C_{in} is the input capacitance of a logic gate or of a path through a logic network. C_{out} is the load capacitance of a logic gate or of a path through a logic network. C_w is the capacitance per unit length of a metal wire.
L	The length of a transistor. In an inverter, L_n is the length of the n-type transistor and L_p is the length of the p-type transistor.
W	The width of a transistor. In an inverter, W_n is the width of the n-type transistor and W_p is the width of the p-type transistor.
τ	The delay of an ideal inverter with no stray capacitance driving an identical inverter.
γ	The ratio of the shape factor of p-type pullup transistors to that of n-type pulldown transistors in the reference inverter: $\gamma = (W_p/L_p)/(W_n/L_n)$. Usually $\gamma > 1$.
r	The P/N ratio of a gate. See P/N ratio.
P/N ratio	The ratio r of the shape factor of PMOS pullup transistors (W_p/L_p) to that of NMOS pulldown transistors (W_n/L_n) in an arbitrary logic gate. For the reference inverter, the P/N ratio equals γ. For a two-input NOR gate, the P/N ratio must be 2γ to have rising and falling delays proportional to those of the inverter.
μ_n	The mobility in n-channel devices.
μ_p	The mobility in p-channel devices.

μ The ratio of n-channel mobility to p-channel mobility: $\mu = \mu_n/\mu_p$. Usually $\mu > 1$. *Warning:* Whereas μ is the ratio of n to p mobilities, γ is the ratio of p to n shape factors.

The adjectives "stage" and "path" are applied to logical effort, electrical effort, effort, effort delay, and parasitic delay. When the adjective "total" is applied to "logical effort," it means the sum of the logical effort per input of all inputs of a logic gate.

Reference Process Parameters

B

Many examples in this book refer to a typical 0.6μ, 3.3v process. Key parameters for the process are listed below. For ease of computation, some parameters used in examples are slightly different than those extracted from simulation in Chapter 5. For example, we use $p_{inv} = 1$ instead of 1.08.

Table B.1 — Process parameters used in logical effort examples.

$\tau = 50$ ps	Basic delay unit
$p_{inv} = 1$	Parasitic delay of an inverter
FO4 delay $= 5\tau = 250$ ps	Fanout-of-4 inverter delay
$\rho = 3.59$	Derived from p_{inv} and Equation 3.25
$\gamma = 2$	Ratio of pullup to pulldown width in inverters
$C_g = 2$ (fF/μm)	Capacitance per micron of minimum-length gate
$C_d = 2$ (fF/μm)	Capacitance per micron of contacted diffusion
$C_w = 0.2$ (fF/μm)	Capacitance per micron of narrowest metal1 wire

Solutions to Selected Exercises

C.1 —— Chapter 1

1-1 $F_a = 8$; $F_b = 10$; (a) is faster; $x = 2.12C$; $y = 3.16C$

1-3 Yes. The stage efforts are not equal and are too large. $\hat{N} = 5$. Add two inverters and adjust the effort of each stage to be 3.6.

1-5 $T = 80\tau$

C.2 —— Chapter 2

2-1 $\hat{D} = 6(2.96H)^{1/6} + 9.0$. Figure C.1 shows that more stages are beneficial to drive larger efforts. Design (b) is always better than (a).

2-3 Initial (extra) inverter: 10. $x = 35.2$; $y = 15.5$; $z = 27.3$. Four-stage delay $= 21.1$. This is 5% faster, which is probably not significant.

2-5 A NAND gate is faster than a NOR gate.

2-7 There are many possible solutions. The design of Figure 2.6 more than meets the delay constraints. Sizes could be reduced to reduce area and power while still achieving adequate delay.

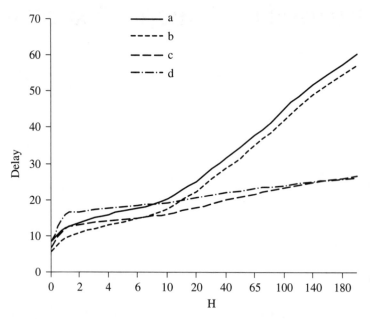

Figure C.1 — Graph of Exercise 2-1 solution.

C.3 —— Chapter 3

3-1   A current source has current $I_i = I_t \times \alpha$. $d_{abs} = \kappa_2(C_{out} + C_{pi})/I_i$ for some constant κ_3. Define an effective resistance $R_t = \kappa_3/(\kappa I_t)$ and substitute this effective resistance to obtain Equation 3.6. The other equations of logical effort flow from this form.

3-3   By induction. Obviously true for one stage. Given truth for N stages, prove for $N + 1$ stages. Suppose the path effort is F and the first stage has effort f_1. The remaining N stages must have equal effort as already proven, an effort of $f = (F/f_1)^{1/N}$. Write the delay equation and take a derivative with respect to f_1 to prove $f_1 = f$ for minimum delay.

3-5   After the gates, assuming the path must drive a reasonably large load. Inverters have low logical effort, so they serve as good buffers with high electrical efforts. Thus, the other gates can be smaller, consuming less area and power. Of course, sometimes it is beneficial to place one inverter before the gates and use DeMorgan's law to convert NOR to NAND gates, reducing the logical effort of the path.

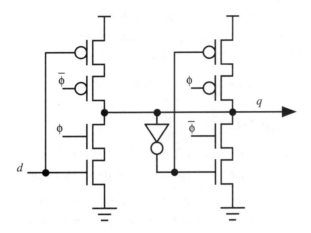

Figure C.2 — One approach for Exercise 4-1 solution.

C.4 —— Chapter 4

4-1 See Figure C.2 for one approach. The additional staticizing transistors should be small to minimize area and parasitic loading while supplying just enough current to counter leakage from the latch; minimum-sized devices are generally adequate. The staticizer places no extra load on the d input, so the logical effort is unchanged. The $\phi*$ bundle effort increases by the ratio of the total new clock capacitance to the original clock capacitance; this increase is minimized with small transistors in the staticizer feedback circuit.

Staticizing can also be done with cross-coupled inverters on the output. The feedback inverter fights the transition at first and therefore increases the delay. If the inverters are sized proportionally to the rest of the latch, say 1/10 the size, they decrease the average latch output current by a fixed amount and increase the logical effort inversely. The extra loading of the feedforward inverter also increases the parasitic delay of the gate.

4-3 The inverter and feedback transistors should be minimum size because they serve only to combat leakage. The logical effort is still 2 because the output drive does not change, but the parasitic delay increases due to the loading of the inverter and the feedback transistor diffusion capacitances.

4-5 Not possible for two-input gates.

4-7 $g = 32/9$ on each input bundle. This design is thus preferred when the electrical effort is large and many stages are required. The single-stage design is better when few stages are required.

4-9   See Table 5.5 for some processes.

C.5 —— Chapter 5

5-1   Your results will depend on your process. If they differ from the data in this chapter by a factor of two or more, be suspicious.

5-3   Connect together the outputs of two NAND gates. Connect a to input 0 of one NAND and input 1 of the other. Connect b to input 1 of the first NAND and input 0 of the other. Now the circuit is perfectly symmetric.

C.6 —— Chapter 6

6-1   Without loss of generality, assume $g_f = g_a$ and $g_u = g_b$. Substitute these into the left side of Equation 6.5 and simplify.

6-3 $D = 2\sqrt{\frac{336}{54(1-s)}}$

6-5   The cost of making the latch static is the additional branching effort, $1/r = (C_q + C_f)/C_q$. This increases the path effort. There is also an increase in parasitic delay due to the diffusion loading of the feedback gate.

6-7   The middle two gates. Yes, the degree of asymmetry depends on the electrical effort because the sizes of the middle gates, and the branching effort they add, depends on path electrical effort.

C.7 —— Chapter 7

7-1   See Figure C.3.

7-3   For each gate in Figure 7.4 undergoing a critical transition, the output current is equal to that of a regular skew inverter. The logical effort is the ratio of the input capacitance to that of a regular skew inverter. For the HI-skew inverter with $2 + 1/2 = 5/2$ units of input capacitance, the logical effort is thus $(5/2)/3 = 5/6$. The other logical efforts of critical transitions are derived in a similar fashion. For the noncritical transitions, the output current is only half

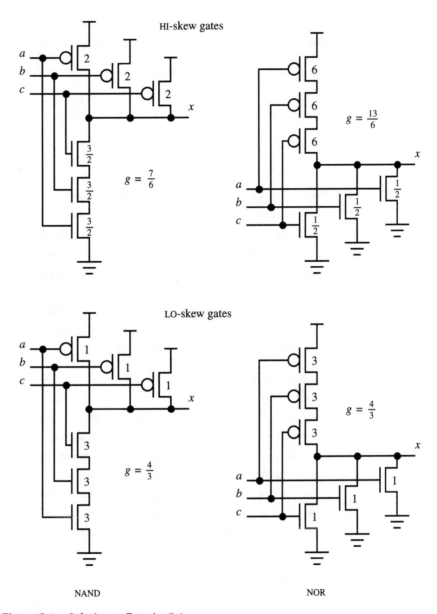

Figure C.3 — Solution to Exercise 7-1.

as great, so the logical effort is twice that of the critical transition. The average logical effort is the average of the rising and falling efforts.

7-5   Compute $\partial d/\partial r$ of Equation 7.11 to be $1 - k\mu/r^2$. Setting this to zero and solving for r gives Equation 7.12.

C.8 —— Chapter 8

8-1   Each gate is sized with a pullup of $2/3$ so the pullup current is $1/3$ that of a unit inverter and each is sized with a pulldown chosen so that the net pulldown current equals that of a unit inverter. Therefore, the pulldown must be $4/3$ as strong as a unit inverter because part of its current is lost to fight the pullup. For gates with s series transistors, the pulldowns are $4s/3$ wide. Because the pulldown current equals that of a unit inverter, the logical effort for a falling transition is the ratio of the input capacitance to that of a unit inverter, or $(4s/3)/3$, giving the data in the table. The pullup current is only $1/3$ that of the net pulldown, so the rising logical effort is three times as great. The average is the average of rising and falling logical efforts.

8-3   Use three inverters in parallel. In the worst case, two inverters are pulling up against one pulling down. Therefore each pullup should be $1/8$ as strong as each pulldown. Size the NMOS transistor $4/3$ and each PMOS transistor $1/3$ for this ratio with pulldown drive strength equal to that of a unit inverter. The total input capacitance is $5/3$. The falling logical effort is therefore $(5/3)/3 = 5/9$. The pullup current comes from three transistors in parallel and is thus $3 \times (1/3)/2 = 1/2$ of that of a unit inverter. Thus the rising logical effort is twice that of the falling, or $10/9$. The average logical effort is $5/6$, which is the same as a two-input symmetric NOR and better than either a pseudo-NMOS gate or static CMOS gate.

8-5   The following proof is unfit for polite company. Let $\rho(1, p)$ be the value of ρ satisfying $p + \rho(1 - \ln \rho) = 0$. Let $\rho(g, p)$ be the value of ρ that is the best stage effort when additional stages may have logical effort g and parasitic delay p. We will differentiate Equation 8.1 with respect to N to solve for $\hat{N}$ that gives the minimum delay. Given the best number of stages, we know the stage effort $\rho(g, p) = (Fg^{N-n_1})^{1/N}$. We can substitute this into the derivative to reach our result:

$$\frac{d\hat{D}}{dN} = (Fg^{N-n_1})^{1/N}\left(1 + \frac{n_1 \ln g}{N} - \frac{\ln F}{N}\right) + p = 0$$

$$0 = \rho(g, p)\left(1 - \ln(Fg^{-n_1})^{1/N}\right) + p$$

$$= \rho(g, p)\left(1 - \ln\frac{\rho(g, p)}{g}\right) + p \qquad \text{(C.1)}$$

We will now assume that Equation 8.2 is true and substitute it into this equation. We will show that the result is still true, indicating that the substitution was valid:

$$0 = g\rho\left(1, \frac{p}{g}\right)\left(1 - \ln\left(g\rho\left(\frac{1, \frac{p}{g}}{g}\right)\right)\right) + p \qquad \text{(C.2)}$$

$$= \rho\left(1, \frac{p}{g}\right)\left(1 - \ln\rho\left(1, \frac{p}{g}\right)\right) + \frac{p}{g} \qquad \text{(C.3)}$$

QED.

8-7 The logical effort depends on the size of the inverters as well as the transmission gates. A design is shown in Figure C.4 with logical effort of 3 on each data input, 8 on s_0*, and 4 on s_1*.

C.9 —— Chapter 9

9-1 Solve

$$N\left(\frac{H}{2\beta}\right)^{1/N} + Np_{inv}$$

$$= (N + 1)\left(\left(\frac{H}{2(1 - \beta)}\right)^{1/(N+1)} + p_{inv}\right)$$

$$= (N - 1)\left(\left(\frac{H}{2(1 - \beta)}\right)^{1/(N-1)} + p_{inv}\right) \qquad \text{(C.4)}$$

for H and β for each value of N.

9-3 The original design achieves a minimum delay of 42.2 with a final inverter size of 212. The improved design replicates the final NAND gate and achieves a

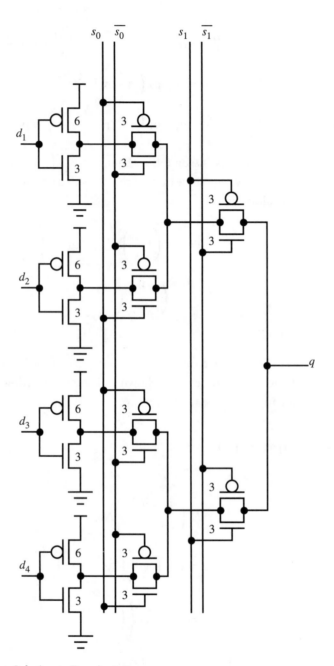

Figure C.4—Solution to Exercise 8-7.

minimum delay of 40.2 using NAND gate sizes of 69 on the 1-leg and 46 on the 2-leg.

C.10 —— Chapter 10

10-1

$$\frac{F_1}{C_1} = D - P$$

$$\frac{F_2}{C_2} = \left(\frac{D - 2P}{2}\right)^2$$

Hence,

$$D^3 + D^2 \left(-F_1 - 5P\right) + 4D \left(PF_1 - F_2 + 2P^2\right) + 4 \left(-F_1 P^2 + F_2 P - P^3\right) = 0.$$

The delay $D + P$ obtained by using Equation 10.5 is 2–11% longer than the delay using the exact equation over a reasonable range of F_1 and F_2 with $P = 1$, as can be verified with a spreadsheet.

10-3 May the force be with you!

C.11 —— Chapter 11

11-1 By DeMorgan's law, a NOR gate can be built from a NAND gate and inverter with inverted inputs. The NAND form uses parallel PMOS transistors and a tapered series string of NMOS transistors, followed by output inverters. The true and complement inputs are swapped. The logical effort per input is lower than for the NOR form for $\gamma \geq 1$:

$$G(n) = 2^{n-1} \left(\frac{\gamma + \left(\frac{1 - \frac{1}{2^n}}{1 - \frac{1}{2}}\right)}{1 + \gamma}\right) \tag{C.5}$$

11-3 See Figure C.5. Notice that, relative to Figure 11.13, the vertical line moves left because the parasitic delay cost of the extra inverter decreases, justifying a two-stage design for smaller electrical efforts. The top curved line moves up because the lower parasitics indicate that there is less need to break the multiplexer into multiple parts to reduce parasitic delay. The sudden jump in

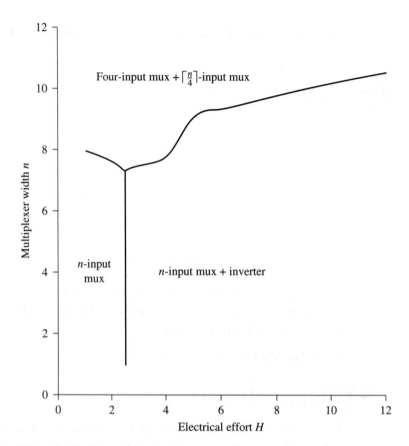

Figure C.5 — Solution to Exercise 11-3.

the top line comes from the discontinuity in the ceiling function as the second multiplexer jumps from two to three inputs.

Bibliography

[1] Bakoglu, H. B. *Circuits, Interconnections, and Packaging for VLSI*. Reading, MA: Addison-Wesley, 1990.

[2] Harris, D., and M. Horowitz. "Skew-Tolerant Domino Circuits." *IEEE J. Solid-State Circuits*, 31(11):1687–1696, Nov. 1997.

[3] Horowitz, M. *Timing Models for MOS Circuits*. Ph.D. thesis, Stanford University, Dec. 1983. TR SEL83–003.

[4] Johnson, M. "A Symmetric CMOS NOR Gate for High-Speed Applications." *IEEE J. Solid-State Circuits*, 23(5):1233–1236, Oct. 1988.

[5] Leblebici, Y. "Design Considerations for CMOS Digital Circuits with Improved Hot-Carrier Reliability." *IEEE J. Solid-State Circuits*, 31(7):1014–1024, July 1996.

[6] Lyon, R. F., and R. R. Schediwy. "CMOS Static Memory with a New Four-Transistor Memory Cell." *Proc. Stanford Conf. on Advanced Research in VLSI*, March 1987.

[7] Mead, C. A., and L. Conway. *Introduction to VLSI Systems*. Reading, MA: Addison-Wesley, 1980, p. 12.

[8] Sproull, R. F., and I. E. Sutherland. "Logical Effort: Designing for Speed on the Back of an Envelope." *IEEE Advanced Research in VLSI*, C. Sequin (editor), MIT Press, 1991.

[9] Visweswarian, C. "Optimization Techniques for High-Performance Digital Circuits." *Proc. IEEE Intl. Conf. Computer Aided Design*, Nov. 1997.

[10] Weste, N., and K. Eshraghian. *Principles of CMOS VLSI Design*, 2nd ed. Reading, MA: Addison-Wesley, 1993, p. 219.

Index

Related Titles from Morgan Kaufmann Publishers

HARNESSING ENERGY · HARNESSING ENERGY · HARNESSING ENERGY

NUCLEAR POWER

BY DIANE BAILEY

CREATIVE PAPERBACKS

HARNESSING ENERGY · HARNESSING ENERGY ·

TABLE OF CONTENTS

PEACE AND WAR. WEALTH AND POVERTY. PROGRESS AND SETBACKS. HISTORY HAS BROUGHT HUGE SWINGS IN THE HUMAN CONDITION, AND WITH EVERY CHOICE PEOPLE MAKE, THERE IS THE POTENTIAL TO MOVE FORWARD OR STEP BACKWARD. AT THE CORE OF THIS CONTINUAL STRUGGLE HAS BEEN THE QUEST FOR ENERGY. ENERGY GAVE HUMANS POWER AND MOTIVATED THEM TO DO GREAT THINGS — WITH BOTH POSITIVE AND NEGATIVE EFFECTS. WITHOUT ENERGY, PEOPLE WOULD NOT BE ABLE TO DRIVE CARS, OPERATE COMPUTERS, OR POWER FACTORIES. WARS ARE FOUGHT TRYING TO DOMINATE SOURCES OF ENERGY. FORTUNES ARE MADE AND LOST DEPENDING ON HOW THAT ENERGY IS MANAGED. THE LAWS OF PHYSICS STATE THAT ENERGY CANNOT BE CREATED OR DESTROYED. THAT IS TRUE, BUT ENERGY CAN BE HARNESSED AND DIRECTED. IT CAN BE WASTED, OR IT CAN BE COAXED INTO EFFICIENCY. CIVILIZATIONS AND TECHNOLOGIES HAVE LEAPED FORWARD — AND SOMETIMES BACKWARD — AS HUMANS HAVE TAPPED INTO EARTH'S SOURCES OF ENERGY.

Nuclear power's explosive nature has made it controversial.

Collectively, the energy stored inside trillions of atoms—and released through trillions of collisions—has the ability to power cities, send spacecraft billions of miles from Earth, and even to heal cancer. Yet it can also kill the people who use it. If something goes wrong, the consequences can be deadly. Nuclear energy literally exploded onto the world stage in 1945, when the United States dropped two nuclear bombs on Japan to effectively end World War II. The aggressive nature of nuclear power would forever influence its future. Some people wanted to use it for electricity generation, transportation, and medicine. Others saw it as a force of destruction—or even evil—that was best left alone. Such controversy haunts nuclear power today.

CHAPTER ONE

TWO BIG BANGS

"EVERYTHING OLD IS NEW AGAIN." That saying is especially true when it comes to nuclear energy. Of all the types of energy that people use today, nuclear is both the oldest and the newest. The first nuclear **reactions** likely happened billions of years ago, when many scientists think the universe was created in a hot, dense state of expansion called the "Big Bang." But it's been less than a century since the second big bang—when people learned how to generate nuclear energy on their own.

According to the Big Bang theory, the universe burst into particles of energy from a single point in space.

In the 1800s, scientists were studying the idea that all matter consisted of tiny particles called atoms. They started to research these atoms—how they combined with other atoms and how they moved. Some atoms, it turned out, were more energetic than others. Marie Curie was a French-Polish chemist and physicist who noticed that when atoms of **elements** such as uranium and thorium decayed, they changed into other elements and gave off tiny particles of energy in a process called radiation. In Britain, nuclear physicist Ernest Rutherford speculated that, if that energy could be harnessed, "Some fool in a laboratory might blow up the universe unawares."

Marie Curie's discoveries made her a pioneer for women in science.

Scientists made great strides toward understanding nuclear energy during the 1920s and 1930s. They worked to figure out how to split atoms on purpose. This is called fission. The nucleus, or center, of an atom contains protons and neutrons. In a fission reaction with a radioactive substance such as uranium, extra neutrons bombard the nuclei of its atoms. The nuclei become too heavy and unstable, and they break apart. When these atoms split, it frees up the neutrons that were bound inside the nuclei. These neutrons then collide with the surrounding uranium atoms in a chain reaction. This releases a tremendous amount of energy in the form of heat. One atom's splitting doesn't provide much energy, but many splitting at the same time do. Nuclear energy actually comes from billions of fission reactions that happen within a fraction of a second. The number of fissions that occur during the explosion of a nuclear bomb numbers more than all the grains of sand in the world!

A cartoon of Leo Szilard demonstrates the tremendous power nuclear scientists were developing.

Hungarian-American physicist Leo Szilard came up with the concept of a nuclear chain reaction in 1933. (According to legend, the idea occurred to him as he began walking across a street, and he'd figured it out by the time he reached the other side.) Szilard began experimenting to test his **hypothesis**. What kind of element would work best to achieve a chain reaction? He needed one that would be likely to free up neutrons and release energy, and thought indium or beryllium might be the answer. Neither worked. After several attempts, Szilard got discouraged and gave up. But other scientists believed there was something to Szilard's idea. German chemist Otto Hahn and Austrian physicist Lise Meitner tried their luck with uranium. In 1938, Hahn and another German chemist, Fritz Strassman, showed that the nucleus of a uranium atom would split when bombarded with a neutron and sustain a chain reaction.

Uranium is incredibly energy-dense. A pound of uranium produces almost 4 million times as much energy as the same amount of coal. Uranium is a fairly common element. It's found worldwide in mineral deposits and in the ocean. Although there's a lot of uranium, it isn't all useful. An isotope is a variation of an element containing a different number of neutrons. Uranium-238 is a common isotope, but it won't work in nuclear reactions because it is not fissile. Fissile means that something breaks apart easily and can sustain a fission chain reaction. Uranium-235 is a different story. It is fissile. But it is also rarer. It makes up less than 1 percent of a natural uranium sample. Before it can be used as fuel in nuclear **reactors**, uranium must be enriched to increase the amount of U-235 it contains.

If nuclear energy had been developed 30 years earlier, or 30 years later, people might use it much differently today. But in the **heyday** of nuclear development (the 1930s and 1940s), much of the world was engulfed in World War II. German scientists had greatly advanced the understanding of nuclear energy, and government officials in the United States worried that such knowledge might be used against the **Allies**. In 1942, the U.S. secretly launched the Manhattan Project with the goal of building a nuclear bomb. Within only a few months, Italian physicist Enrico Fermi had built the first nuclear reactor in Chicago. By 1945, a team of scientists, including Fermi and American physicist J. Robert Oppenheimer, had successfully completed the

J. Robert Oppenheimer strove to educate others on scientific problems.

project's mission. In August 1945, the U.S. bombed the Japanese cities of Hiroshima and Nagasaki. Nuclear energy helped end the war, but it opened a Pandora's box of power struggles around the world.

Although the first use of nuclear energy had been for war, the next decade saw a shift to use it as a peaceful power source. In 1953, U.S. president and former Army general Dwight D. Eisenhower started a program called "Atoms for Peace." He wanted countries to share information about nuclear technology. Eisenhower said, "It is not enough to take this weapon out of the hands of soldiers. It must be put into the hands of those who will know how to strip its military casing and adapt it to the arts of peace." Within a few years, the U.S., the

Soviet Union, Great Britain, and France all began producing electricity from nuclear power.

Nuclear energy use grew steadily over the next two decades, but it wasn't just for the arts of peace. "Dual-use reactors" made electricity, and they also made plutonium, which forms when uranium fissions. Plutonium is an extremely fissile radioactive element ideal for building bombs. The world's two superpowers, the U.S. and the Soviet Union, were hostile toward one another during a period known as the **Cold War**. Both countries built and stockpiled nuclear weapons in case the other attacked. This weapons **proliferation** helped spur anti-nuclear protests in the 1960s. For two weeks in 1962, the U.S. and the nearby island nation

A 1955 U.S. postage stamp featured phrases from Eisenhower's optimistic "Atoms for Peace" speech.

During the Cold War era, the U.S. government warned citizens to prepare for a nuclear attack.

of Cuba were in a tense political standoff. Cuba was an ally of the Soviet Union, and the Soviets had placed nuclear missiles there. Although the incident was resolved peacefully, the threat of nuclear missiles being launched from Cuba remained. The Cuban Missile Crisis reminded everyone how close the world could come to nuclear war.

The relative instability of a nuclear reaction also posed the danger of a large-scale accident. "The China Syndrome" supposed a scenario in which a nuclear reactor malfunctioned and melted through the earth—straight to China. Such an event is impossible, but it illustrates how people were fearful of nuclear accidents. A movie called *The China Syndrome* was released in March 1979. Two weeks later, a real-life nuclear accident occurred at the Three Mile Island nuclear power plant in Pennsylvania. There was no **meltdown**, but enough radiation was released to put people on edge. A few years later, in 1986, a far more serious accident occurred. A reactor at the Chernobyl plant in the Soviet Union exploded. Dozens of people were killed immediately, but the worst death toll came later: Radiation released into the environment at the time of the blast has been blamed for thousands of deaths in the years since. It may cause still more.

A number of factors led to the accidents at Three Mile Island and Chernobyl. The reactor at Chernobyl was poorly designed, without sufficient shutdown equipment, and operators were not properly trained about how to respond in the case of an accident. At Three Mile Island, instruments that indicated a problem were difficult to read, so workers did not recognize the problem in time. The thought that a simple mistake—or an intentional plan— could kill thousands gives people pause. Nuclear energy is powerful but terrifying. Is it worth it?

People were evacuated from the Chernobyl area and were too fearful to ever return.

CHAPTER TWO

DIFFERENT PATHS

IN THE 1970S, THE U.S. WAS PREPARED TO BUILD A LOT OF NUCLEAR POWER PLANTS. It wanted to reduce dependence on oil that had to be imported from the Middle East. However, after the accident at Three Mile Island, many of these plants were never built. Instead, people became more energy efficient. New resources of oil and gas were found. The great nuclear expansion never happened in America.

At the same time, France faced a choice. Or did it? A national **slogan** declared, "no oil, no coal, no gas, no choice." (The country also had no uranium, but it had ties to former **colonies** in Africa that did.) The French government launched a huge nuclear power program. France and the U.S. took two very different paths, representing the opposite opinions about nuclear power that still persist today.

Containment buildings housing nuclear reactors at power plants are reinforced to confine radiation.

Concern about weapons development made even the types of nuclear reactors that were built controversial. In the 1960s and '70s, most new nuclear plants were classified as light water reactors. These are still the most common type today and operate either by boiling water or by pressurizing it. Either way produces high temperatures for making steam. In both types of reactors, light water—which is just ordinary water—is used as a coolant. The coolant transfers the heat energy to electrical generators after the reaction, making it a relatively efficient means of energy transfer. Light water reactors use uranium as fuel, but not all the uranium gets used up during a reaction. A lot gets wasted. As William Hurt, an American nuclear engineer, explains, "The way it's done now, our power-plant reactors use the once-through method—the open fuel cycle. That's like burning the bark off a log in your fireplace and then throwing the log away."

A more fuel-efficient type of reactor is called the fast neutron reactor. Neutrons produced from fission move very quickly, but faster neutrons actually create fewer fission reactions. In a traditional reactor, certain substances are used to slow the movement of neutrons, in order to create more fission

A power plant's cooling towers transfer heat into the atmosphere.

reactions. In a fast neutron reactor, however, the neutrons are not slowed down. Although they cause fewer reactions, they can use non-enriched uranium-238 as fuel, because fast neutrons are good at changing it into plutonium-239, a fissile isotope which can also be used as fuel. Fast neutron reactors can also be designed to be fast breeder reactors, meaning that plutonium production is optimized so that these reactors produce more fuel than they use. In a fast breeder reactor, a core of plutonium is surrounded with a layer of uranium. The plutonium leaks into the uranium and causes another fission

reaction that then "breeds" more plutonium. As a result, far more of the original fuel is used than in the once-through uranium cycle.

Very few fast breeders are in operation, however. That's mostly because of concern that the plutonium created by the reaction could be used to make weapons. To get the plutonium, it must be reprocessed, or isolated from the rest of the waste. The original point of reprocessing, during World War II and in the following decades, was to separate plutonium for weapons development, not for fuel. That has made many people wary of using reprocessed plutonium at all. In

Now a repository for radioactive waste, Washington's Hanford Site made plutonium in the 1940s and '50s.

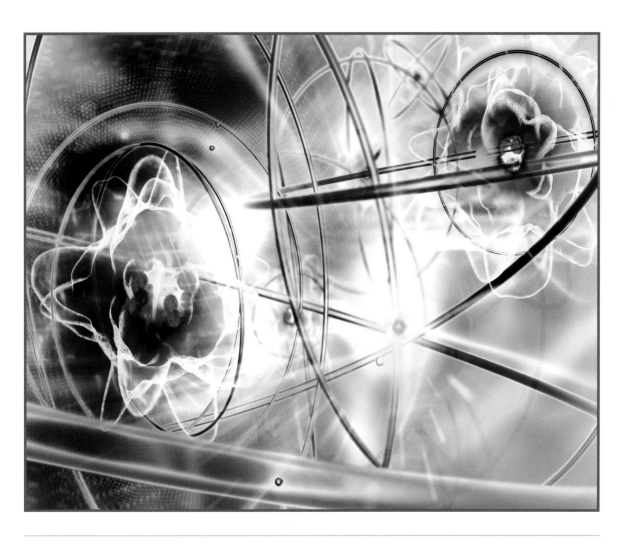

Researchers often use computer-generated artwork to show how atomic reactions release energy.

1977, U.S. president Jimmy Carter banned reprocessing so that plutonium could not be harvested for weapons. In Europe and Russia, though, reprocessing is routine. That continues to create political tension over the use of nuclear power. Even though the type of plutonium that can be extracted from a fast breeder is different from what is used in weapons, any amount of plutonium is considered dangerous.

Although the word "nuclear" often brings up chilling thoughts of war, most nuclear energy today is used nonviolently. In addition to reactors that generate power,

there are many research reactors in use that produce fission reactions on a much smaller scale. These reactors can do a number of things, including making radioactive isotopes of certain elements. These are then used in medicine to diagnose and treat certain diseases. Neutron capture therapy is a process used in fighting brain tumors and certain types of cancer. First, the patient is treated with a substance that absorbs neutrons, such as boron. Then, neutrons are fired into the cancerous cells. The boron absorbs the neutrons, producing a reaction that destroys diseased tissues.

If the New Horizons *spacecraft arrives on schedule in 2015, it will be the first probe to travel to Pluto.*

You won't find nuclear energy powering an ordinary car (yet), but it does come in handy on some fancier types of transportation. Nuclear-powered submarines were developed by the U.S. Navy in the 1950s and are still used today. A nuclear submarine uses a fast breeder reactor, so it doesn't have to refuel for 20 to 30 years! Ships that travel to the Arctic or Antarctic use nuclear power to break through ice sheets. In 2006, the U.S. decided to let nuclear energy take the spacecraft *New Horizons* on its nine-year trip to Pluto. The sheer power of a nuclear reaction was needed to get the craft up to its cruising speed of 36,000 miles (57,936 km) per hour.

Coal-fueled power plants provide 40 percent of global electricity.

The biggest use of nuclear power today is to produce electricity. The heat from fission reactions is used to heat water into steam. The steam power turns a **turbine**, which powers an electric generator. The electricity is then delivered to people's homes and businesses. With about 440 nuclear power plants around the globe, nuclear power provides roughly 13.5 percent of the world's electricity. That is less than coal or natural gas, but more than any single **renewable** source such as hydropower, wind, or solar. Nuclear usage is not evenly distributed, though. For example, in 2012, France got about 75 percent of its electricity from nuclear power plants. The U.S. relied on nuclear for about 20 percent. The entire continents of Africa and South America, which have few nuclear power plants, used virtually none.

Part of the problem is money. Nuclear power is extremely expensive. It costs between $5 billion and $10 billion to build a nuclear power plant, and construction takes years. Not surprisingly, investors aren't rushing to finance new plants. The global trend is for most nuclear power plants to be partially financed by **subsidies** from national governments.

In addition, nuclear reactions produce radioactive waste that can

In the Chernobyl region of the late 1980s, some children born with deformities were abandoned in institutions.

be deadly to humans. Although people are exposed to radiation all the time in the environment, the body can withstand only a small amount. In large doses, radiation can kill people within hours. In smaller doses, it can cause sicknesses that may linger for years as well as diseases such as cancer and **genetic mutations**. While some symptoms can be treated, no cure to absolutely reverse such diseases' effects is known. Even worse, radioactive material lasts for a long time. It takes thousands of years for it to decay enough to become nonreactive and harmless.

Despite nuclear power's drawbacks, by the 1990s, concern about **climate change** had prompted some people to predict that a "nuclear **renaissance**" was close at hand. One reason for this was the demand for cleaner energy. In contrast to pollution-causing, **greenhouse gas**-producing **fossil fuels**, nuclear power is "clean"—sort of. It does not technically burn fuel, so it produces no pollution. Nuclear power does not contribute to **global warming**, either, but it still has enough muscle to satisfy much of the demand for energy. It seemed like a good solution to environmental problems.

A year after the 2011 Fukushima plant disaster, Tokyo protesters demanded an end to nuclear power usage.

However, the renaissance was put on hold. Even though many countries, especially in Asia, were building their nuclear industries as of 2013, a lot were cutting back. When a recession rippled around the globe in the 2000s, it became difficult for anyone to scrape up a few billion dollars for new reactors. Meanwhile, budget-minded consumers became more likely to choose lower-priced natural gas.

And then there was Fukushima. On March 11, 2011, a powerful 9.0 (out of 10) magnitude earthquake shook the coast of Japan. It triggered a **tsunami** that hurtled 45-foot (13.7 m) waves over the country's east coast. Power was knocked out at the Fukushima Daiichi nuclear power plant. Backup generators failed to keep the reactors cool, and all three reactor cores melted down. Dangerous levels of radiation were released into the air. That event revived fears over nuclear disasters. The earthquake may have lasted only a few minutes, but when it ended, the entire future of nuclear power was left on shaky ground.

CHAPTER THREE

GENERATIONS OF POWER

UNTIL THAT FATEFUL DAY IN 2011, JAPAN DEPENDED HEAVILY ON NUCLEAR POWER. By the next year, the country had closed almost all of its nuclear power plants. It also announced that it did not plan to re-open them. Such a decision will mean a huge shift for a country that once depended on nuclear power for roughly 30 percent of its energy. Switzerland also has plans to phase out nuclear power. So do Germany and Venezuela. A week after the Fukushima disaster, Israeli prime

A nuclear power plant overgrown with ivy has become a symbol for finding alternative energy sources.

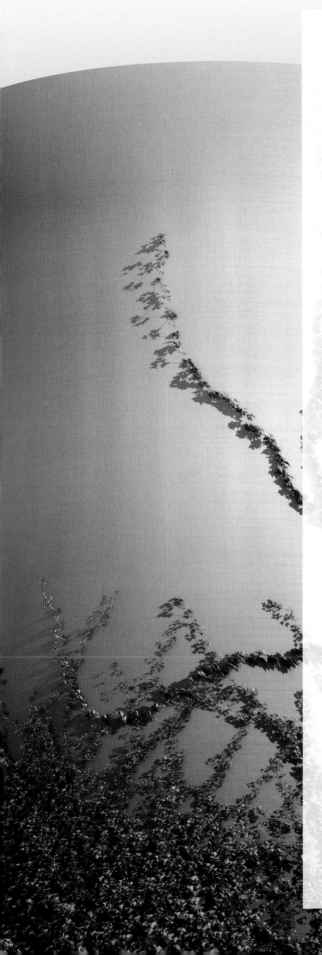

minister Benjamin Netanyahu bluntly said, "I think we'll go for the gas. I think we'll skip the nuclear." Several new plants were planned in the U.S. in the early 2000s, but progress slowed, and some have been canceled. Even France, which has long been a world leader in using nuclear power, announced that it would try to scale back nuclear power from about 75 percent to closer to 50 percent in the aftermath of the Fukushima disaster.

It's not clear whether such resolve against nuclear power will last, however. In the early 2000s, Germany announced that it planned to stop using nuclear power by the 2020s. But in 2012, chancellor Angela Merkel admitted the country was behind schedule in switching to renewable sources of energy. Japan pledged to phase out nuclear power after Fukushima—but then it approved the building of reactors that had already been scheduled.

Even as some countries attempt to cut back, others are eager to increase their dependence on nuclear power. The attitude toward nuclear is very different in developing areas, especially in Asia. China and India are the world's two largest countries. Their populations and economies are growing quickly, and so is their demand for electricity. As they explore options for keeping the lights on (and adding new ones), nuclear power presents an attractive solution. The Middle East is another growing market for nuclear. In 2009, the United Arab Emirates (UAE) selected a group of South Korean companies to build four reactors in the UAE, citing South Korea's experience with nuclear power and its ability to do the job quickly and efficiently. Plans to build a new plant in Turkey were announced in 2012.

Some people are troubled by the timing of this growing interest in nuclear power. The U.S. and Russia are reducing their collections of nuclear weapons just as countries such as Iraq, Iran, and North Korea are building them. These countries have unstable governments, and that has other nations worried. Although nuclear power could be used for civil purposes, such as generating electricity, it's possible it could also be used for a weapons program.

Even without the threat of weapons, nuclear power faces huge obstacles involving cost and safety. To help overcome some of those issues, since 2000, scientists have been working on new types of reactors called Generation IV reactors. These designs were still on the drawing board as of 2013, but if they were built, they could increase fuel efficiency, reduce nuclear waste, and operate more safely. Many of these new models are simpler than existing designs. They have fewer moving parts and less chance of breaking down. More safety features are also being incorporated. For example, cooling water could be stored in a reservoir built high in the reactor. Then, if there was a power outage, the water could flow into the reactor core using simply the force of gravity. Another reactor design is called the pebble-bed reactor. It uses pellets of fuel about the size of a tennis ball. These reactors burn hot but cool down naturally, so they are less prone to meltdowns.

Future reactors could use different kinds of fuel. Uranium is the most common nuclear fuel used today, but it's not the only possibility. Some experts think that fast breeder reactors, using plutonium, could make a comeback. U.S. physics professor Robert Laughlin writes in his 2011 book *Powering the Future*, "[G]overnments have dragged their feet at developing full-blown

In 2013, protesters called on South Korean officials to take precautions against a nuclear accident.

India planned to build several reactors powered by thorium pellets and become energy independent.

breeding technology ... But the risk calculus will be very different when the world's coal is nearing its end. No government will oppose breeding if the alternative is no electricity."

Another potential fuel is thorium. Those who favor it say that thorium is cheaper, safer, and more common than uranium. Thorium is not fissile. Instead, it is **fertile**. That means it can easily capture neutrons and breed a fissile isotope of uranium. However, thorium still produces waste, and it would also be expensive to retrofit uranium-specific equipment for thorium's use. Thorium research was largely abandoned decades ago

when the U.S. Navy chose to pursue uranium over thorium. However, some experts predict uranium shortages in the future. That could drive the price up and make thorium more desirable. In India, thorium research has a head start. In the 1960s, the U.S. and Canada helped India set up a reactor. India promised to use it only for research, but instead, the country also built nuclear weapons. When it tested a nuclear weapon in 1974, other countries cut off India from buying any more nuclear materials. India had no uranium of its own, so it started developing a nuclear program based on thorium.

Germany's nuclear fusion reactor, the Wendelstein 7-X, was named after a mountain in the Bavarian Alps.

Currently, all commercial nuclear power comes from fission. But there is another way to harness nuclear energy. Fusion is the opposite of fission. In this type of reaction, atoms are forced together instead of split apart. Fusion has some advantages over fission. Its active ingredient is hydrogen, which is plentiful. The byproduct of the reaction is helium, which is harmless. Without radioactive uranium or plutonium to deal with, disastrous accidents and leaking nuclear waste wouldn't happen. An advertisement for fusion would boast that it's nontoxic and produces more energy than fission. But the small print at the bottom of the page would reveal its downside: man-made fusion is nearly impossible to achieve for more than an instant.

A joke about fusion is that it is the energy source of the future—and that it always will be. A fusion reaction requires that the nuclei of atoms bombard one another at extremely fast speeds and extremely high temperatures—about 180 million °F (100 million °C). Scientists don't have the technology to easily achieve or maintain such temperatures. Developing that expertise may take 30 or 40 years, in part because it's vastly expensive to experiment with such conditions.

No one company, or even one country, can take on such a project. However, research is underway. The International Thermonuclear Experimental Reactor (ITER) project is a joint initiative among several countries. The ITER organization is in the process of building a giant fusion reactor called a tokamak in France. Tokamaks use enormous magnets to spin a mix of hydrogen isotopes at incredibly high temperatures—10 times hotter than the sun. At that point, the atoms fuse to form helium, producing heat in the process. However, it's enormously difficult to keep the reaction going, and then harness the heat to be used for power. Another approach to fusion is to blast lasers at small pellets of hydrogen fuel. The lasers compress the pellets, creating enough heat and pressure to trigger a fusion reaction. Scientists hope fusion technology can eventually produce 10 times as much energy as what goes into the reaction. However, so far, they've managed to capture only two-thirds of the energy that went in. Commercial applications of fusion seem to be at least a half century away.

People aren't likely to put their electrical demands on hold while fusion research proceeds, however. They want to power up their refrigerators and TVs now. Technologically, the immediate future of nuclear power lies in fission. The bigger question remains as to whether money and politics will let nuclear have a future at all.

ITER technicians wear full-body suits to avoid contamination.

CHAPTER FOUR

REACHING THE BOILING POINT

NUCLEAR POWER HAS BEEN DESCRIBED BY CRITICS AS A FANCY WAY TO BOIL WATER. Their point is that the end result is nothing more than boiled water, and that can be done in ways that are potentially easier, cheaper, and less dangerous.

The reactor accident at Three Mile Island in 1979 did not kill anyone, but it did release radiation into the environment. It reminded people that they were largely powerless in the face of a nuclear accident. Seven years later, the far more serious

Empty classrooms and homes near Chernobyl are present-day ruins, decades after their evacuation.

incident at Chernobyl happened. One of the most sobering aspects of this accident was the Soviet government's response. Afterward, officials refused to talk much about it. Hoping to avoid a panic, they did not immediately evacuate the surrounding city, Pripyat. That exposed residents to radiation. As it tried to avoid criticism from the international community, the government also wasted time before seeking outside help. In 2007, an earthquake in Japan started a fire at a nuclear plant. Some radiation was released, but the damage was minor. However, that incident was only a wake-up call for what happened four years later at Fukushima.

These events grab headlines. When nuclear power goes wrong, it goes devastatingly wrong. Shortly after Fukushima, a briefing of the event in *The Economist* magazine concluded, "Simply put, you can't trust the stuff. Somewhere, eventually, reactors will get out of control.... Nuclear power thus looks dangerous, unpopular, expensive and risky."

But proponents point out that those events are few and far between, and that nuclear energy has a better safety record than other industries. In his book *Atomic Awakening*, U.S. nuclear engineer James Mahaffey writes, "You have more chance of

Once a city of almost 50,000, Pripyat, Ukraine, now stands abandoned.

*High levels of radiation from the first atomic bombs
remain at the Trinity test site in New Mexico.*

getting killed or injured on the job if you are a real estate agent or
a stockbroker than if you are a nuclear-plant worker, and yes, that
includes death by cancer."

Setting aside the risk of a nuclear accident, nuclear's biggest
problem is spent fuel, otherwise known as radioactive waste. This
is the stuff that glows green in the movies (though not usually in
real life). It has labels with skulls and crossbones warning people
to stay away. It's dangerous stuff, and it can stay dangerous for

thousands of years. Not surprisingly, few people are excited about
the idea of a pile of nuclear waste being buried near their homes.
It's not that there's even that much of it. Suppose someone got
all his power needs from nuclear energy. Over the course of his
lifetime, the waste would fit into a soda can and weigh about two
pounds (0.9 kg). The amount of waste from coal, for one lifetime,
is almost 70 tons (63.5 t). The sticking point, of course, is that
they are different types of waste.

Nuclear fuel is radioactive and dangerous, but *used* nuclear fuel
is hundreds of times more so. High-level waste accounts for only
about 3 percent of the total volume of nuclear waste but about 95

percent of the radioactivity. It must be carefully handled and stored in special tanks. Currently, most nuclear waste is stored at the power plants themselves, but some people would like to see a sort of "nuclear landfill." In the 1980s, the U.S. made plans to build a disposal facility under Yucca Mountain in Nevada. It was supposed to open for business in 1998. However, the project has lost funding and been subjected to several legal challenges. Its future is still unknown. Another way to reduce waste is through reprocessing. This allows the uranium to be used several times, cutting down on how much is left at the end. The problem, however, is that this fuel system requires plutonium, and in that lies the potential for producing weapons.

In 1970, the Nuclear Non-Proliferation Treaty (NPT) went into effect. This was an international agreement among several countries that committed to using nuclear technology for peaceful means and limiting the spread of weapons. Nonmember NPT countries are, in theory, prevented from gaining new knowledge about nuclear technology from those that are members. Almost all the world's nations have signed the treaty. However, as of 2013, India, Pakistan, Israel, and South Sudan have not agreed to the terms. North Korea joined but then dropped out in 2003. Other countries, such as Iran and Libya, did sign, but later were discovered to have broken the treaty's terms.

Another concern with nuclear power is the potential for terrorist use. If terrorists got their hands on uranium or plutonium that was intended for fuel, they could possibly use it to make bombs. And the nuclear reactors themselves are targets. If terrorists were able to blow up a plant, it could release huge amounts of deadly radiation. The likelihood of a successful attack is debated. Critics say that security around nuclear plants is inadequate. Other experts say that there are plenty of built-in safety measures at a reactor. Even a direct attack would be unlikely to trigger a full-scale explosion or meltdown. However, safe does not mean foolproof. There are no guarantees.

Known as the Cerenkov effect, spent nuclear fuel glows blue from electromagnetic radiation.

Nuclear plants are also shockingly expensive. They cost far more than a fossil fuel plant, and they tend to go significantly over budget. Investors often shy away from nuclear plants because of the expense, so much of the development must be subsidized by governments. This means that taxpayer money is used to help pay for them. Critics also argue that companies are often too optimistic about how much power a plant can produce and how long it can remain in operation. Finally, there is the cost of **decommissioning** them once they're too old. That's typically in about 40 to 50 years. In the U.S., many operating reactors are scheduled for shutdown within the next two decades. It will cost money to properly dispose of the remaining radioactive material, and such costs must be figured into the overall price of the electricity generated by nuclear power.

Is nuclear even doing the job it's supposed to? The main selling point of the so-called nuclear renaissance was that it was a clean source of power because fuel is not burned

as it is with oil, coal, or natural gas. That means that no greenhouse gases are released. While this is true, producing nuclear power doesn't begin and end with the reaction itself. First, uranium must be mined, shipped, and refined. All of that takes energy, and a lot of it comes from fossil fuels. Put everything into the equation, and nuclear gets a lot dirtier. Because of this, some scientists do not believe nuclear power can really fight climate change.

Few people argue that the world should not start phasing out fossil fuels. Most agree that technologies should be developed to make renewable energy a more practical possibility. What some disagree on are the particulars of when that should happen, where, how, and how much. Most significant is the question of who should pay for it. But nuclear is a special case. Experts on both sides offer compelling arguments as to its place in the world's energy mix. As some countries build nuclear plants and others close their doors, it's clear that nuclear power divides more than just atoms.

Between 2010 and 2040, global energy usage is expected to rise by 56 percent.

Things just didn't add up. In the early 1930s, English scientist James Chadwick noticed the atoms he was studying were heavier than they should have been. At that time, there were only two known parts of atoms: protons and electrons. Chadwick began looking for another particle in the nucleus of the atom. He believed it wouldn't affect the magnetic charge of the atom because it was neutral. However, it still had mass and thus affected the atom's overall weight. Chadwick named this hypothetical particle a "neutron." He proved its existence in 1932. Soon, scientists discovered neutrons were ideal candidates to start fission reactions.

The batteries in a few of today's flashlights probably generate more power than the world's first nuclear power plant did. When scientists in Arco, Idaho, got Experimental Breeder Reactor-I running on December 20, 1951, it churned out only enough electricity to turn on four light bulbs. Things improved, though. By the next day, the plant produced enough electricity to power the whole building. It wasn't until 1954, though, that nuclear-powered electricity was generated for civil use. At that time, the Obninsk nuclear power plant in the Soviet Union was connected to the power grid. It produced enough electricity for about 2,000 homes.

With Chadwick's discovery of the neutron, scientists gained a complete image of the atom (above), its nucleus, and its subatomic particles: electrons, protons, and neutrons.

How much is enough? Most scientists working on the Manhattan Project in the early 1940s were in agreement that bombs should use only nuclear fission. However, Hungarian physicist Edward Teller supported the development of a fusion bomb that used hydrogen. He called it the "Super." It was about 500 times more powerful than a fission bomb. Other scientists felt wielding such power was unnecessary. However, president Harry Truman sided with Teller, and Teller continued his work. With input from Polish-American mathematician Stanislaw Ulam, the fusion bomb, nicknamed "Ivy Mike," was constructed and successfully **detonated** in 1952.

It's a National Historic Landmark, but the USS *Nautilus* has nothing to do with land. Instead, this submarine was cast off one day in 1955 with the never-before-heard message, "Underway on Nuclear Power." The idea of using nuclear power in submarines was championed by U.S. Navy captain Hyman Rickover. He became known as the "Father of the Nuclear Navy." Several technical hurdles were overcome by Rickover and his team. They had to make a reactor small enough to fit on a submarine, for one, and take into account the different pressures and temperatures they would encounter underwater.

The first of its kind, the 319-foot (97.2 m) USS Nautilus *(above) could dive to 700 feet (213 m), carry more than 100 people, and stay underwater for upwards of 2 weeks.*

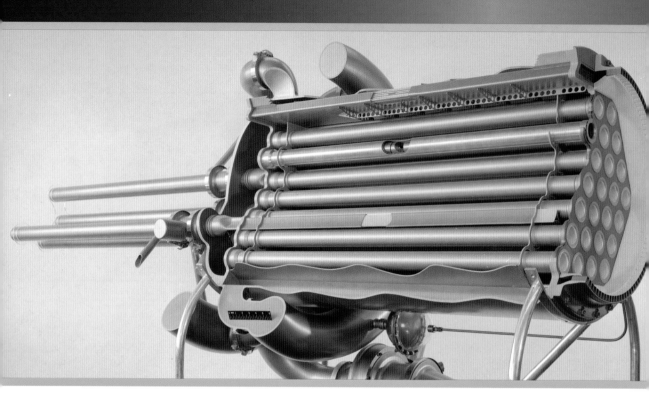

Sundown in outer space can last a long time. Nights on the moon are long, and planets far from the sun have little access to solar power. In these areas, spacecraft need another source of energy for electricity. In 1965, the U.S. launched the first nuclear reactor into space. SNAP-10A was a little bigger than a toaster oven but weighed 650 pounds (295 kg) because it was filled with uranium to be used as fuel. The reactor worked, but it had to be shut down after 43 days when another problem with the system occurred. SNAP-10A was the only nuclear reactor launched by the U.S., but the Soviet Union used several from 1967 to 1988.

Call the detectives. In 1972, French workers discovered some of the uranium they had been working with was not as pure as they'd expected. That meant some of it was missing. Fearing it had been stolen, the French government launched an investigation. The responsible party was not a clever criminal. It was the earth itself. It turned out that 1.5 billion years earlier, at a mine in Oklo, Gabon, in Africa, where the uranium originated, some of it had spontaneously launched a nuclear reaction. It probably lasted several hundred thousand years. Scientists have studied the event to learn more about how nuclear reactions are naturally regulated.

NASA's Systems for Nuclear Auxiliary Power program produced compact nuclear reactors and radioisotope thermal generators (RTGs) that powered spacecraft (above).

Get a lot of important people talking, and see what happens: In 1985, U.S. president Ronald Reagan and Soviet leader Mikhail Gorbachev met at the Geneva Summit and settled on an idea. They agreed to cooperate on a large project to develop nuclear fusion for peaceful means. Today, the U.S., Russia, the European Union, Japan, China, South Korea, and India are all committed to the International Thermonuclear Experimental Reactor (ITER) project, which is being built in France. Construction on the facility began in 2008. The reactor is expected to begin operation in 2019.

In 1974, India detonated an atomic bomb. Other nations strongly opposed this act. For 30 years, India was cut off from a lot of international help with developing nuclear technology, even for peaceful means. That changed in 2006. U.S. president George W. Bush signed an agreement with India that allowed the nation to collaborate with the scientific community. Bush's decision was controversial. India was one of only four major countries that had not agreed to the 1970 Nuclear Non-Proliferation Treaty (NPT) to prevent the spread of nuclear weapons. Under the terms of the 2006 agreement, India can still pursue a nuclear weapons program.

At Italy's Consorzio RFX facility, one of the research and testing sites used for the ITER project, researchers perform experiments in plasma physics and thermonuclear fusion.

GLOSSARY

Allies—the countries, including France, Poland, the United Kingdom, the Soviet Union, the U.S., and China, that banded together during World War II to fight the Axis powers, the German-led opposition that also included Italy and Japan

climate change—a phenomenon in which weather patterns undergo significant and long-term changes

Cold War—the period from 1945 to 1990 when the U.S. and the Soviet Union experienced hostile political relations characterized by the threat of war

colonies—regions that are geographically separated but politically and economically tied to a mother country

decommissioning—formally shutting down, removing from service; for nuclear reactors, referring to the taking apart of reactors and decontaminating them to make them safe

detonated—caused to explode

element—a basic substance that cannot be broken down chemically

fossil fuels—fuels formed by decaying plants and animals over millions of years

genetic mutation—a change in DNA structure that causes an organism to develop improperly

global warming—the phenomenon of Earth's average temperatures increasing over time

greenhouse gas—a gas that builds up in Earth's atmosphere and prevents the release of heat

heyday—the most important or productive time in something's development or popularity

hypothesis—a suggested explanation for how or why something works, based on observation but not proven

meltdown—the occurrence of a nuclear reactor core becoming too hot and experiencing an uncontrolled reaction

proliferation—a continued increase or buildup of something

reactions—in chemistry, the reconfiguration of atoms and molecules, either by combining or splitting, to produce different substances

renaissance—a period of rebirth or revival

renewable—able to be replenished and used indefinitely

slogan—a motto or saying

subsidies—money supplied by a government to help pay for something

tsunami—a large ocean wave triggered by an earthquake

turbine—a machine that is driven by water, steam, or a gas flowing through the blades of a wheel

SELECTED BIBLIOGRAPHY

Cooke, Stephanie. "After Fukushima, Does Nuclear Power Have a Future?" *New York Times*, October 10, 2011.

Ferguson, Charles D. *Nuclear Energy: What Everyone Needs to Know*. New York: Oxford University Press, 2011.

Hore-Lacy, Ian. *Nuclear Energy in the 21st Century*. London: World Nuclear University Press, 2006.

Laughlin, Robert B. *Powering the Future: How We Will (Eventually) Solve the Energy Crisis and Fuel the Civilization of Tomorrow*. New York: Basic Books, 2011.

Mahaffey, James. *Atomic Awakening: A New Look at the History and Future of Nuclear Power*. New York: Pegasus Books, 2009.

Niemeyer, Kyle. "Chain Reaction: The (Slow) Revival of U.S. Nuclear Power." ArsTechnica.com. March 6, 2012.

Shrader-Frechette, K. S. *What Will Work: Fighting Climate Change with Renewable Energy, Not Nuclear Power*. New York: Oxford University Press, 2011.

Sovacool, Benjamin K. *Contesting the Future of Nuclear Power: A Critical Global Assessment of Atomic Energy*. Singapore: World Scientific Publishing, 2011.

NeoK12: Nuclear Power

http://www.neok12.com/Nuclear-Power.htm

A collection of videos on this site explores various aspects of nuclear power, including the processes of fission and fusion, how a nuclear reactor operates, and nuclear applications of the future.

U.S. Energy Information Administration

http://www.eia.gov/kids/energy.cfm?page=nuclear_home-basics

This section of the U.S. Energy Information Administration's website provides information on nuclear power's history, how it works, and where it's used.

NOTE: *Every effort has been made to ensure that the websites listed above are suitable for children, that they have educational value, and that they contain no inappropriate material. However, because of the nature of the Internet, it is impossible to guarantee that these sites will remain active indefinitely or that their contents will not be altered.*

READ MORE

Claybourne, Anna. *Who Split the Atom?* Mankato, Minn.: Arcturus, 2010.

Gunderson, Jessica. *The Energy Dilemma*. Mankato, Minn.: Creative Education, 2011.

Morris, Neil. *Nuclear Power*. Mankato, Minn.: Smart Apple Media, 2010.

Oxlade, Chris. *Energy Technology*. Mankato, Minn.: Smart Apple Media, 2012.

————. *Nuclear Power*. Mankato, Minn.: Smart Apple Media, 2010.

Royston, Angela. *Sustainable Energy*. Mankato, Minn.: Arcturus, 2009.

Solway, Andrew. *Resources*. Mankato, Minn.: Smart Apple Media, 2010.

HARNESSING ENERGY • HARNESSING ENERGY

Published by Creative Paperbacks
P.O. Box 227, Mankato, Minnesota 56002
Creative Paperbacks is an imprint of The Creative Company
www.thecreativecompany.us

Design and production by The Design Lab
Art direction by Rita Marshall
Printed in the United States of America

Photographs by Alamy (epa european pressphoto agency b.v., Dino Fracchia), Corbis
(Pallava Bagla, Bettmann, Peter Ginter/Science Faction, Nodoka Ishida/Demotix, Karen
Kasmauski, Igor Kostin/Sygma, Matthias Kulka, Lebrecht Music & Arts, David Pollack, Roger
Ressmeyer, Paul Souders/WorldFoto, Eric Tschaen/epa, Rufus Wondre/Science Photo
Library), Dreamstime (Olivér Svéd), NASA, Shutterstock (AlexanderZam, Sissy Borbely, Oleg
Golovnev, Dariush M, posztos, Roman Sigaev, tinta, Tomas1111, vasakkohaline, Wlad74)

Library of Congress Cataloging-in-Publication Data
Bailey, Diane.
Nuclear power / Diane Bailey.
p. cm. — (Harnessing energy)
Includes bibliographical references and index.
Summary: An examination of the ways in which nuclear reactions have
historically been used as energy sources and how current and future energy
demands are changing their technical applications and efficiency levels.
ISBN 978-1-60818-411-8 (hardcover)
ISBN 978-0-89812-997-7 (pbk)
1. Nuclear engineering—Juvenile literature. 2. Nuclear energy—Juvenile literature. I. Title.

TK9148.B35 2014
621.48—dc23   2013035755

CCSS: RI.5.1, 2, 3, 4, 8, 9

First Edition
9 8 7 6 5 4 3 2 1